The Theological Roots of Christian Gratitude

Pathways for Ecumenical and Interreligious Dialogue

Series Editors: Mark Chapman and Gerard Mannion

Building on the important work of the Ecclesiological Investigations International Research Network to promote ecumenical and inter-faith dialogue, the Pathways for Ecumenical and Interreligious Dialogue series publishes scholarship on ecumenical and interreligious dialogue and encounters in relation to the past, present, and future. It gathers together a richly diverse array of voices in monographs and edited collections that speak to the challenges, aspirations, and elements of ecumenical and interreligious work. Through its publications, the series allows for the exploration of new ways, means, and methods of advancing the wider ecumenical cause with renewed energy for the twenty-first century.

The Theological Roots of Christian Gratitude
Kenneth Wilson

The Ecumenical Legacy of the Cappadocians
Edited by Dumitraşcu Nicu

The Theological Roots of Christian Gratitude

Kenneth Wilson

THE THEOLOGICAL ROOTS OF CHRISTIAN GRATITUDE
Copyright © Kenneth Wilson, 2015.

All rights reserved.

First published in 2015 by PALGRAVE MACMILLAN® in the United States—a division of St. Martin's Press LLC, 175 Fifth Avenue, New York, NY 10010.

Where this book is distributed in the UK, Europe and the rest of the world, this is by Palgrave Macmillan, a division of Macmillan Publishers Limited, registered in England, company number 785998, of Houndmills, Basingstoke, Hampshire RG21 6XS.

Palgrave Macmillan is the global academic imprint of the above companies and has companies and representatives throughout the world.

Palgrave® and Macmillan® are registered trademarks in the United States, the United Kingdom, Europe and other countries.

ISBN: 978-1-137-53691-4

Library of Congress Cataloging-in-Publication Data is available from the Library of Congress.

A catalogue record of the book is available from the British Library.

Design by Scribe Inc.

First edition: October 2015

10 9 8 7 6 5 4 3 2 1

Contents

Preface   vii
Also by Kenneth Wilson   viii

1. Introduction   1
2. The Theological Roots of Gratitude   13
3. A Christian Theological Understanding of the Self   31
4. Becoming Response-Able: Learning to Be Responsible   51
5. Inheritance and Legacy: The Open Power of the Present   69
6. Compassion   89
7. The Gift of Service   109
8. Learning to Give Attention   127
9. Sharing: Building Together   147
10. The Beauty of Holiness   167
11. Picking up the Pieces   187
12. Conclusion: A Way Forward   207

Bibliography   227
Index   237

Preface

The opportunity to engage with the matter of gratitude from a theological perspective came about through Dr. Jack Templeton's desire to honor the memory of his father, Sir John Templeton, the centenary of whose birth fell in 2012. The coincidence of Dr. Templeton's ambition with the Diamond Jubilee of Queen Elizabeth II led to conversation between the Templeton Foundation and a group of British scholars, the outcome of which was the establishment of The Jubilee Centre for Character and Virtues at the University of Birmingham.

The Jubilee Centre is engaged in research and development over an initial period of ten years, with the intention of contributing to the renewal of British character and virtues in the context of the family, education, and the professions. Its website offers a great deal of material for reflection and practical relevance: www.jubileecentre.ac.uk.

I have discussed the subject of this book with a very large number of people during my professional life. Latterly, James Arthur, the director of the Jubilee Centre, and its members have been important—most particularly, Professor Kristján Kristjánsson, whose friendship and interest has been most insightful.

Unsurprisingly, family and friends have been an inspiration whenever I have been daunted by the task as it unfolded. Humor may not figure as one of the major virtues per se, but it certainly plays a major role when things get tough.

Kenneth Wilson, Lent 2015

Also by Kenneth Wilson

Making Sense of It

Living It Out

Freedom and Grace, ed. Ivor Jones and Kenneth Wilson

The Experience of Ordination (ed.)

Focus on God, Kenneth Wilson and Frances Young

Governance and Authority in the Roman Catholic Church, ed. Noel Timms and Kenneth Wilson

Christian Community Now, Paul M. Collins, Gerard Mannion, Gareth Powell, and Kenneth Wilson

Learning to Hope

Dying to Live

Methodist Theology

Chapter 1

Introduction

My purpose in this book is to set our experience and understanding of gratitude within a Christian theological framework. Could a sense of gratitude turn a society often dominated by envy and suspicion into one inspired with a desire to inquire, to sympathize, and to care? I shall argue that attention to the theological roots of gratitude opens us to the breadth and depth of what we can be grateful for. Moreover, gratitude for the Christian has intellectual, emotional, and moral dimensions, all of which are vital in exploring what human flourishing involves. In particular, an appreciation of what we can be grateful for will, I believe, lead to a recovery of vocation, inform personal and professional relationships, and enhance the reputation of the professions, trust in which has been threatened by recent scandals.

It is a significant fact that after a period of neglect, the emotions and their relationship to the moral life have once again become a focus of interest to philosophers and psychologists. The Vienna Circle dismissed the practical import of philosophical inquiry while existentialism, the predominant continental philosophy, was rooted in absolute freedom. The situation has now changed dramatically. G. E. M. Anscombe, Alistair MacIntyre, and Martha Nussbaum, following Aristotle, consider the emotions to have cognitive significance. Virtue ethics, with a particular focus on emotion and the virtues, has burgeoned through the important work of scholars such as Robert C. Roberts (2013) and Kristján Kristjánsson (2010). This is paralleled by developments in psychology, which has moved from a Freudian preoccupation with disorders to a focus on the positive virtues. There is indeed empirical evidence to support the view that gratitude reduces stress, contributes to an individual's well-being, and promotes prosocial behavior (Emmons, 2007).

My assumption that gratitude has roots in religion is not intended to imply that every dimension of gratitude is, in principle, religious in origin; rather, a Christian theological framework offers an open and nourishing perspective with which to explore the nature of gratitude. The focus here is naturally on the Christian theological tradition, since the moral character of Britain and the West has been based in Christianity. For the British people, it provides their metaphysical perspective, the moral and religious framework for the unwritten British Constitution, ongoing political debate, the emerging British legal system, and the ethics of personal relationships. However, gratitude features as a key element in the thinking of each of the Abrahamic faiths, and given the contemporary diversity of British society, the conversation will in the future need to embrace contributions from Judaism and Islam.

There is much debate about the nature of gratitude, which I shall explore as appropriate in due course. To begin with, I take it to be a virtue in the sense that to be grateful is a dimension of personal life that helps shape character and leads to greater self-understanding. However, it expresses itself in feelings that are not simply concerned with acknowledged past benefactions but are future-orientated; it stimulates future behavior and encourages a sense of community and the desire to contribute to the well-being of others. It is, as Aristotle pointed out with regard to all the virtues, a reflective habit, which suggests that it may be possible (and if so, desirable) to educate a person to be more grateful. The point is that it is not sufficient to express gratitude from time to time; one must be an overall grateful person.

The Dynamic of Christian Theology

Christian theology is not literal or static: it is dynamic and developing as I hope will become apparent in what follows. It is sufficient at this point to note that a dimension of the use of theological language is performative; to employ the language is to *do* something that is more than passively recognizing and acknowledging a state of affairs (Austin, 1962). The Christian is grateful to God for creation, God's unmerited, gracious gift; we are grateful to God for the gift of curiosity, which offers the opportunity to learn about the world of which we are a part, and to employ our understanding to enhance human well-being. We are grateful for what we inherit from the past and the desire to enter into the conversation of the generations with a view to what we might leave as a legacy. We are also grateful that the misuse of God's gifts and the betrayal of our inheritance do not lead God to abandon us: there is always the divinely renewed gift of new opportunity.

The incarnation of Jesus Christ is the doctrine in which Christians state their belief that God has committed and does commit *himself* to the future perfection of the creation that he will never neglect. Moreover, the absolute continuity of God's gracious presence is explored through the gifts of the Holy Spirit, which include holiness, freedom, authority, justice, understanding, wisdom, and above all, love. The dynamic relationship of God with creation and his interaction with humankind (itself a part of that creation) explains why Christians use the term "Trinity" to refer to God. By saying it, they attempt to express the mutually interactive dynamism of love, which informs the relationships within the Godhead of the Persons of God himself—Father, Son, and Holy Spirit—and the model that offers to the active perfecting of all human relationships, personal and societal.

All of this means that theological inquiry is not static: it is an eternal search for wisdom that finds its life within a world that is diminished if it excludes the horizon of God. Humans flourish when they are essentially (the word is used deliberately) grateful, not only for the fact of God's gracious gift of the world, but also and especially for God's loving gift of God's self. The exploration of what this means for human self-understanding and human relationships, for our knowledge of the creation and what use we can rightly make of that knowledge, is a key ingredient of theological inquiry. The virtue of gratitude frees persons, communities, and societies to love the world and one another because they know themselves to be flourishing in the love of God.

This, I believe, has powerful relevance for personal life and professional practice, which it is often said have come to be concerned with narrow conformity to external standards rather than energized by moral sensitivity. My intention is to explore the concept of gratitude as it emerges in the Christian tradition and is explored in Christian theology to see whether it is indeed a virtue that, if grasped in its fullness, could inform a renewal of both personal life and professional practice. I shall argue that professional persons, grateful for what they inherit and for the trust that society and the client place in them as responsible persons, will find themselves liberated both as persons and as professionals when they realize the wholeness of the context in which they live, move, and have their being. The deeper the awareness of the lively context, the greater the chance that the professional will accept the opportunities and responsibilities open to him or her. My purpose is practical in the sense that I believe theological reflections on the theological underpinnings of gratitude can inform the mind of the professional in practice. The professional, I shall emphasize, remains a "person-in-relation" (a term used by Macmurray [1961] to express the interconnectedness of persons; no professional can cease to be a person-in-relation), even as he or she engages with the client. In fact, this is disguised in the development of the professions and their ability to exercise power. Temptations have come with this.

The Professional Society

It was Harold Perkin (1926–2004) who made us aware of the emergence of what he called "the professional society" (Perkin, 1989). He argued that social changes brought about by the Industrial Revolution led to the emergence of a new class that challenged the old preindustrial aristocratic society: it was based on entrepreneurialism and had triumphed by the mid–Victorian era in England. By this time, acquired wealth, or movable capital rather than inherited wealth based on land, had come to be the basis of power nationally and especially in local communities.

A further transformation of society came about by what he called "the forgotten middle class," the noncapitalist professionals. They established themselves, both personally and as communities of interest, so thoroughly in the middle of the nineteenth century that we can now regard ourselves as a professional society. The professions wielded power and enjoyed a prestige through which, by diligent organization, they transformed society.

But what is a profession? Sidney and Beatrice Webb believed that a profession was a vocation to provide advice and service to society at large, without regard to personal gain, in return for a reward that was defined and agreed upon by both client and professional in advance. This raised the question of how the professions could turn a service into an income-yielding property. On the face of it, the investment of time and intellectual energy in the acquisition of knowledge and expertise, which is then enhanced through practice, might seem a sufficient explanation. However, knowledge and expertise per se do not explain the whole picture: they might give a person the opportunity of some regular income, provided there is not oversupply and provided the expertise is in demand, but education does not, of itself, give an educated person the intellectual resources on which he or she can rely to build up capital. What is required is, as Perkin points out, "professional control of the market" (p. 7). With a view to this, the professions have organized themselves into professional bodies whose purpose is to control admission, limit membership numbers where possible, determine fees, set and regulate standards and personal behavior, and devise, publish, and implement approved codes of conduct. The personal aspect of professional practice and the sense of vocation can be lost when this happens.

Professional Practice and Compliance

How does society currently value the professions? Actually, they are the subject of much criticism and a focus of public concern and suspicion. They are accused of protectionism, of setting themselves apart from society, of self-aggrandizement, and of financial exploitation. No profession seems exempt from attack, including the media, education, accountancy, banking, the clergy, the medical profession, the police, the military, and so on. While of course there are many good professionals, there is sadly evidence in the public domain to justify the opprobrium.

The loss of trust in the professions is all the more significant when one considers that their evolution and growth hitherto has often been a major influence for good in the transformation of British and Western society following the Industrial Revolution. Until at least the close of the Second World War in 1945, the professions were looked up to and generally trusted. They provided a solid foundation for the British way of life, offering services to society based on tradition and dispassionate judgment, sound knowledge, and courteous attention to the interests of clients, patients, pupils, or parishioners. The term "vocation" was then commonly used and widely accepted as an appropriate designation for a professional person: he or she was called to serve the interests of society at large without fear or favor.

The growth of professional societies has had a political aspect, as they compete with one another for clients, most especially in times of austerity for state support. In turn, this stimulates competition between public and private sectors, for the latter believes it pays the taxes on which public services rely. In the face of a straightened economy and the consequent need for austerity, which Britain, the European Union, and the United States currently face, there has developed internal competition, even between the professions engaged in public services. Who among the professions education, police, social welfare, defense, transport, and health is to have the lion's share of government expenditure? Which will public opinion favor?

Rivalry between the professions for public recognition led them increasingly to protect their interests rather than embrace their essential common purpose to provide counsel and service to society by promoting the common good. Income generation, cost reduction, and performance related pay were valued above service in the eyes of many an employer, whether in the public or private sectors. In the face of such self-regarding behavior and *dis*order, government has sought to impose regulation in order at least to determine minimum standards. Furthermore, given that professional organizations, such as banks and accountancy firms are international in their activities, regional and international bodies, such as the European Union and the United Nations, are in the process of trying to develop and enforce standards of their own. But it must be emphasized that whatever standards are brought to bear by whatever national government or international authority, they can only be minimal with the consequence that professional practice tends more and more to be a matter of compliance. The idea of vocation is seriously threatened.

If and when compliance becomes the ultimate standard of professional practice, the client, the patient, the pupil, the member of the general public will suffer. When the professional lacks awareness of the moral perspective, the client's interests cease to be the central focus, and personal relationships suffer; even the language of communication is compromised and the quality of personal experience diminished. Indeed the very *persons* who are really involved in the professional relationship fade out of the picture: the characters of both client and professional are reduced to that of a functionary.

So where do we go from here? Is there any way back, or do we simply have to accept that a patient is a case on the doctor's computer, a pupil a statistic on a school's inspection record, a suspect a note on a police file, and a client no more than an opportunity on whom to practice the dark arts of extracting fee income?

A Way Back or a Way Forward?

The first thing to recognize is that in social terms, there is never "a way back" to the "good old days" if such a time ever actually existed; it is impossible to put evolution into reverse. However, that does not mean that the current situation is closed to the possibility of transformation: the contrary is the case. It is in everybody's interest, the professions' and the public's, to find a positive way forward.

To begin with, we all know that the quality of personal relationships is the key to contentment and opportunity in society; it is also the key to successful professional practice. My argument is that gratitude informed by an inclusive theological framework offers a coherent, inclusive virtue that will transform and reaffirm the essential values of personal and professional practice.

We have not, of course, lost sight of the virtue of gratitude; rather, we seem to lack the courage to express it publicly. To some, it implies weakness; to others, it is simply embarrassing. I focus on the virtue of gratitude in relation to professional practice because it assumes the mutuality that properly informs both the personal and the professional character of every good professional relationship. Moreover, it will widen appreciation for what the professions, in their diverse traditions, inherit from previous generations, their interdependence, and perhaps above all, their dependence for their future prosperity on the way society values their services. In thinking this through, one must also remember that prosperity is more than financial security, and the value that society places upon the professions' services is more than those that can be calculated in cash. There are personal ingredients integral to the quality of good relationships that will characterize good professional practice.

Each profession is naturally concerned about its autonomy as it faces up to its responsibilities. Threats to professional autonomy in the case of medicine are examined in an interesting article by Hoogland and Jochemsen. They argue that professional autonomy can only be maintained if members of the profession continue to critically reflect on the values that regulate today's medicine and subject their activities and decisions to critical evaluation by other members of the profession and by their patients (Hoogland and Jochemsen, 2000, pp. 457–75). The same could be said of all professions. Mere compliance threatens autonomy because it places professional practice at a distance from its essential moral purpose. It is important that each profession maintain its autonomy but not at the expense of cutting itself off from other professions, from its clients, or from the general public, the values of which need to be taken into account if a profession is to fulfill its proper role in society.

Gratitude seems, at first sight, to be such a simple idea—something intuitively understood, easily expressed, and readily accepted. On the one hand, gratitude, the expression of thanks to another for a kindness, can be a very local matter if the range and depth of its reach is not appreciated. It is easy to say, "Thanks," but the intuitive gesture is hardly noticed in the ordinary course of events. On the other hand, if fully appreciated, an expression of gratitude can transform a situation, stimulate a greater sense of oneself, and open up the imaginative perspective that is relevant to a fuller understanding of what one is actually thankful for. It builds relationships, affirms community, and is appreciative of people's interdependence and indeed their total environment. But even this does not wholly explain what is really meant by "gratitude," what it says about our humanity, what it means to be a grateful person, where our understanding of it comes from, whether it can be cultivated, and if so, how.

Christian Theological Roots of Gratitude

In order to uncover what gratitude means and what is involved in being grateful, I shall explore its roots in Christianity. This in itself may seem to constitute a difficulty because religion has been pushed to the margins of life to such an extent that most people find it hard to recognize that the values informing their everyday lives are grounded in religious practice and theological exploration. As for theological inquiry, the creative expression of faith in practice, even the language in which such issues are discussed, has fallen into desuetude. I call theology "the creative expression of faith in practice" in order to distinguish the lively orthodox tradition of faith from the dry, absolutist, and uninformative doctrinal statements with which it is all too frequently associated in the public mind. Considered as such, it is hardly surprising that many consider theology to be a set of self-referential propositions we have grown out of in the light of subsequent developments in human knowledge.

Some theologians have colluded: they affirm the truth of their theology and try to cocoon it from contamination by any other area of discourse because it has been directly revealed by God. Other theologians have wanted to justify it by focusing on one aspect of life that they believe to be fundamental to human flourishing—an aspect in which religious practice and personal concern coinhere, such as the desire for freedom. This led to theology becoming identified with political action and to the emergence of political theology and what came to be known as "Liberation Theology." It interprets the teachings of Jesus as challenging unjust political, economic, and social systems and marks Jesus out to be a revolutionary freedom fighter (Gutierrez, 1973; Sobrino, 1994). Liberation Theology is a reductionist version of Christian theology; it may have been a stimulus to new thinking in the circumstances of its time in South America, but it is an incomplete understanding of Christian Faith and the person of Jesus. What is required is not Liberation Theology but *the liberation of theology* so that it can freely engage in conversation with the whole of human life in all its dimensions, disciplines, emotions, understandings, fears, and ambitions.

Donald MacKinnon claimed that genuine theology could not live apart from the challenge of public life, where it is tested and argued with. The seminary, he argued, provided the security of confessional commitment for the training of future ministers or priests, whereas in the university, theological inquiry has to face the inquiring minds of other disciplines from the point of view not merely of its truth but of its worthwhileness or even its seriousness (MacKinnon, 2011, pp. 1–9).

In beginning to look at the theological roots of gratitude, focusing on the Christian tradition, it is necessary to take into account several dimensions, historical, moral, and social, since the Christian Faith has been and, I would claim, still is the foundation of the understanding that underpins the common life of British and American society. This is not an exclusive claim and certainly cannot be so for the future. They have, for centuries in fact, been multicultural societies in the sense that more than one religious tradition has flourished here: Jewish communities and more recently Muslim communities have been present. However, they hitherto have not had the public profile that they currently enjoy. It will be important to see whether and, if so, to what extent the traditions of Christianity, Judaism, and Islam share an understanding of gratitude and could offer a common expression of what it means to be grateful to society at large. Perhaps the subject of gratitude is one in which the Abrahamic faiths would find it worthwhile to invest some mutual effort; doing so could help them develop a dynamic understanding of gratitude that would inspire the future of British and American society (Solomon, Wilson, and Winter, 2014). We could ask, as a community of religious traditions, to whom are we grateful, what are we grateful for, and how can we best express this so that others can come to share our gratitude? Could it be revelatory of, or at least inform, a new moral coherence? Moreover, as I understand it, while the roots of gratitude are theological in principle, the virtue of gratitude is something that, if coherently expressed, could become a vision for the whole society, whether or not it shares a common faith.

The Christian tradition may be said to be grounded in gratitude; Martin Luther referred to gratitude as the basic Christian attitude. In a recent article, William J. Byron said, "I've said it often and would argue the point anytime, that if I were pressed to reduce the entire meaning of religion to one word, that word would be gratitude" (Byron, 2012).

Yet despite this, in the mistaken belief that it would protect the Christian tradition from abuse, believers have often colluded in a pattern of thinking that has moved religious belief and theological thinking from the center of life.

In fact, the engagement of theological inquiry with the major intellectual developments in human understanding has been a regular feature of Christian history. St. Thomas is misunderstood if he is regarded as offering a set of propositions not open to inquiry because their truth is guaranteed by revelation. In fact, it was he who opened up the Christian Faith when he took theology into conversation with the philosophy of Aristotle, the Judaism of Maimonides, and the Islam of Averroes. In the twentieth century, Lonergan recognized the need to bring theological inquiry into relationship with the most celebrated current style of thinking: empiricism. He spent his life engaged in the enterprise (Lonergan, 1970).

The Christian tradition of theological inquiry does not establish a moral theory or system so much as what we might call a moral framework, which is the responsibility of Christians to explore and apply. The experience gained from trying to think through the moral implications of Christian Faith will lead to renewed reflection on the human situation and the acceptance of further challenges. In this study, the intention is to engage theological inquiry with the character of British society and to do so by challenging the limited perspective of compliance that seems currently to be replacing moral judgment as the criterion of good behavior. "If it is permitted, then it is reasonable to do it" is a wholly inadequate way to express what it means to be human.

Conclusion

In some ways, it is not surprising that compliance should have come to be so prominent since it is obviously important; one's first duty is to comply with the law. But it is too limited to be a complete picture of what makes a person or a society flourish. If all one focuses on is compliance, then what one is doing is protecting one's self, company, institution, or profession with the consequence that one is most likely to have taken one's eye off the overall professional responsibility for the interests of the client, the moral health of the good society, and human well-being in general. Gratitude is a quality of a whole person in response to what he or she owes to other people. When properly understood, as I hope to show, gratitude opens up the whole matter of relationships—with God, with the world, and with our peers.

I am more optimistic than some about the future of our society: the opening up of the context of professional practice to include the

Christian theological framework provides nourishing soil for confident development. Richard Brinsley Sheridan has it that the British society of his time was *A School for Scandal*. The collusion between Mr. Snake and his little world of intrigue with society is not one to be shared. The deceitful Mr. Snake is embarrassed that a good deed might ruin his reputation: he begs that it be kept secret and is assured that it will be. The whole tenor of this book is to the contrary. Public gratitude for what is good will confirm the deep desire of all to contribute to the common good.

In the following chapter, I shall explore the Christian theological framework, with its insights into the loving nature of God and the potentially infectious vitality that it has to illuminate the intentional reality of personal and professional relationships.

Chapter 2

The Theological Roots of Gratitude

Introduction

The Christian Faith is characterized by gratitude, a feeling of delight and intellectual excitement that our world is not only created by God but nourished by his gracious presence. God encourages us to reflect on what this means for our attitude toward creation, toward one another, and toward ourselves and inspires us to take risks in order to grow as grateful persons in relation to him.

Christian theological inquiry, I believe, opens up a lively understanding of gratitude that can inform the character of personal and professional relationships. Christian theology provides a framework within which the virtues are grounded: it is not a system from which ethical conclusions can be deduced. Aristotle helpfully distinguishes between what is clear and knowable to us because we have created the terms in which a point of view is stated and what is "clearer and more knowable by nature," by which he means what lies behind and within what we claim to know but is, albeit intelligible and informative, nonempirical—that is, metaphysical (Aristotle, 1984c, *Phys.*, 184a). The Christian theological framework shares this character: it lies behind and within what we claim to know; it is intelligible and informative but not empirical.

Gratitude from a Philosophical and Psychological Perspective

Gratitude is currently exciting both philosophers and psychologists. Research into the beneficial influence of gratitude has boosted interest in positive psychology. The results of empirical inquiry have provoked philosophers to look again at emotions and reconsider such ideas as free will, intention, mind-body relationship, consciousness, happiness, and faith.

Gratitude is the virtue that engenders a positive emotion in response to a gift or benefaction from another. As Robert C. Roberts affirms, gratitude is triadic; I am grateful to you for X (Roberts, 2004, pp. 58–78). In my opinion, it is insufficient simply to appreciate a benefaction; in so doing, one depersonalizes and objectifies what is implicitly a personal relationship. Indeed it is awareness of the benefactor and trust in his or her motivation that stimulates the beneficiary's personal transformation. This is particularly the case, I shall argue, when gratitude is placed in the Christian theological framework.

Adam Smith distinguishes three relationships that may stir the emotion of gratitude (Smith, 1976, pp. 94–97). One may have a favorite wallet and be grateful for it, but one knows that it does not value one's appreciation. Second, one may have a faithful dog whose companionship is a comfort. In this case, one acknowledges a relationship by the way one physically expresses one's appreciation. The dog will respond and show its "gratitude" by wagging its tail. But this is still unsatisfactory and incomplete for one is not confident that the expression of "gratitude" is self-consciously and freely offered. Predictability of behavior is insufficient. Thus, third, a benefactor is not appreciated because of the fact of his or her benefaction but because the benefaction is a free expression of unmerited personal commitment on the part of the giver. A shared moral purpose is a necessary condition if the beneficiary is justified in having the highest regard for the motives and virtuous character of his or her benefactor.

A doctor who offers his services out of a sense of professional duty may, of course, earn my gratitude. But this behavior is best considered an event involving doctor and patient that is objectively appreciated. In my view, an essential feature of a situation meriting gratitude is self-awareness of the mutual relationship between the benefactor and the recipient of the gift. The personal relationship of the beneficiary and benefactor encourages their physical and mental health and helps each experience what it means to *be* a grateful person.

Empirical research conducted by McCullough and Emmons supports this view (Emmons and McCullough, 2004). They suggest that a grateful person who appreciates what he has and is grateful to his or her benefactors is more content and less inclined to suffer from depression. Gratitude, they suggest, enlivens deeper relationships, enhances social confidence, and encourages altruism. In each case, however, it appears that the perceived motives and implied character of the benefactor are crucial, since it is not simply the benefaction for which gratitude is expressed but the benefactor to whom the beneficiary is grateful.

This raises in my mind the question, to whom can one be truly grateful without question and for what gifts? Is there anyone of whom it can truly be said that he or she ought to be grateful if he or she is to realize the full potential of his or her human life? Notwithstanding the illuminating work of moral philosophers and empirical psychologists, it is within religions especially, but not exclusively those of the Abrahamic faiths, that gratitude is most fully expressed to God, for it is he and only he who is understood to be absolutely good, loving, and eternally present. In the case of Christianity, for example, God is said to create freely by grace, not just to have "caused" the world to come into being; he is conceived to have committed himself personally to his creating. Thus appreciation of the world's natural beauty and attention to its nature, in all its delightful complexity, is inadequate; one is invited to know the person of the Creator as revealed in Christ and to enter into a relationship with him. To want to know God and to choose to seek him is to embrace the possibility of transforming one's life after the pattern of God's image. The gratitude that one feels for this is profoundly expressed in the practice of the Faith, worship, attention to the well-being of others, and care for creation.

The triadic relationship between benefactor, benefaction, and beneficiary underpins our understanding of the nature of gratitude. It grounds the account of how it comes about that gratitude is so affirmative of the human qualities that give meaning and purpose to personal life and community living. The practice of faith makes explicit an implicit awareness of what we owe to God. Actually, "owe" may not be the right term, because it suggests indebtedness and obligation, which gives the wrong impression of the generous, freely given, gracious, and affectionate relationship that God offers to humankind.

THEOLOGICAL INQUIRY AND THE MEANING OF GRATITUDE

Tillich refers to God as "the Ground of our Being"; St. Thomas Aquinas calls God "the first of all causes," Creator, "the world's *active* source." More recently, Cottingham has focused on what he calls the metaphysical puzzle "of explicating the sense in which God is thought by the religious adherent as the source of value and meaning in human life" (Cottingham, 2005, pp. 46–49). Adams claims that "the realm of value is organized around a transcendent Good" who is God (Adams, 1999, p. 50). Each of these views of the divine nature holds together the essential matters of *praxis* and *theoria*. In God, "being" and "doing" are one and the same thing: there is no ambiguity in his nature. Interestingly, Iris Murdoch, from her Platonist perspective, suggests that "God was (or is) a *single perfect transcendent non-representable and necessarily real object of attention*" whose essential characteristics moral philosophy should attempt to retain (Murdoch, 1970, p. 55). For human beings, made in the image of God, gratitude must hold together doing and intending. Gratitude expresses itself in word and action.

Christian theology provides the ground from which the virtue of gratitude flourishes. Behind and within Christianity, there lies a profound appreciation of all that God has done and does to inform everything that contributes to the quality of human experience and the inherent beauty of creation. First, we are grateful for creation, with which there comes our desire to explore it in practice. The gift is of God's grace, by which we mean that God takes sheer delight in bringing a world into being to share his love—an unmerited and unconditional gift. Second, we are thankful for the personal character of creation, for God commits himself to making a success of what he has begun. We recognize this in Christ and the liberating forgiveness he offers, which encourages us to give of ourselves for the world's salvation. Salvation in this context is salvation *for* good, not simply salvation *from* evil. There is a moral quality inherent in the beauty of the world as Christians understand it (de Gruchy, 2001). Thus, third, despite apparent evidence to the contrary, creation is essentially good; in it, we experience the holding together in God of the divine gifts of creation and redemption. One might say that God's commitment of himself is redemptively creative: redemption is the manner of God's creating. The world is therefore, by God's grace, a generous environment; it is good in an active, healing sense, constantly evolving and capable of being understood by human beings who themselves share the world's life while at the same time being self-consciously aware of their own distinctive nature.

We are grateful too for God's encouragement to explore and understand the world and live with affectionate concern for it and for one another. Most especially, the Christian wonders at and is grateful for the Spirit's incitement to accept God's invitation to share with him or her a responsibility to work toward the world's emerging perfection. In our thinking and doing, we too can be "redemptively creative" and thus reveal the world of God's creation to be a generous environment.

Human beings are in an important sense called to be cocreators with God. These dimensions of the human experience of God in creation inform the theological development of the Christian perception and understanding of God as Trinity. The term expresses the nature of God's unity in the loving intimacy of the Divine, experienced by human beings as Creator, Redeemer, and Encourager. The Orthodox tradition uses the term *perichoresis*: each Person of the Trinity acts of himself but in an affectionate mutuality in the unity of the Godhead.

Gratitude in the New Testament

Gratitude is a wide-ranging theme of the New Testament. It is apparent, for example, in Jesus's feeding of the five thousand, the only miracle found in each of the four Gospels (Matt. 15:36; Mk. 8:6; Lk. 9:16; Jn. 6:11). We in our contemporary culture have difficulty with the physical miracles; what exactly is happening? The key to understanding the miracle is not the physical increase in the food but the context of gratitude in which Jesus sets it. By giving thanks to God and by blessing the bread and fish, Jesus acknowledges God's presence with his world and with his people. His thankfulness liberates him to make good use of God's gifts in feeding all those who have followed him into the desert. God's gifts, free for all, are sufficient for all—and more. Hence, according to Luke, there is an immense superfluity of food left over. God's gifts never come to an end.

We with our limited perspective, like the crowd in St. John's account, may miss the point. Our understanding is confined to the physical world; we do not appreciate the moral character of the world that Jesus reveals is characterized by God's presence. In a different sense, those in the crowd that followed Jesus into the wilderness were also focused on physical events: they mistook the signs and thought he was the Messiah who would overthrow Roman rule. But as John writes, "When Jesus realized that they were about to come and take him by force to make him king, he withdrew again to the mountain by himself" (Jn. 6:15). Jesus's gratitude for all that God had given him frees him both to make best use of the resources at hand and to satisfy the crowd's hunger, but also to show God's intimate concern for them in their sociopolitical situation. Physical force would not liberate them; they were foolish to think they could take their future into their own hands. Only an awareness of the gracious presence of God would nourish their deep desire for peace and freedom.

St. Luke underlines the crucial role of thankfulness in his account of Jesus's healing of ten lepers. Only one, and he a heretical Samaritan, returned to give thanks; the rest presumably took it for granted and misunderstood the context. Luke writes, "Then Jesus asked, 'Were not ten made clean? But the other nine where are they? Was none of them found to return and give praise to God except this foreigner?' Then he said to him, 'Get up and go on your way; your faith has made you well'" (Lk. 17:17–19). It seems from the latter remark that Jesus believed the man's gratitude was a dimension of his healing. Jesus is not looking for thanks himself; rather, he wants us to recognize that the source of true health is God. So the miracle here is the Samaritan's return, "praising God with a loud voice" (Lk. 17:15–16). Bodies may be healed, but without recognition of God's presence, lives will not be transformed. The Samaritan may indeed thank Jesus, but the miracle is the transformation of his life through his gratitude to God.

The centrality of gratitude in the practice of Christian Faith is underlined in Jesus's celebration of the Passover meal with his disciples on the eve of his Crucifixion. He thanks God for bread and wine, thus transforming them into signs of God's presence. Only then does he share them (Matt. 26:27; Mk. 14:23; Lk. 22:17, 19). This is especially significant as the meal is the foundation of the Eucharist (the Service of Thanksgiving), also known as the "Last Supper," or more commonly, "the Mass." This will be discussed later, for it is the focus of Christian worship summing up in word and action the Christian celebration of the intimacy of God's gracious relationship with his world.

Gratitude is prominent too in the writings of St. Paul. He thanks God for his success in drawing people to be faithful to the vision of God revealed in Jesus Christ and grounds his hope in the joy of God's presence as celebrated in the Eucharist (Rom. 1:8; 1 Cor. 1:4ff.; 1 Thess. 1:2; 2 Thess. 2:13; 1 Cor. 11:24). In particular, he begins every request to God with thanksgiving: "Rejoice in the Lord always: again I will say, Rejoice. Let your gentleness be known to everyone. The Lord is near. Do not worry about anything, but in everything by prayer and supplication with thanksgiving let your requests be made to God. And the peace of God, which surpasses all understanding, will guard your hearts and minds in Christ Jesus" (Phil. 4:4–7). This is a classic statement of the place of the virtue of gratitude in the practice of the Christian Faith. First, remind yourselves of God's presence with gratitude, Paul advises the Philippians, because you may then find your world transformed by the discovery that everything you need is within your grasp.

St. Paul continually recalls the enormity of the gift that he believes the world receives from God in Christ; in his letters, he encourages the churches to share the thrill of their faith. "Give thanks in all circumstances," St. Paul urges his readers in the first surviving piece of Christian literature (1 Thess. 5:18). It is interesting that Islam should share the same perspective: "At the heart of Islam is the teaching that one should praise and be thankful to God in every circumstance" (Mobin-Uddin, 2002). Paul's instruction is all the more powerful because the situation of the Thessalonian Church was far from easy. Founded in about 315 BC and conquered by Rome in 168 BC, Thessalonica became the capital of the province of Macedonia in 146 BC. It grew to become an economic, political, and commercial center, attracting a large cosmopolitan population. Archaeological research has uncovered physical evidence of the presence of conflicting religious traditions, which potentially threatened public order.

St. Paul came to Thessalonica probably in 50 AD, following his expulsion from Philippi. The Jewish community was sufficiently established enough to have built a synagogue where Paul preached with some success, thereby arousing the opposition of the Jews (Acts 17:1–2). The epistle itself suggests that the majority of the Christians in Thessalonica were in fact gentiles. Paul was prevented from returning to visit the community, but prompted by reports from Timothy of theological confusion, he wrote to encourage them. They questioned the fate of those who had died, and Paul tried to assuage their fears. Thankfulness characterizes the letter; however, it is thankfulness not to the Thessalonians but to God for their willing reception and acceptance of the Good News of Christ notwithstanding their difficulties.

Paul's thankfulness is obviously not based on material prosperity; there is nothing naive or superficial about it. His focus is God (1 Thess. 1:2; 2:13; 3:9). It is God who has transformed their lives and opened their minds and hearts to the reality of God's presence in Christ. They live in a challenging religious environment, they suffer for their faith, they are theologically puzzled, and from time to time, they do not see eye to eye. But despite these concerns and doubtless many others, they must settle themselves with the thought that because God is with them, who can be against them (Rom. 8:31–39)? Paul knows the truth of this for himself but is encouraged when he recalls the faith he has received and gives thanks to God for it (2 Cor. 11:21b–27). Faith is encouraged when, aware of God's presence, we know we can and should give thanks in all circumstances. It is an experience many professionals enjoy, whatever the sheer complexity, ambiguity, and personal perplexity they may frequently find themselves in.

Gratitude in the Christian Tradition

The centrality of the virtue of gratitude is evident in all Christian traditions and across all denominations. St. Augustine is concerned in his *Confessions* with his sins, but we misread what he has to say if we think these are his ultimate focus. In fact, careful attention reveals an underlying awareness of and deep thankfulness to God. For God, despite Augustine's ignorant and gross misbehavior, never took away his God-given delight in friendship and the desire for truth. He may only later have appreciated these and put them to the creative use for which they were intended, but God was present with him all the time (Augustine, 1907, I, 31). Aquinas affirmed gratitude to be a virtue since it was an aspect of justice with respect to the gifts of all benefactors—above all, to God, whose range of unmerited gifts he believed flowed from his personal commitment of himself to his creation (McDermott, 1989, p. 238f.). Martin Luther claimed that gratitude was "the basic Christian attitude."

The virtue of gratitude is integral to the Christian theological framework that informed the spiritual practice of the fourteenth-century English mystic Julian of Norwich. She paradoxically enjoyed a profound optimism because of, not despite, awareness of her sin. Without the actual experience of "losing" God, Julian believed she would not have become aware of the reality of his presence. This is expressed in the words attributed to her, "All shall be well, and all shall be well, and all manner of thing shall be well." Jonathan Edwards (1703–58), the American Reformed theologian and preacher, regarded love and gratitude as basic signs of religion.

Examples could be adduced from the writings of theologians, hymn writers, and poets and from the prayers of simple believers throughout the centuries. They bear witness to lives transformed by feelings of gratitude toward God for all that they enjoy and can share with friends, who in principle include all people.

The *Our* Father

Christ, whose life was lived aware of the presence of his Father, asks all Christians and indeed all humanity to pray with him to his and our Father in heaven. When we pray in Christ the prayer Jesus taught his disciples, we assume something fundamental to all prayer, God's presence prompting and encouraging us. And we are grateful: "The Christian is a person whose mind is dominated by thankfulness" (Ward, 1967, p. 20). "Prayer is not properly petition, but simply an attention to God which is a form of love" (Murdoch, 1970, p. 55). Moreover, when Christians pray the Our Father, they attend to God with Christ on behalf of all people. "*Our* Father," as an expression, is utterly inclusive, and so it should be, for God created all humankind, not just a privileged few: "So God created humankind in his image, in the image of God he created them: male and female he created them" (Gen. 1:27). This reveals the personal and communal challenge of praying the prayer.

The Kingdom of God for which we long is one that all may share, not just believers. So in praying for God's rule ("Thy will be done, on earth as it is in heaven") Christians eschew personal power—not *my* will but "*thy* will be done." The demand is vividly expressed in the petition, "*Give* us this day our daily bread." This is not a local request for me and my family. When we pray this prayer with Christ, we do so on behalf of all people, including the 1.2 million whom it is currently estimated are starving; "Give *us* this day our daily bread." As cocreators with God in bringing the world to perfection, we share in his redemptive creativity. And given that God is eternally present, there will undoubtedly be things we can do—that is, if we want to, if we try. Anscombe suggests surely rightly that the primitive sign of wanting is "trying to get" (Anscombe, 1957, p. 67). There is food for all in God's good creation. No wonder the following words from the Our Father ask for forgiveness: "We know that we could do more but fail because we have no sense of the Real Presence of God in Christ." Gratitude, as Aquinas says, is the essential virtue that is missing if justice and equality are to prevail; to be a grateful person is to live with the knowledge of one's capacity to love others (Aquinas, 2006, II.II, qs. 57–58). Word and action, as I have mentioned, are inseparably one.

The Christian's attention is focused on God as the one to be thanked: Christians believe God offers a transforming relationship that reveals the true human condition, informs the inner life, and stimulates the desire to respond to God's sacred presence. God is the added dimension to the three aspects of gratitude explored by Adam Smith, to which reference was made earlier. The God of the Christians is not an object like a stick, a lively companion like a dog, or merely another person with whom one can have a friendly relationship. The Christian God is infinitely desirable, affectionate, and utterly committed to human well-being; his nature is always to love the world he is creating. There is no one and nothing more trustworthy or full of grace; the Christian declares him to be revealed in the life and work of Jesus—crucified, resurrected, and ascended—and sustained by the work of the Holy Spirit.

It is important to emphasize that the gift of gratitude is not confined to Christians, as Christians themselves clearly recognize. St. Augustine, for example, believed that generosity was practiced outside the Church "because of the common bond of a shared human nature" (Brown, p. 559, ft. 44). However, whereas the rich Roman would, on the whole, restrict his or her generosity to fellow citizens, who might compose no more than a third of the population, the Christian considers every person to be a potential "citizen of the Kingdom of heaven" and therefore to be served as a fellow. Moreover, the motivation is different: the Roman wants the honor of the people; the Christian seeks to express by his or her service to manifest the love of God for all his people.

The World of Homer and Aeschylus Contrasts with That of Christianity

The world of Homer and the Olympian gods stands in stark contrast to the intimacy of the relationship between God and the world in the Christian tradition. In Homer's world, the gods are external, disengaged: the good life is one of gratitude for the "luck of the gods," and "success" is concerned with honor.

Dreyfus and Kelly discuss the Greek perspective on what it means to be human and the qualities that contribute to it. They draw attention to the notion of *arete* that lies at the heart of the Greek understanding of human beings. In contradistinction to the Christian ideal, *arete* lacks a moral perspective but expresses a sense of the sacred that is outside the world and beyond human control: "Excellence in the Greek sense involves neither the Christian notion of humility and love nor the Roman ideal of stoic adherence to one's duty. Instead, excellence in the Homeric world depends crucially on one's sense of gratitude and wonder" (Dreyfus and Kelly, 2011, p. 61). Moreover, "gratitude is more than simply the appropriate response in Homer's world; it is essential to a well-lived life" (p. 64).

It was therefore, in Homer's polytheistic world, vital to identify which god was responsible for the particular lucky event that had brought one success or salvation, since lack of gratitude was regarded as "one of the surest signs that a character is deficient" (p. 72).

In the *Oresteia*, Aeschylus pursues no new moral ideal but dramatizes the way of life with which the Greek was already familiar. The chorus says in words, and particularly in dramatic performance, what it understands life to be about. It "shows" how it was for them: the audience would recognize themselves and their relationships and be drawn in to laud and confirm the virtuous character in practice. They were grateful for the experience, as it involved them, but the last thing they expected or wanted was to be challenged by something new. This is what brought Socrates into trouble with the authorities as the dialogues of Plato demonstrate: his questioning threatened to disturb and mislead the younger generation.

Aristotle's perspective is intriguing. He affirms that the "proud man" judges himself correctly to be worthy of great things: "The proud man since he deserves most, must be good in the highest degree; for the better man always deserves more, and the best man most" (Aristotle, 1984b, *N.E.*, 4, 3). For the proud man to feel gratitude would be a weakness, since everything that he has is deserved. Aristotle continues his account of the proud man: "And he is the sort of man to confer benefits, but he is ashamed of receiving them" (4, 3). On the other hand, in his later discussion of friendship, Aristotle contrasts the proper return for services required by contract with those freely offered: "But where there is *no* contract of service, those who offer something for the sake of the other party cannot (as we have said) be complained of (for that is the nature of the friendship of excellence), and the return to them must be made on the basis of their choice (for it is choice that is the characteristic thing in a friend and in excellence)" (Aristotle, 1984b, *N.E.*, 9, 1). For Aristotle, it seems that the proud man is incapable of gratitude because to require any gift would be a denial of the just basis of his pride, whereas a friend is precisely free to enjoy a personal relationship that is the ground of genuine gratitude.

Reconfiguration: Development of Doctrine

Theological development is a hotly debated matter, but there can be no doubt that it actually occurs—something that many hostile critics of religion fail to recognize. Dreyfus and Kelly suggest there are moments in history when human experience, as commonly interpreted, is challenged by events or ideas and needs to be reconfigured (Dreyfus and Kelly, 2011, pp. 104–7). Reconfiguration presumes the existence of accepted background practices that offer some initial understanding: there is no question of a totally new beginning, for human beings cannot extricate themselves from the continuous historical process and begin *ab initio*. Thus the Second Vatican Council took seriously the concept of "beginning again," but this was assumed to be taking up the tradition again, not a going back as if they could deny where they had come from (Flynn and Murray, 2012). Of course, a person whose life and teachings challenge accepted ideas and offer a radical new life will be deemed dangerous and arouse opposition. This person may strike a chord with some who will struggle to find a language in which to explore the ideas and a drama in which to enact them. Ultimately, in the face of continuing misunderstanding, the radical will have to *embody* his or her vision in the hope that others will catch on and, through trying to live it, begin to develop in conversation a fruitful new language (Moore, 1967).

In this event, the articulation of a new language usually follows the death of the reconfigurer because the reconfigurer "loses" himself or herself and lacks the language with which to state plainly what he or she has glimpsed. Jesus is in this sense a radical who lacked a persuasive language with which to articulate the truth he embodied. He confused his disciples and was misunderstood by the public, so the authorities took steps to remove him; like Socrates, he appeared to be a threat because what he was doing and saying challenged the accepted background framework with which they were familiar. Neither in theory nor in practice could they make any sense of the vision he presented. Hence the Gospels show Jesus trying to get himself across and engage his disciples through storytelling in parables and the sign language of miracles. There was no alternative to involving the disciples and others in sorting it out for themselves. Ultimately, he had to be the message himself, to enact the truth of what he said he enacted in the Last Supper and did when he "gave" himself on the Cross.

Dreyfus and Kelly may be correct to suggest that Jesus was aware that his successors would do the reconfiguring, not he. Certainly he grieved over the failure of the disciples to understand but never despaired that they would eventually "get it" because he believed God, the Father of all, was committed to the well-being of humankind. Thus, as I suggested previously, Jesus taught his disciples to join him in the prayer to his Father, the *Our* Father. Jeremias wants to translate the Aramaic *Abba* as "Daddy," which underlines the stark reality of the intimate life that Jesus was revealing and the new language that shocked many who heard him. Jesus is, Christians believe, the embodiment of what it means to live a life in gratitude for the presence of God.

Reconfiguration is a continuous process: it never ends. Hence the Church and theologians, in the light of what they have inherited, continue to seek wisdom (Wilson, 2006; Ford, 2007). Central features of the new way of life will consistently be practiced once they have been established—for example, the Eucharist. However, much of the language of interpretation will develop as the tradition learns wisdom through conversation with new insights from the physical sciences and technology, the arts, the social sciences, and so on. Nothing is without a potential illuminating impact on the way in which theological understanding develops and the way in which Christian life is thought through and ultimately lived.

Through it all, there is the presence of God. The never-ending reconfiguration of Christian theological understanding reveals new insights into God's relationship with his creation. The result is the extension of the ways in which the Christian is able to partner with God in creating and the deepening his or her sense of gratitude, which in turn continues to transform the Christian's sense of self and open him or her up to the possibility of further reconfiguration.

Gratitude for the Wonder of Creation

The virtue of gratitude is stimulated when humankind realizes that creation is a gift from God and not a mere happenstance. It is therefore assumed to have order, be intelligible, be capable of being understood, and above all, be responsive to love. It excites wonder and curiosity, which arouses an awareness of its liveliness and promise and the human desire to contribute to the never-ending process of its perfecting. We shall explore the implications of this in Chapter 4. Implicit in this and inseparable from it is an awareness of the liberty into which God delivers us, which enables us to be grateful in the first place and to live freely and creatively in all that we do and are. Indeed we are uniquely that dimension of the creation that is free to recognize what is worthy of our gratitude and the person or persons to whom it is proper to be grateful.

The expression of gratitude for the things that are worthy of it and to God, who is worthy of our thanks, is a transforming experience because, as Jesus revealed, it brings us into a right relationship with God. It reminds us of the context that makes sense of the fact that we can have good relationships with the world and with our fellow human beings. Humankind lacks its full potential when it fails to realize the presence of God and to develop in conversation a theological language with which to explore what it means to be grateful.

I discuss what this implies for our understanding of the self, which can be grateful more fully, in Chapter 3. But first, I shall explore further the central act of Christian worship, the Eucharist, in which God's giving of himself is associated and celebrated alongside the believer's offering of himself or herself to share in God's creating.

The Eucharist

The Eucharist is the thankful celebration of God's presence with his people in Jesus Christ. The celebration is not a *repetition* of an ur-event; instead, time is collapsed into the eternal moment in which creation and redemption are thankfully expressed in Christ's life, death, Resurrection, and ascension. To share in it, to celebrate it with Christ, is to be a thankful person committed to working toward what that means for one's treatment of the world, of other people, and indeed of oneself. One emerges from the event of the sacrament *in Christ*, free to serve the world with love in peace and justice. As the priest says at the conclusion of the service to all those assembled (and to all Christians wherever they are), "Go forth in the power of the Spirit to live and work to God's praise and glory."

The form itself is instructive. The Eucharist begins when one presents oneself, for by one's bodily presence among members of the community of faith that Christians call the Church, the believer acknowledges the presence of God, or at least, he or she acknowledges that he or she is committed to exploring what it means to remember and celebrate God's presence. The thought is brought to mind that we come into God's presence; his presence preceded ours. Our presence, let alone our moral worth, did not cause God to be present. We are responding to, grasping, an invitation that he graciously offers. When these thoughts are taken with the seriousness they merit, they open questions that stir the heart as well as puzzle and intrigue the mind. And they raise, above all, the fundamental question, who am I that God should choose to associate himself with me and with the rest of this community among whom I find myself? Indeed, who are we as humankind that God should choose to associate himself with us and all those among whom we find ourselves? What is this world in which we are set, and how does God come into the picture?

These questions provoke a sense of our incompleteness, inadequacy, and unworthiness, as well as the need for greater self-knowledge, remorse, the confession of sin, and a desire for forgiveness. The term "sin" is open to gross misunderstanding, probably due to the Church's comparatively recent practice of encouraging regular—even weekly—confession to a priest, which developed into a silly recalling of trivial matters of no real consequence. It reinforced a vision of God as always on the brink of withdrawing his affectionate concern and encouragement. Nothing could be further from the truth. In the sacrament of penance, we are made aware of God's continuing, forgiving presence, not of our failures.

The fact is that, as St. Augustine realized, but for God's eternal presence, there would be no sense in life at all, let alone the appreciation of the good things one already knows, such as the nourishing experiences of love and friendship. Herein lies the background in which a new language of faith is developing. The celebration flows naturally through the "Gloria" (the voicing of gratitude to the Trinitarian God), followed by readings from Scripture that reflect the development of Christian religious experience drawn from the Jewish Scriptures, the earliest Christian writings of the Epistles and the Gospels. The theme is taken up in a sermon by the priest, who attempts to reconfigure our common experience in the light of Christ's vision of God's presence in a world he is creating. All is gathered together in intercessory prayer, where the health of the whole world is brought to mind and commended to God's gracious care. A sign of peace is then exchanged along with the offering of the whole of creation in the matter of bread and wine, which is then consecrated by Jesus's words on the occasion of the Last Supper. This culminates in the solemn sharing of the bread and wine, the body and blood of Christ, and Christ's sending of the Church out into the world to bear witness to God's presence as it shares its thankfulness with all people.

Certain claims are implicit in the celebration. It is not simply the persons who are present at a particular celebration who are involved but all God's people—past, present, and future. The celebration is therefore what we may call a sanctification of time and a recognition of the vital importance of the historical process. As I have said, there can be no such thing as repetition: each time the Eucharist is celebrated, it is the one and only event of Christ's sacrifice and Resurrection with which the whole Church associates itself; indeed the one and only celebrant of the Eucharist is Christ himself, represented in the person of the priest, whose ordination is specifically for this purpose.

The event of the Eucharist culminating in the dismissal is a dynamic, living celebration of the true nature of human experience, dependent as it is on God's relationship with his creation, and the acceptance of the authority that flows from God's commitment of himself to the perfection of the world. The celebration is therefore proleptic—concerned with a future in which the whole Church, on behalf of all humanity, is to take its part in transforming the world so as to make real God's relationship with his creation.

Thankfulness, like faith itself, is proleptic, as it anticipates and enacts the future in principle and in practice: "Faith is the substance of things hoped for, the evidence of things not seen" (Heb. 11:1). This seemingly blind confidence expressed by the writer of the epistle to the

Hebrews in fact makes it plain that the person of faith is an intentional actor in the process of transformation, not a passive observer of something achieved by an outside agency. God is not an external power but a present authority with whom the believer is invited to cooperate. Gratitude is likewise a transforming power that effects a future change of direction and brings about a new state of affairs. There is plenty of evidence to confirm this, which makes mere compliance unsatisfying and personally unrewarding. Hence, as Ward wrote, "It is important for understanding the Christian way of life to cultivate the faculty of gratitude and nourish it as much as one can" (Ward, 1967, p. 20). This raises the very interesting question of whether gratitude can be nourished and, if so, how. It surely can. It is a question to which attention should be given in every person's education and in the education of the professional.

Is there any other ritual in which we can share that will remind us of the importance of gratitude and will actively increase our capacity to be grateful? Actually, it seems that humankind cannot do without rituals. Humans may or may not be religious, but whether they are or not, they will still, I suggest, draw their strength from traditional practices that are recognizably religious. For example, the Communist Party in the German Democratic Republic (DDR, Deutsche Demokratische Republik) adopted a ritual—the *Jugendweihe*—which had been developed by secular societies in the nineteenth century as a substitute for the confirmation found among Roman Catholic and Protestant Churches. Authorities in the DDR required even Christians to take part or suffer in education and employment. The ceremony, normally at 14 years of age, involved promises to serve the state and all socialist peace-loving peoples, to deepen friendship with the Soviet Union, and to fight in the spirit of proletarian internationalism to defend socialism against imperialism. In response, the initiates were accepted formally "into the great community of working peoples, which, under the direction of the working class and its revolutionary Party, united in will and action, is building the developed socialist society in the German Democratic Republic" (World Heritage Encyclopedia, 2014). One cannot miss the flavor of confirmation in the public ceremonies that the state had developed: they too were proleptic in their determination to create a society of people committed to "making a difference" through acting with others in the party to make peace and build the DDR. The contrast with Christian initiation is striking: in the Marxist world, the promised transformation was a result of human action, whereas within Christianity, it is the consequence of bearing witness, in word and action, to the way the world is when seen as characterized by the gracious presence of God.

Ward interestingly remarked, "It is Christian conviction that life in itself is neither meaningful nor holy, but that it can be made meaningful and holy. Thankfulness consecrates it, makes it meaningful and holy" (Ward, 1967, p. 21). This honesty needs to characterize all our relationships, whether they are with God or with our fellow human beings, including, therefore, those that flow from our professional responsibilities.

But Is Not Religion Irrelevant?

Given the presumed lack of interest in religion in the Western world—and indeed the positive opposition to religious belief among many who regard it as not only false but dangerously destructive to human well-being—is not a Christian theological framework beside the point? What can it possibly add to the consideration of moral values and their reconfiguration in the face of the current tendency to confine ethical judgment to mere compliance?

Three things can be said. First, religious belief is not as rare as it is often represented to be: formal church attendance may be falling (indeed it certainly is in the West), but that is a far cry from the assumption that religious belief is declining. The same may be said in response to those who point to figures suggesting that the numbers of those who say they believe in God lessen each year. Even if true, which I doubt, the world of spiritual life is of profound importance to a large proportion of the population. Indeed there are atheists, such as Alain de Botton, who intuit that there is something in Christian Faith that is of real significance for human well-being and needs to be cultivated (de Botton, 2012). Second, the universal ontological nature of a theological grounding for the role of gratitude provides a uniquely dynamic and encouraging perspective for human experience of the world. It assumes that the whole creation, including human life itself, is the gift of a God who is personally committed to its well-being. This has implications for every aspect of the virtuous life. The narrative of religious faith is one into which we can enter and take up the story for ourselves. Third, we have not yet come to the end of theological inquiry; it is encouraged and stimulated by engagement with contemporary developments in human understanding (Ford, 2011; Wilson, 2011). Certainly the claims of some scientists have not removed it from serious discussion (Hart, 2011). There is a never-ending quality about this that we would be foolish to abandon as

Donald MacKinnon observed in an introduction to John Henry Newman's *University Sermons*.

For Newman, such openness, as the empiricist temper counsels, is something in which men could discern a parable of the sort of openness of mind that faith demanded. What faith demanded of course was unique, but men could only harden their hearts the more against understanding the nature of that demand if they imprisoned themselves in the doubtless comforting womb of their own established assurance that the secrets of the world were known to them, at least in principle, the methods required for their perfect study at their fingertips (MacKinnon and Holmes, 1970, p. 21).

Conclusion

Christians are grateful for all the gifts implicit in God's gracious gift of creation and his commitment of himself to its perfection. In subsequent chapters, I shall explore the creative implications of this for our understanding of what it means to be human and what it means for a person's life and professional practice. Suffice it to say at this point that professional life is also proleptic, concerned as it is with anticipating the transformation of the world. The point is that a member of a profession has a vocation to serve the common good by focusing on a client's need. The conception of society involved is not confined to the here-and-now; it is necessarily anticipatory of the needs of future generations insofar as they can reasonably be understood. But that will only occur if he or she opens himself or herself to the virtue of gratitude and learns to be thankful.

In order to appreciate the wholeness of our world, which is conceived to be alive with the presence of God, it is necessary for me in later chapters to draw attention to some of the dimensions of our capacity to be curious, the need to be grateful for our human inheritance, the awakening of compassion, the reality of personal community, the desire to be of service, the possibility of new beginnings, the experience of relationship that comes from learning to give attention, a growing understanding of what we have to share and how we learn to share it, and the knowledge and opportunity to learn. But first, we must attend to the matter of the human self. Who or what is this self that knows what it means to be a grateful person with all that flows from that experience?

Chapter 3

A Christian Theological Understanding of the Self

Introduction

The relationship of a professional with a client has two dimensions: the personal and the professional. Both are vital, for when a lawyer is counseling a client, he is a human self as well as a professional drawing on his knowledge and experience. But what is a human self? I shall argue that the language implicit within the Christian theological framework inspires an understanding of the self that fruitfully informs both the personal and professional dimensions of professional practice.

The concept of "self" is distinguished from that of "person" and, following Kristjánsson, those of "personality" and "character" (Kristjánsson, 2010, pp. 25–28). "Personality" covers our moods, dispositions, and habits, which are the products of "conditioning," whereas "character" is concerned with moral worth and therefore subject to development by reason. The term "person" is both more general and more particular than the term "self." There is also the question of the relationship between the term "soul" as Christians conceive it theologically and the term "self" as discussed more generally in philosophy. I begin with some reflections on "person."

"Person": Some Approaches in Philosophy

P. F. Strawson regards "person" as a necessary, irreducible concept without which we would be unable to do justice to our first-person experience. "M-predicates," Strawson argues, refer to the material body (e.g., finger, brain), but they inadequately express what we believe about ourselves; there is, Strawson says, an essential role for "P-predicates" (e.g., in such sentences as "I remember," "I am warm"; Strawson, 1959, pp. 87–116).

The concept of "person," including both M- and P-predicates, has for some philosophers a substantial reality in contrast with that of "self"—the very existence of which is contentious. Thus one may point to a person: "He's over there, the person in the brown suit." One cannot, on the other hand, point to a self: "Who is that self with the red tie?" The self is an interior, first-person reality to which, according to Plato, I have exclusive access. This is disputed by Aristotle, who points out that friends may show me features of myself of which I was previously ignorant and thus enable me to make more equable moral judgments. However, since I am the person who knows whether or not what friends tell me is true, notwithstanding the fact that I may learn something about myself from interacting with others, I have access to my self, which no one else possesses. Thus I have a responsibility for myself, which I share with no one.

But is there such a thing as the self, and if there is, what is it? Hume rejects the very idea of the self as an object of perception; the self is an illusion because when he looks into himself, he has no firm and consistent impression of his self, only a series of impressions and ideas that he imagines to have reference (Hume, 1951, pp. 46–52, 251–52). But while Hume claims that each time he looks into himself, he has a new impression that brings into question the persistence of the self, he nevertheless later suggests that experience leads him to feel that he is a moral self—the product of emotional experience and subject to consistent development (Hume, 1951, pp. 275–90; Kristjánsson, 2010, pp. 46–52).

Searle affirms the reality of the self:

> In order to understand my visual perceptions, I have to understand them as occurring *from a point of view*, but the point of view itself is not something that I see or otherwise perceive . . . The point of view has no substantive features . . . it has to be that point from which my experiences take place . . . Now similarly the notion of a self that I am postulating is a purely formal notion but it is more complex. It has to be an entity, such that one and the same entity has consciousness, perception, rationality, the capacity to engage in action, and the capacity to organize and reason, so as to perform voluntary actions on the presupposition of freedom. If you have got all of that, you have a self. (Searle, 2004, p. 297)

Other views attract interest. Oliver Sacks (1985), Daniel Dennett (1992), and Owen Flanagan (2002), base identity of the self in personal narrative; this approach Galen Strawson contests (Strawson, 2004, pp. 428–52). However, while arguing that personal experience implies the existence of the self, which is a subject of experience, it does not, in his opinion, exist in any material sense because even mental "things" are physical (Strawson, 2009, pp. 281–85). But does this matter when I recognize that I have indubitable knowledge of myself as a subject of experience? Both Galen Strawson and Peter Strawson consistently deny that M-predicates deal adequately with our experience. For Galen Strawson, however, there are "S-predicates" as well as P-predicates and M-predicates. Both Strawsons affirm the idea of free will.

Any narrowly physical perspective is apparently inadequate to cover the concept of "person"; to refer to the person involves more than simply pointing to a body. When I refer to Johnson as *personally* responsible, I mean more than that Johnson's material body was the physical cause of the accident. There is a person, we believe, who knows what it means to accept moral responsibility. The whole person may be taken to be body, mind, and spirit, but even that is insufficient to satisfy what the Christian tradition means by imputing selfhood or "soulness" to a person. When one refers to a person, one is identifying a subject and an object that should both be treated with dignity. P. F. Strawson makes this clear when he holds together P-predicates and M-predicates in coming to terms with the ordinary experience of being a person (Strawson, 1959, pp. 104–6). For the Christian, however, person is more than body but less than self, which involves the notion of "soul."

Made in the Image of God

The Christian concept of the self is complex and even beyond words. But as Wittgenstein revealingly remarks, "Perhaps what is inexpressible (what I find mysterious and am not able to express) is the background against which whatever I could express has meaning" (Wittgenstein, 1980, p. 16e).

The Christian concept of the self, however, is countercultural, for its meaning is rooted in the essential relationship between humankind and God found in the biblical tradition. Discussion of the biblical material will be brief, but key perspectives will I hope become clear for our purpose. What we want is a sense of what Christians mean by "a grateful person" and what Christians understand this to suggest for "the practice of the Faith" and therefore also for professional practice.

I say "suggest" advisedly, since much debate takes place about the relation of theological inquiry and ethics. The idea that theological propositions straightforwardly imply moral certainties is generally rejected. Nevertheless, while there may be no deductive relationship between theology and ethics, an interactive coherence must be continuously worked for because, as I have argued, doing and saying are intimately connected. Christian theology offers a moral framework in which to think through ethical judgments, not a moral system from which they can be deduced (Roberts, 2013, pp. 13–17). One might put it this way: how do the theologically explored insights of Christianity grasp ethical principles on which we can rely when, as faithful selves (souls), we want to live with moral integrity?

The Christian understanding of the human self flows from the claim that humankind is made in the image of God:

> Then God said, "Let us make humankind in our image, according to our likeness; and let them have dominion over the fish of the sea, and over the birds of the air, and over the cattle, and over the wild animals of the earth, and over every creeping thing that creeps upon the earth." So God created humankind in his image, in the image of God he created them. God blessed them, and God said to them, "Be fruitful and multiply, and fill the earth and subdue it; and have dominion over the fish of the sea and over the birds of the air, and over every living thing that moves upon the earth." (Gen. 1:26–28)

There is no space here to discuss the multitude of scholarly interpretations of "made in the image of God." But the idea is central to Christian anthropology, a matter of current theological discussion and included in the catechisms of Catholic, Anglican, Orthodox, and Protestant traditions. The question of its meaning cannot be dodged.

The Hebrew word *tselem* has been translated as "likeness" with the implication of similarity, but it carries the sharper sense implied by "image": humankind is made in the *image* of God—that is, it "carries God's stamp." We cannot here be talking in physical terms, which "likeness" may suggest; the idea is irrelevant, since God has no material form. The better approach affirms that God's character informs the true character of humankind. Indeed God's creation of humankind implies its special relationship with him, since the Hebrew verb *bar'* is exclusively used of God's creative authority. Thus the clue to the nature of the human self lies in the nature of God, by whose gracious act humanity was brought into being and whose mark it bears. So what, if anything, can we usefully say of the nature of God?

First, God exists in "aseity"—that is, the nature of his being depends on nothing and no one but himself. God knows himself absolutely, but the mystery of his presence is beyond human grasp because of the very absoluteness of his being. He is therefore without external constraint or interior stress, free to commit himself to the well-being of his creation without anxiety that its existence and development will constitute a challenge to the knowledge he has of who he is in himself. God chooses out of his grace to create the world; he is not compelled to do so nor constrained by external circumstances in the manner of his creating.

Second, in the profoundest sense, God loves the world that he is making and pronounces it good. Thus we say that God, in his creating, is graciously redemptive; God continuously makes and renews the world in order to bring it to itself. He is eternally himself and acts with authority in accord with his own nature.

Third, there is no end to the lengths to which he is willing to go in order to seek the essential participation of creation in its own coming into being. God crowns creation with humankind made "in his image," endowing it with the freedom to know itself, the created world, and him whose creation it is.

Fourth, God identifies himself in Christ with his creating in order to show absolutely that nothing can separate him from his creation and its coming to perfection.

There is a wholeness about the human self as thus conceived, at least potentially, that is compatible with the wholeness of God himself. The human is not a divided being any more than God and therefore cannot be understood as divided into body, mind, and spirit. Linguistic usage in the Bible makes this plain. The Hebrew word *nephesh*, often translated as "soul," refers to what one is in oneself, not to something one possesses—a perspective closer to Aristotle than Plato, as Aquinas perceived. And what one is, a soul, is the result of one's relationship with God, one's Creator (Pedersen, 1926, pp. 99–181). We are capable of knowing not simply *that* we exist, but *who* we are by virtue of our relationship with God, for it is through God's gracious gift of the spirit (*nephesh*) that we are who we are. To turn away from God is to be a fool, to lack any sense of oneself as a self and behave as if there were no limits to what one can do or who one can become. To deny one's nature as a human being and in one's pride neglect to search for wisdom is to suffer with the ungodly (Ps. 14:1–7; Prov. 1:20–22). The human being is profoundly a unity, a soul.

St. Paul's use of anthropological terms is an insightful expression of this conviction (Jewett, 1971). Whatever human relationships St. Paul is exploring, he is clear that he is talking of the totality of human selfhood: the human self is indivisible. Thus, when a person sets his or her mind (Gk., *nous*) and heart (Gk., *kardia*) on God, the person *is* a soul (Gk., *psyche*); when he or she abandons that dimension of aspiration and focuses on satisfying mere bodily needs and desires, the person's whole self becomes subject to corruption and is, in Pauline terminology, "flesh" (Gk., *sarx*). Paul on two occasions refers to the "inner man" (Gk., *eso anthropos*), which he identifies with the human heart (Gk., *kardia*), the term that Paul used to symbolize the whole person as daily renewed by God's spirit (Gk., *pneuma*). In each case, a person remains "body," a whole person capable of relationships with himself or herself and other persons and therefore of commitment to God in faith; a human being is a subject with a personality who really exists (Gk., *soma*; Bultmann, 1952, pp. 192ff.). Hence, when talking of Resurrection, Paul cannot imagine a "future life" without "body." Interestingly, it seems neither could Strawson (Strawson, 1959, p. 116). Personhood is an object of perception that identifies the individual as a persistent entity; the Christian notion of the self is dependent on the reality of God's presence and is affirmed by God's grace. The human being is free to take responsibility for himself or herself in relationship with other people, with the world, and with God. What that amounts to is a matter of serious concern.

Let Them Have Dominion

In *Genesis*, the divine making of humankind in God's image is followed by God's giving humankind dominion over creation. Sometimes Christians have mistakenly assumed that the natural world has been handed over to humanity to use for its own purposes. John Passmore offers a trenchant critique of this point of view. He is particularly hard on those approaches that draw upon the biblical tradition to justify a despotic attitude by humans toward nature (Passmore, 1974, pp. 3–27). It is true that influential traditions of Christian belief still flourish that expect the imminent end of the world and therefore see no reason to care for the environment, let alone to safeguard it for future generations. The notion of stewardship is foreign to their thinking.

Such a view is a gross misunderstanding of God and his relation to creation. He cannot "hand over" to humankind the care of his creation. Nothing could be further from the truth. In fact, the orthodox

Christian attitude toward God's creation is that God saw that it was good and committed himself to its well-being. In view of what we know about the natural world, the potential devastating impact of human activity, and the fact that humankind is itself a part of nature, we need to think carefully about what it means for *God* to have dominion and therefore the nature of the dominion that he urges humankind to exercise in his name, with his authority. Humankind has no independent authority.

How does God exercise authority? What would it mean for humankind (made in the image of God) to act with the same character. What qualities inform God's exercise of authority, and how will humankind act in conformity with the authority God has given it? It is easy to conceive of God's authority on the analogy of human power as if, in contrast with the limitations we experience, there is nothing that God in his omnipotence is prevented from doing. This is not only false as an understanding of God but totally misleading as far as human behavior is concerned.

God does not model himself on human behavior. On the contrary, God acts in accord with his own unique character. When he acts, he reveals *himself*. Were he to behave in an authoritarian manner, he would be false to his nature of love, since he would deny his creation any possibility of self-awareness: it would only exist insofar as it was possessed by God. But we know that the Creator and the creation are not to be confused. In order to be himself, he will therefore need to exercise his authority courteously by affirming the real being of creation. God's authority is not demonstrated by the exercise of power over others, though logically it may be the case that God has such absolute power. But that is the point: God chooses to exercise power not over others but over himself. God is therefore omnipotent in the sense that he uses his power to rein in any temptation (if one may use that term of God) that he may have to lose control of himself, be other than who he is, and serve his own interests rather than those of the world he is graciously creating. In other words, God's exercise of his authority in creating depends on the fact that he liberates creation to act freely of itself in the persons of humankind. God's authority is authoritative, not authoritarian.

To claim that humankind is created in God's image is to acknowledge that the fullness of human life will be expressed not in an authoritarian manner but in an authoritative one. Moreover, God has, in his grace, granted to humankind the freedom to control the temptation it naturally has to act in its own interests, ignorant of the nature of the world and without regard to its relationship with God. In fact, humans may choose to neglect this opportunity and so fall into what Christians call "sin." Even so, as Aquinas affirms, the graced nature of humanity is not wholly erased: freedom to be oneself remains a possibility. When humankind treats the world of creation as a resource to be possessed and spent wantonly on human prosperity, it mistakenly denies the world of creation any independent value of its own. In so doing, humankind not only mistakes the nature of God's creation but chooses to act contrary to its own nature. As Paul might say, such behavior reduces a human being to flesh, whereas in reality, he or she is a soul, a self with self-knowledge, capable of exercising self-discipline because of the reality of the relationship that he or she can enjoy with God.

The human acceptance of the authority of God must be freely and responsibly undertaken. It is more than following orders—"Do as I say because I say so." If humankind is to grow in the awareness of what it means to be made in the image of God and what that means for the life of humankind, the response to that relationship must be voluntary. After all, there are precious few, if any, "commands" of God whose meanings are transparent; they all need to be interpreted and lived out in responsible experimentation. Nevertheless, it is clear that the biblical tradition affirms that humankind is called to be obedient to the will of God; indeed Jesus asks his disciples to join him in his prayer to the Father: "Thy will be done in earth as it is in heaven" (Deut. 11:26–28; Jer. 7:23–26; Matt. 6:10).

Willing obedience implies understanding the situation in which one finds oneself, and to that end, humankind is endowed by God with the gift of curiosity about the world and about humankind's role in it. The account of Isaiah's vision refers to God's calling of the Israelites and their rebellion against him. He rejects the various japes that they have adopted in order to try to ignore him and the authority they thought it possible to exercise but affirms their continuing relationship by inviting them to "argue it out." If they do, then they will find God and themselves and enjoy "the good of the land" (Is. 1:17–20). An analogous point of view is found in Jesus's parable of the talents. Humankind has the capital—namely, its natural curiosity and the freedom to invest it profitably. The servant who buried his talent failed because of laziness or a mistaken assumption that he could take advantage of the initiative of others (Matt. 25:14–30). Parables are often wrongly interpreted as threats of punishment; they are better considered stories of failure to accept responsibility.

Persons in Community

Humans depend on one another in their pursuit of wisdom and responsible behavior. We are not private individuals who have to find others to make community. On the contrary, people will only identify their selfhoods insofar as they recognize that they are born into community—indeed into many communities—which include the graced world of physical creation, family, nation, and all the many communities of which they are members and that they inherit through collective memory and explore in conversation. Human curiosity and human inquiry are not lonely matters but cooperative enterprises shared through experiment, memory, discourse, and fellowship.

All knowledge is the result of teamwork, not limited to the contemporary community of scholarship, but including the results of generations of human experience and inquiry. St. Paul's anthropology implies that humankind, born in the image of God, is capable of self-knowledge through inquiring about the world with others. In so doing, we become self-consciously aware of the freedom we have to partner with God and undertake a special role in creation. The selves that we become are products of habitual behavior encouraged by our attention to God, who constantly reminds us that notwithstanding our tendency to give up, behave like fools, and follow false gods, we can behave so as to reveal to ourselves and in ourselves the image of God. The Christian's habitual praying of the Our Father reminds him or her of the rigor of the demand while at the same time recalling God's courteous pouring out of his spirit in renewal so that he or she can still realistically aspire to be in the image of God despite all evidence to the contrary. Such a life, lived dutifully and affectionately, will lead and nourish the Christian's soul so that he or she really is in the eye of God; ultimately, it will enliven the Christian's awareness of the vision of God, for whom in fact he or she longs and in whom he or she lives. In so doing, the Christian fulfills his or her calling to share the character of God and give himself or herself for the world's sake.

This is the ultimate ground for gratitude: a feeling and a cognitive experience that informs one's awareness of oneself as a child of God.

Christ, the True Image of God

God reveals himself in Christ's humanity, the Word of God through whom all things were made and by whose life and death is revealed the wholeness of God's presence. He is the true image of the Father

(Jn. 1:1–5). Theologians fashionably talk of Christ as if that were possible without "standing on secure doctrinal ground concerning God" (Turner, 2013, p. 100). I have tried to avoid that here. In one sense, there is nothing "new" in Christ; he reveals the true nature of creation and embodies the authoritativeness of God's power in the world by his unassertiveness. His life, teaching, example, Crucifixion, death, Resurrection, and ascension confirm that God's love for his creation will never be withdrawn: He is *really* present, immovable. He always has been, is, and will be. His love is offered unconditionally without prejudice, though what is meant by unconditionality needs to be carefully attended to, for it calls us to follow the painful, self-giving example of Christ and focus our selves upon loving God for his sake, not for what we can get out of it.

Those who recognize this enter into the divinely given freedom of Christ, and even as they try to understand what it means to be obedient, they are able to love creation and all other creatures without fear through giving themselves to its flourishing. This is what it means to be made in the image of God. Each human being is capable of becoming a self who, through coming to know the intimacy of the love that God has for creation, is able to be a member of the Body of Christ and partner with God in caring for his world. It is vital to keep in mind that this is true of all people, not simply those who call themselves Christians; there is no limit to God's loving authoritativeness or therefore to the potential self-giving love of which humankind is capable (Gen. 1:27; Gal. 3:27–29; Rev. 21:1–4). In all circumstances, we can be the selves we truly are because we know that we belong to the creation of the loving God who will not abandon us to our own devices.

I previously alluded to the importance of habit in forming good dispositions of behavior. Jesus taught his disciples to pray regularly *with him* the Our Father. The fact that Christ asks his disciples to pray *with him* his prayer to his and their Father reminds them of the capacity they have to act in the image of God with the freedom to give themselves to the "other" without regard for reward. In fact, they can be *real* human beings.

The central claim of Christian anthropology is that the entity that is the human "self" is characterized by an open relationship with the world, with other people, and above all, with God, in whose image the human being is created. The Christian concept of the self is real only insofar as it takes its reality from its relationship with God.

The Christian Self

There is much in common between the Christian and the Aristotelian notions of the self with respect to the reality of its existence. The Christian position is that the human self is real, not illusory; it is "a willing and knowing self," which can be orientated in a particular direction when it chooses to be "led by the divine spirit" (Bultmann, 1952, p. 207). For Aristotle, the human self is "capable of forming intentions to honour objective moral properties, and to do so, over time, by developing stable, self-shaping, virtuous dispositions" (Kristjánsson, 2010, p. 128). However, whether this takes form in a person's life, according to Aristotle, depends on early intervention through education, the influence of virtuous friends, and having one's attention focused on excellent models on which one can base one's thinking and behavior. For the Christian, however, the self is not defined by reference to a limited *moral* dimension. As I have suggested previously, "self," as the Christian understands the term, implies an ontological dimension that follows from the intimacy of the commitment of God's self to his creation and the capacity of humankind to seek to bear fruit as it comes to love God and grows to understand its calling to *be* in the image of God. For the Christian, the excellent model for moral guidance is Christ. But this is not because he is simply a good moral guide; there are others, such as Socrates. Christ is only a good moral guide because he is "of one being with the Father," the only Son of the Father who embodies the character of the Living God. The Christian "self" is real in the sense that he or she exists through God's grace; he or she expresses himself or herself in the created world of common experience in psychological terms and moral behavior.

Actually, the term "self" is rarely used in theological discussion; when it is, it normally refers loosely to personal identity, by which is meant more than mere physicality but does not exclude the body. The more usual theological term is "soul," but that is frequently misunderstood, associated as it is in the public mind with some supposed additional feature possessed by the human being. "Has a human being a soul?" is a misleading question, for as we have seen, when God gives the spirit to humankind, it is not something added to or poured into the body; it is what makes humankind human: the event affirms that what it means to be human assumes a relationship with God. In Christian theology, the soul is who one really is in relation to God. The self is an embodied soul, not an illusion.

However, it is also true that I may not know myself for who I really am and may be deceived by my weakness of will into behaving in ways that, in the event, I would wish that I had not. I may in fact be subject to the Aristotelian condition of self-deception and take my idea of myself at a given moment to be all there is to who I am. That would be false and indeed destructive. The "calling" of God, hints of his presence, and a sense of the worthwhileness of seeking to understand and respond to him can potentially open or reopen dimensions of one's experience and of one's self. The self, looked at from the point of view of Christian Faith, is indeed capable of development and is free to change with the possibility of a growing maturity in relationship with God. The self will grow through knowledge of the world as creation, cooperation with others, and above all, seeking God.

Moreover, in whatever particular experience one is involved, the Christian self/soul is multifaceted in its capacity to learn: it is open to learning through the emotions, the intellect, moral awareness, aesthetic appreciation, and religious experience. There is no valid Christian position that is reductionist—repositioning oneself so as to take into account further dimensions is always possible. To leave out any of the ways in which experience is open to us is to live an incomplete life; their neglect cuts off not just experience of the world as it really is but a part of the self. One might almost say that such a self is handicapped, incapable of full expression, because it lacks openness to the range of experience that feeds the soul and nourishes a potential relationship with God. It is vital to keep this in mind when planning a school curriculum or the education of a professional: there is always more to it than one imagines.

In fact, it is much more complex than even this. For each of the facets of what it means to be a self, a soul, interacts with all the others. Thus, for example, Kristjánsson affirms with regard to Aristotle, "Aristotle could not have implicated emotions in moral virtues if he had not presupposed that emotions have a cognitive component amenable to rational and moral evaluation—and, if necessary (if it turns out to be irrationally formed, morally unjustified or both), liable to criticism and change" (Kristjánsson, 2010, p. 14). The converse is also true. Many a conclusion of rational inquiry causes unease because while it may not be false, there is more to be said if one is to grasp the whole picture. The civil engineer who, indifferent to local needs, builds a road through the middle of a community is simply a bad engineer. Good engineers want to see the situation in the round. Furthermore, aesthetic appreciation can transform what one is engaged with and open one's eyes to a moral depth of which one previously had been ignorant or to a wholeness that one's focused attention had missed.

The religious framework will bring together cognitive inquiry, moral sensitivity, and aesthetic appreciation and thus stimulate an awareness of the wholeness of things and their interrelatedness. But none of them individually or together reveals things as they are in themselves: their aseity keeps them free from our possession with lives of their own, forever presenting new opportunities of knowledge. Merleau-Ponty, in his analysis of perception, is fully aware of this: we can never "possess" what we perceive, for by so doing, we would destroy it. "If the thing itself were grasped," he says, "it would from that moment be arrayed before us and stripped of its mystery. It would cease to exist as a thing at the very moment when we thought to possess it. What makes the 'reality' of the thing is therefore what precisely snatches it from our grasp. The aseity of the thing, its unchallengeable presence and the perpetual absence into which it withdraws, are two inseparable aspects of transcendence" (Merleau-Ponty, 1962, p. 233).

I suggested previously that the Christian understanding of the human self, as described in theological language as the "soul," is currently countercultural. Iain McGilchrist offers an explanation as to why this should be so in terms of the physiology of the brain (McGilchrist, 2009). Every activity of the brain involves both left and right hemispheres, yet evolution has preserved a difference between them in how they work, which one can assume therefore has a value. They are complementary, but one of the hemispheres may come to dominate through habitual use. This is the case, McGilchrist believes, with the left hemisphere, which is focused on the formation of theories and their application to develop practical solutions to problems. The reduction of the influence of the right hemisphere of the brain, which is open to new experiences and the world of the imagination, has reduced our awareness to what our manageable "theories" allow us to consider.

McGilchrist believes the consequence is that we have become socially and emotionally insensitive, with an impaired understanding, for example, of beauty, art, and religion. This has even distorted our appreciation of scientific inquiry and encouraged the thought that we can possess and control things that are inevitably beyond our control. The fact is, he argues, that the right hemisphere is unconsciously alive to all dimensions of experience and provides information that the left hemisphere can include in its experimenting. However, we are now handicapped because we have so conditioned ourselves to live within the world as presented by the left hemisphere that we are inclined to neglect the stimulating world of the imagination and any sense of being aware of the "wholeness" that is open to us. Yet the self who is learning is me, or you, or us; the knowledge that we gain is personal knowledge. A Christian understanding of the self implies that its maturity depends on the full functioning of both hemispheres of the brain.

The idea is fleshed out further by Michael Polanyi, whose brilliant insights are often neglected (Polanyi, 1958; 1966). He argued a point with which Wittgenstein would have agreed: we humans can know more than we can tell. The activities of both the right hemisphere and the left hemisphere are essential if we are to take up the ever-present opportunity to be ourselves in community. Polanyi practiced as a medical doctor and later as a physical chemist. He thus had the experience of dealing with the personal world of patients and the inanimate world of scientific inquiry. Of course, he did not argue that one opposed the other; the one was incomplete without the other. In both, he believed he was involved as a person and aware of the knowledge that his intellectual passion gave him through sympathy, interest, and emotional focus on what he was attending to. He called it "personal knowledge" and claimed that it was an essential ingredient of successful science and all other forms of human inquiry. Maurice Merleau-Ponty, from his phenomenological perspective, shares something of the same point of view when he refers to the body as expression and as speech. What the body is, he said, is what it says (Merleau-Ponty, 1962, pp. 174–99).

Love: The Wholeness of Commitment

The potential wholeness of a personal and participatory relationship with God, with the world, and with other people is the key to the understanding of the Christian perception of the self. So where does this take us when we as Christians try to come to terms with our selves as responsible persons? The self is *real* insofar as it seeks to grow in relation to God and in its knowledge of the world, of which it is a dimension and within which it is set, and as it works in responsible cooperation with other people. These are not independent functions or attitudes. On the contrary, we are whole persons in each case, not divided beings; we find ourselves in relation to God through affectionate attention to the well-being of creation and with others in the loving acceptance of responsibility for creation's movement toward perfection. Being and doing are one in the case of God: to live in his image is to aspire to share the same coherence. However, human distinctiveness means that we are aware of the gap between our human being and human doing to which it is necessary to attend.

The wholeness of the Christian understanding of the human is illuminated when we consider the crucial relationships implicit in the experience of love. The challenging nature of what it means to be a loving person is plain when put alongside the Christian belief that humankind is made in the image of God. Christians believe God's loving purpose is to create a world capable, through human beings, of freely acknowledging his loving authority. The fulfillment of God's purpose demands, in gratitude, the total commitment of the faithful person's whole self to creation's well-being. The incarnation—the loving presence of God in Christ—expresses this: the world of God's creation can accept the wholeness of what it means for God to be God without threat to the nature of God or the world of human being. The Crucifixion points to the utter reality of God's commitment: here in Christ is the wholeness of God, not a dimension of the Divine. The Resurrection and ascension point to the eternal, indelible, ever-present character of God's love.

In order to stimulate a free response to work with God in fulfilling his purpose, God imbues humankind with a sense of its own independent identity. The world is thus given the freedom to live a life of gratitude in response to God's love through the self-offering of humankind. The Church, the community of faith, reminds itself of this in each celebration of the Eucharist, when it gratefully celebrates and identifies itself with the fact of God's living and loving presence with his people. Just as God is not divided in his commitment of himself to creating the world, the response of each human being in gratitude to God involves his or her whole self. Each dimension of human experience—intellectual, emotional, aesthetic, moral—contributes to the life of the whole person, not to an aspect of it. It inspires a personal curiosity to explore the world with others and, above all, to know him who is the loving Creator.

Grateful Selves

Every dimension of what it means to be a loving person needs to be placed within the Christian theological understanding of God and the reciprocity of the love that God has for humankind and that humankind can have for God. The Christian acknowledgment that human beings are made in the image of God indicates that as whole persons united in themselves—as souls in fact—they are at liberty to follow the example of Christ. In so doing, Christians express their gratitude to God for all they have received and all they are when they give themselves in service to the well-being of the world, their neighbors, and society at large. This has implications for every human being who wants to contribute to "the common good," which I assume includes every professional. The professional who knows what it means to be grateful to God is free to take account of other selves and to give attention to the client's personal well-being, as well as his or her professional concern. In so doing, both professional and client are helped toward self-conscious maturity. There is no professional responsibility that is free from value judgment. Compliance and moral concern arise together and are in mutual support of one another. This is a fact that is true for everyone, though the Christian will ground it in the particular human relationship with God.

To sum up, my discussion of the Christian concept of selfhood has shed the following light on the concept of gratitude as understood in the Christian tradition. In the beginning, there is the wholeness of the commitment of God's self to the world's well-being. Our understanding of ourselves is rooted in our gratitude for this gift; the wholeness of humankind's gratitude is expressed in the personal quality of its relationship with God, creation, and other people. God's creative authority is apparent in his desire to reveal himself graciously rather than to demand attention, let alone unthinking obedience, to his commands. Hence he is said in Genesis to have taken care to see that the world was good (Gen. 1:31). The Hebrew word *tobh* covers a wide range of meanings but is commendatory in principle like the use of the English word "good." In the case of the creation, the book of Genesis declares that God pronounces each day's work to be "good," which gives what he does special significance. I suggest that it implies that God was satisfied that his creation was capable of bearing the stamp of his loving presence and encouraging the character of human response in his image.

If that is indeed the character of God's world, it can therefore be understood and, above all, enjoyed by humankind, since it will naturally encourage an analogous (if not identical) character and the emergence of a reciprocal quality of love. This is a key aspect of what it means to be human when looked at from the Christian perspective: humankind is blessed with the capacity to give and receive love. God profoundly realizes this in the person of Christ: "God so loved the world that he gave his only Son that whoever believes in him may not perish but may have eternal life" (Jn. 3:16). I take "eternal life" here to imply "eternal awareness of the loving presence of God." For those who have eyes to see, for those who have faith, the world *does* express the loving presence of God; so clearly is this the case that it can bear the stamp of God himself without threatening the distinct nature of either God or the creation. The invitation to humankind to try to follow the example of Christ and live in the image of God is therefore reasonable and not impossible. It was Pierre de Caussade, SJ, the French eighteenth-century writer on spirituality, who remarked that our Lord would not have commended perfection as a reasonable ambition for human beings if it were impossible. He goes on to say, "Be ye therefore perfect as your Father in heaven is perfect" (cf. Matt. 5:48). It is possible in the moment; unfortunately, pride leads us to aim beyond our strength, which is not God's will. As de Caussade writes, "The duty of the present moment is the only rule" (de Caussade, 1921, p. 57).

However, love is not an exclusive quality of the life of the faithful Christian. The Israelite tradition assumed love to be the central focus of the life of the pious Jew, who prayed the following every day: "Hear, O Israel: the Lord our God is one Lord, and you shall love the Lord your God, with all your heart, and with all your soul, and with all your mind" (Deut. 6:4–5). This must be put alongside the words of the book of Leviticus, "You shall love your neighbour as yourself" (Lev. 19:18). These two commands assume that humankind's love of God embraces all one's senses and the wholeness of creation, including other people. These many aspects of love were held together formally in Christ (Mk. 12:29–31).

Some Comparisons and Contrasts

Debate about what it means to love has led to much confusion. For example, in discussing Christian anthropology there are some distinctions that are often asserted to be crucial to its understanding. I am thinking, for example, of Law and Gospel, *eros* and *agape*, altruism and self-love. Let's briefly take these in turn: first, the supposed distinctiveness of Law and Gospel.

It is often claimed the Christian Gospel replaces the Law with love, whereas Jesus's claim is to have fulfilled the Law, not to have overthrown it: "Do not think that I have come to abolish the law or the prophets; I have come not to abolish but to fulfill" (Matt. 5:17). In effect, he extends and deepens the demands of the Law so that motives, not simply acts, are included. But this is implicit also as we see in the Israelite view of life; indeed it is explicit in the idea of the covenant relationship that the Israelites believed God had established with them. God's demands are on the character of the whole person, not the objective observance of rules and regulations.

Second, a contrast is often assumed to exist between *eros* and *agape*. However, they also need to be explored together: they are not conflicting dimensions of love such that *eros* is to be eschewed and *agape* embraced. Anders Nygren (1890–1978), a Swedish Lutheran theologian, argued that *agape* was, in opposition to *eros*, the only true characterization of Christian love (Nygren, 1969). *Eros* is human love and therefore essentially self-regarding: only God is capable of *agape*, he claimed, because only God is capable of unconditional love. But this is a mistake.

In Genesis, when God is said to have seen on each day of creation that the world was good (Heb., *tobh*), he took pleasure in it and anticipated doing so in the future. The point is that his behavior is always true to his nature of self-giving love so that his feelings are invariably well-disposed toward human well-being and that of the whole of creation. It is thus in contrast to the human situation in which feelings are themselves capable of dominating behavior; indeed Hume was of the opinion that all human behavior was stimulated by the emotions to the exclusion of reason.

Yet humans are made in the image of God and therefore are capable of acting with the same sacrificial self-giving love as God. In any case, *eros* is not simply feelings; both *eros* and *agape* are to be enjoyed. Human beings are one in body, mind, and spirit; to fail to recognize the proper sensitivity of human beings to beauty and the world of the senses is to deny the reality of their bodily presence. That is impossible if one is to be true to oneself.

A third mistaken contrast is made between altruism and self-love. To give oneself to the service of others will not be helped normally if, in so doing, one neglects one's own well-being. Jesus's response to the question, "Teacher, what good deed must I do to have eternal life?" includes, "You shall love your neighbour as yourself" (Matt. 19:16b, 19b). What each believer wants is to commend the love of God to all; this is impossible if we are not at the same time wanting ourselves to love God more. It is to embrace the Christlike understanding of what it means to live in the image of God.

Conclusion

We human beings, made in the image of God, are capable of taking responsibility for one another, for our environment, and for ourselves. A world appreciated as a creation in which God is graciously present is one for which we can be truly grateful and in which we can grow into being grateful persons. As professionals, therefore, we can give ourselves to the well-being of the persons whose interests we share without diminishing ourselves or our capacity to take and accept responsibility for ourselves. This opens up the question of responsibility: how can we become "response-able" and thus learn to be responsible? In the following chapter, I examine what it means to accept gratefully our God-given curiosity and inquire into God's creation, other people, and our own nature.

Chapter 4

Becoming Response-Able
Learning to Be Responsible

Introduction

The world that we enjoy is nourished by God's loving presence. When we appreciate that with gratitude, we are liberated to love God and free to serve the world with gladness. All humans are made in the image of God, who calls them to work with him in creation. We find our true, caring selves as we respond to this call. However, in order to act responsibly, we must know what we are doing and what the assumptions and implications are. Aristotle affirmed human nature to be essentially curious: we want to learn. Christians go deeper; they believe our natural curiosity to experiment and inquire is God-given. God endows us with the talent we need to accept the responsibility to which he calls us. We can learn; by so doing, we become more response-able—that is, better equipped with new knowledge—and therefore liberated to act more wisely and responsibly. However, in order to learn, we must love what we want to understand, whether that is ourselves, another person, our environment, or God. No wonder Christians are grateful to God, not only for the creation, but for their capacity to learn about it and to find it lovable and beautiful. We are free to live in the image of God, to share God's character, and to give ourselves to the world's flourishing.

There are implications here for professional persons who are called to take responsibility for themselves, their clients, and the common good. In order to do so with integrity, they require knowledge and experience based on experiment and inquiry. The responsible professional will pursue knowledge and take the risk of acting upon it with appropriate courtesy as a steward of the world's well-being. In this chapter, I explore some implications of these themes; the meaning of creation, the freedom of love, the experience of community with its diversity, the glue of language, and the promise of wholeness.

CURIOSITY AND CREATION

Curiosity does not begin with the Christian tradition. "All men by nature desire to know," Aristotle observed (Aristotle, 1984a, *Met.*, 980a25, 1552). The extant Aristotelian corpus testifies to the breadth of Aristotle's own inquiry.

The Christian, too, is intrigued and excited by his many-splendored world—its physical nature, social diversity, linguistic complexity, and moral ambiguity. In the case of the Christian, this is all the more true for the very particular reason that he or she believes it to be the creation of God. But what does this mean? God's creating is continuous, not an "event"; moreover, God sees that it is good. "Good" means more than "pretty" or "nice"; it means "fit for purpose." God regards creation, which he endows with a life of its own, as worthy of his loving presence. As Christians see it, God invests himself in his creating.

The loving relationship between God and his creation is expressed in the profound language of St. John's Gospel: "In the beginning was the Word, and the Word was with God, and the Word was God. He was in the beginning with God. All things came into being through him, and without him not one thing came into being. What has come into being in him was life, and the life was the light of all people. The light shines in the darkness, and the darkness overcame it not" (Jn. 1:1–5). The apostle's insight lies at the heart of the Christian understanding of God, of the world as God's creation, and of God's gracious involvement with the world.

The Hebrew Scriptures construe the Word of Yahweh to be the guiding principle of Jewish life in the community (Brown, Fitzmyer, and Murphy, 1995, p. 1292). The Israelites' defiance of God's Word may lead them into trouble, but God's gracious word, spoken in creation and through the prophets, nevertheless reminds them of who they are and what, including their liberty, they owe to Yahweh.

St. John identifies God's Word with Jesus Christ, the embodiment of God's gracious expression of himself to and in his creation. The Word is coeternal with God so that the purpose of God in creating is inherent in his nature as the Creator. Nothing outside the reality of God's Being causes him to intervene in the world to, as it were, put it right by "sending his Son," for he is eternally present. There is neither beginning nor ending to God's caring. Gregersen argues in an illuminating article that the Christian understanding of God is that he is "the ultimate reality, at once the source of all reality and pervasively present throughout time and space" (Gregersen, 2014, pp. 99–129). Furthermore, there is nothing within the world of God's creation that is an alien intrusion, since God's authority is conceived by Christians to be all-encompassing. God's caring for the world can never be extinguished because his love is identical to his eternal Being. God's Being and God's doing are one. For him, to speak is to act: "Then God said, 'let there be light,' and there was light" (Gen. 1:3).

The Christian assertion that God is present to and for creation is neither panentheistic nor pantheistic, for God is independent of the world, and the world is independent of God. God's continuous affirmation of the world means that the Christian rightly talks in terms of creation and not happenstance. Indeed the key to making sense of the Christian claim that God creates the world is to explore the quality of the implied relationship between God and the world and what it means for our understanding of the nature of God and human being. That humankind is free to be curious about this relationship lies at the heart of what humankind is grateful for: it opens a real possibility of "knowing itself" through knowing the Creator.

A vital implication of the relationship that the Christian asserts to exist between God and the world is that no complete understanding of the world—or therefore, of his or her own sense of what it means to be human—can exist that fails to take account of God. The natural curiosity with which humankind finds itself endowed is a God-given gift implicit in creation; it is part of our human nature. Not to accept with gratitude God's invitation to explore the world (including ourselves) amounts to denying our God-given nature and implicitly even his existence. To choose not to be curious is a dimension of human sinfulness, a falling short of the glory of God, a failure to recognize that a full human life is always lived in the presence of God in the Trinity—Father, Son, and Holy Spirit.

Of course, it is ultimately impossible to be a human being and not want to inquire, which is why Aquinas, for example, is right when he points to the fact that the desire for God cannot be ultimately extinguished in human life. Rahner makes a similar point: "Our actual nature is *never* pure nature. It is a nature installed in a supernatural order, which man can never leave, even as sinner and unbeliever"

(Rahner, 1966, p. 183). Wesley, the Founder of Methodism, concurs when in a sermon called "On Working Out Our Own Salvation," he says, "No man sins because he has not grace, but because he does not use the grace which he has"(Wesley, 1872). There is always opportunity to respond to the world as God's creation, to "find oneself" and recover that lively sense of gratitude for one's relationship with God on which one's human nature depends.

Our desire to understand is not limited, as MacIntyre, a key virtue ethicist, makes clear in his vision of our humanity:

> What is distinctive about the theistic view of the nature of things is not only that theists assert the existence of God and that they take the world to be fully intelligible only if understood in its relationship to God, but that they conceive of human beings as occupying a unique position in the order of things. Human beings are on the one hand bodies, having a physical, chemical, and animal nature, inhabiting an immediate environment, located at particular points in space and time. Yet on the other hand their understanding extends indefinitely beyond their immediate environment to what is remote in space and time and to the abstract and universal as well as to the concrete and the particular.
>
> And their aspiration to complete and perfect their understanding of the order of things and of their place within it is matched by an aspiration to achieve a relationship with a fully and finally adequate object of desire, an end to which if they understand themselves rightly (on the theistic view), they are directed by their nature. Yet human beings are not animal bodies plus something else. The human being is a unity, not a duality. (MacIntyre, 2009, pp. 77–78)

Free to Love

"Disinterested intellectual curiosity is the lifeblood of real civilization" (Trevelyan, 1944, p. viii). Indeed it is. But as MacIntyre implies, it is crucially an activity of the whole person. To inquire with affectionate concern is to strive to live in God's image by accepting responsibility with God for the knowledge and wisdom that is the product of one's inquiry. In effect, as the Hebrew tradition has it, the human being is a cocreator with God. He or she, like God, is free to love the world and commit himself or herself to its well-being.

The world is lovable because it can be explored, experimented with, reflected upon, and increasingly understood. The world's intelligibility is a dimension of the fact that God saw that his creation was good, a worthy object of the love of both God and humankind. Humankind therefore "possesses" neither love nor the good; they are divine absolutes in which we participate, even as they transcend us. Their pursuit is a lifetime's grateful work but not just for an individual, for it is set in the context of the pursuit of truth by the whole human race. God's creating presence in his Word guarantees the intelligibility of the world and at the same time, in Christ, expresses the world's capacity to respond to his love.

Of course, words are not incidental; they are necessary if we are to explain, interpret, question, and unpack the meaning of what we think we are beginning to discern through our inquiring. Above and beyond what we see and enjoy—our human commitment to accept responsibility for using what we know in caring for the world (including our fellow human beings, of course)—there is God, with whom we may grow into a relationship, enhancing further our capacity to understand our human nature and the nature of creation. As MacIntyre writes of humankind, "Their aspiration to complete and perfect their understanding of the order of things and of their place within it is matched by an aspiration to achieve a relationship with a fully and finally adequate object of desire, an end to which if they understand themselves rightly (on the theistic view), they are directed by their nature" (MacIntyre, 2009, pp. 77–78).

Christopher Hitchens, a vigorously intelligent atheist, bases all knowledge on empirical inquiry and dismisses the idea of empirical certainties, as if one could arrive at the "end" of inquiring before gathering all the evidence. From his point of view, therefore, an "impermeable faith" is simply not worth having: he looked forward to learning something new every day and hoped to live on the edge with an experimental perspective that was always open to the fact that there is always more to learn than we know (Hitchens, n.d.; 2007). Hitchens offers this as a crushing demolition of religious belief because religions are based on ungrounded (that is, nonempirical) certainties. But Christians are well aware that complete security, in any sense, is beyond human reach. Christians in fact celebrate his view of an infinitely expanding world, which is why we call it a creation: we are always on the way to greater understanding and can never rest with the security that what we think we know is all that there is to be known.

God is the infinitely dynamic Divine Being whose lively presence in creating lures us gratefully to want to know. The seductive attractiveness of the future in God leads us to respond freely to the desire to know and to share what we learn with gratitude. There is of course no compulsion in the "lure" of God's creativity inherent in the world because God's lure of humankind's creative advance is a loving stimulus, not a magical power. David Pailin, a process theologian, writes, "Process views of theism understand God's creative activity not as an irresistible force, compelling and coercing conformation to its wishes, but as the luring influence of love which respects the integrity of the creature . . . It is possible that this model of lure allows the notion of God's activity in relation to the creative advance to be developed in a way that does not impinge upon the relative autonomy of the creature. God may seek in love to 'draw' the creature to ever higher states of aesthetic richness but there is no compulsion" (Pailin, 1982, p. 87).

I agree with Pailin. In contradistinction to what Christopher Hitchens believes, Christian Faith, far from constraining one's thinking and desire to learn, is a profound stimulus to empirical experiment, intellectual inquiry, aesthetic appreciation, and moral commitment. Indeed to recognize that one's desire to understand is a God-given gift and that the world is intelligible and lovable is to be liberated to share in God's life of creating; it is what is implied when the author of the book of Genesis refers to humankind—both male and female—as being made in the image of God (Gen. 1:27). Not only is certainty undesirable; it is impossible. Thank God! God's loving presence delightfully lures humankind, in the end, to God himself.

If we follow the example of Aristotle, there will be no inquiry that lacks interest for us and fails to stimulate discussion of who we are, what we are, and what we are free to contribute to the world's well-being. In each context, greater understanding opens up new opportunities to be cocreators with God: growing response-ability in the light of new knowledge enhances our potential to live wisely and more responsibly. We are fascinated by our immediate physical environment; by the diversity of human societal structure; by the wholeness of human experience, which finds expression in the arts; and ultimately by the question of meaning. But first, I present some remarks about scientific methodology.

The Scientific Method

Our physical environment is intriguingly and delightfully complex. How do we learn to inquire successfully about its nature? Conventional wisdom encourages the belief that our knowledge of the physical world is produced by using "the scientific method." But the "scientific method" is itself a complex matter. Aristotle was the first person to give it serious attention. He was interested in valid inference and believed that in order to provide a clear description of something, one needed to know what it was for—what its goal was. Only then could one build a picture of the essential nature of something related to a hierarchical system of causal propositions, the careful application of which would enable one to deduce the nature of everything else. His authority lasted in the West until the sixteenth century, when Francis Bacon (1561–1626) explained that the scientific method depended on observation, hypothesis, and justification. Yet he envisioned the method to be essentially inductive, a form of argument that falsely assumes that true generalizations can be validly deduced from a set of individual observations. The unreasonableness of induction in the case of empirical inquiry soon became apparent: inference from particular to general goes beyond the evidence.

Karl Popper (1902–94) took a more questioning approach and denied that absolute proof was ever possible in empirical inquiry. Empirical statements must be investigated, he asserted, with a view to their falsification, for they can never be demonstrated beyond doubt (Popper, 1968, pp. 40–42). Thus, while certainty may be out of the question because we can never examine all possible cases, one disproof is sufficient. The best one could hope for was that a hypothesis would be true beyond reasonable doubt, which amounted to a declaration of confidence in the absence of evidence to the contrary. For much scientific inquiry, this is sufficient, as we can see from the profound impact it has made on our culture. The results have been remarkable and are certainly critical to our developing capacity to care for the world and to think through *ab initio* what we understand to be our human nature. I take two contrasting perspectives, which are the subject of continuing research and speculation.

Our Immediate Environment

It seems that every tribe and culture has been curious about its origin and has told itself stories in an attempt not only to place itself in a universal perspective of world history but to uncover means whereby "the gods" may look upon them with favor (Wilson, 1969, pp. 3–155). The attempt to find our place in the natural world, to understand the origins of our universe and in particular the origins of life, not only stimulate the professional scientist but also inspire the popular imagination through books and television programs. Cosmological inquiry has discovered a universe that is almost unimaginably large in space-time. Yet the human imagination is caught by the challenge of "other worlds." Some, like Sir Martin Rees, former British Astronomer Royal, anticipate the colonization of our solar system. He speculates that our world may be one of many—the consequence of an infinity of Big Bangs. He is sure that the future is both exciting and dangerous: humankind has for the first time in its history the opportunity to destroy itself, but he believes that the "far future" evolution of humankind is in its own hands (Rees, 2013). A second absorbing area of inquiry concerns the Human Genome Project, finally completed in 2003. What the human body is made of, how it works, and how it hangs together as a complex, functioning set of organs has always been puzzling. The discovery that the gene is the basic physical and functional unit of heredity was the major step forward. When the project was launched, the expectation was that human genes would number in excess of 100,000, but in fact, it turns out there are 24,000 or so, just a few more than a chimpanzee. However, since genes do not appear to act individually but in consort, factorial 24,000 is a very large number to "manage" if that is what we discover we are dealing with.

In principle, the hope is that such a complete mapping of the genetic structure of *Homo sapiens* will lead to dramatic new developments in the personal treatment of disease via gene therapy. There is indeed the prospect of individualized treatment, though the whole matter of "treatment" and diagnosis has turned out to be far more complicated than was anticipated. We have, as it were, a list of words, but the unpacking of the syntax and grammar essential to understanding, let alone speaking, the language is only slowly becoming secure. Moreover, there are problems to be thought through, both technical and ethical, stimulating work in prospect.

It would be easy to conclude that given the immensities of (possibly) many universes, the slightness of human being hardly counts. However, there is more to be said. Size is not all that counts if one is to have an impact. An African friend pointed me to the African saying, "If you think you are too small to make a difference, you have never spent a night with a mosquito!" Our curiosity has led us profitably to enhance our understandings of both the origin of the universe and the genetic foundations of our physical human being. The opportunities that our new response-abilities offer to our capacity to love the world and share in God's creating are infinite. They range from the opening up of the universe to human exploration, eventual colonization, and managing the far future of our evolution to stem cell research and the design of personal gene therapies for the condition of an individual patient.

As a result, we have to rethink our perception of our place in the universe and what it means to be human: the stimulus will never end.

But the exciting fact is that the human brain is so constituted and has so evolved that it can, at any rate and in a formulaic pattern, conceive of the hugeness of the world and the minute complexities of the physical biochemistry of which we are constituted. To put that very simply, the human being has the wonderful capacity to hold together, in one whole system, what he or she believes about the world and his or her relationship to it. And moreover, human beings have the capacity to be sufficiently dissatisfied with the result so far, to want to go on responding to God's lure to know more. It is no wonder that the study of the brain is attracting more and more interest.

Fr. Chris Corbally, SJ, president of the National Committee for Astronomy in Vatican City, was surely right to say in a lecture at the University of Charleston, "God gave the universe freedom to explore, and that's the wondrous thing. So that scientists can go back and see all the various galaxies and star systems and life forms and extinctions that are, because of the patience of God to allow for the freedom of creation . . . It's a much more satisfactory relationship with God than one which dictates every step of the universe" (Corbally, 2013). Grateful people appreciate the opportunities opened up by the God-given gift of curiosity and the freedom they thereby enjoy to engage in conversation with God.

Living and Working in Community

Not only are we curious about the nature of our physical world and able to benefit from it, but we can also learn from contact with diverse societies across the world whose social structure is influenced by geology, meteorology, fauna, flora, climate, and landform, among many others.

The example of the Azande is a classic case of a much-studied tribe. Actually, to call it "a tribe" is misleading; it is a collection of peoples who live in a territory that now covers the Sudan, the Central African Republic, and Zaire. Evans-Pritchard studied their religious and witchcraft beliefs, showing that it was through these that they maintained their values and the stability of their institutions, including that of the family group (Evans-Pritchard, 1934). Interestingly, he also showed that these practices were never applied in contexts where either party would have an interest in denying them.

Jared Diamond's recent work on the culture of tribal life in New Guinea offers a critical perspective on social relationships in our society. The traditions he identifies cannot, of course, be directly applied to twenty-first-century Western communities, but he suggests that careful attention to the motives, styles of thinking, and attitudes of tribal societies can help us refocus on crucial matters of universal human concern that we may be failing to deal with sensibly or even neglecting altogether (Diamond, 2012). What are their attitudes to birth, to bringing up children, to disease, to conflict, to old age, and to the inevitability of death? Are there qualities of the life of the complex communities of the Azande and the tribal traditions of New Guinea that could inform the qualities, traditions, and values of our society? Learning from them in order to translate them into patterns of living that would profitably influence the way we live could be very desirable. One might say that it is a matter of translation: learning to express in one societal structure the principles one learns through examining the structures embedded in another.

It is important also to realize that there are other communities than the natural ones of family and tribe. Scientific inquiry is itself a communal effort: the process is too complex for one mind to embrace everything relevant to a research project. We know, for example, that the world's growing population will require more food, more energy, and above all, better management of water resources if humankind is to flourish. The disciplines of inquiry involved if we are to tackle the complexities of the problem are immense. The ordinary person assumes that there is a serious shortage of food; after all, there are estimated to be more than one billion hungry people and an unknown number who are malnourished out of a total world population of some seven billion. Crop research has an important role to play, employing both traditional breeding techniques and genetic modification. But is this the whole solution?

Greenpeace notes that most hungry people live in countries where there is a food surplus, not a food shortage. If true, this means that distribution, price, and human greed are more to blame than actual shortages. In any case, government policies—for example, those in India and China—are focused on urban development and industrialization because they produce taxes. The reduction in biodiversity with the consequent reduction in the number of species increases susceptibility to disease. The terms of international trade tend to keep primary producers poor, thus reducing the availability of finance for investment in infrastructure, agriculture, and manufacture. Even this minimal list of the issues involved points to the need for collaborative research in agronomy, transport, international relations, economics, politics, and ethics.

To these problems must be added those of climate change and global warming. What research is relevant to the investigation of their causes and likely consequences? What will be the impact on sea levels? What will happen to the distribution of flora and fauna across the world? What changes will occur in crop production? How can the poorest countries be protected?

And what are the causes of climate change? Is human activity to blame, or is it the consequence of the natural cycle of events—perhaps associated with the activities of the sun? To what degree is it influenced by changes in the flow of ocean currents, or is it the case that such changes are themselves the product of other as yet unknown causes apparently unconnected with climate change? Whatever our research discipline, we shall need to take account of the work of others in order to put together a more complete picture than we could effect on our own.

The fact that all these issues, and the very many others associated with the task of facing up to these problems, have attracted our curiosity is a matter for gratitude. We are free to inquire and thereby to become, as a result of our increased response-ability, potentially more responsible in the ways we choose to behave.

One Human Nature in Diversity

There are two further dimensions to take into account: human prejudice and self-regard. Conversation is necessary if we are to form a clear idea of the practical questions facing us but also so that we may bring to our attention underlying prejudices that may unconsciously misdirect our perceptions and confuse our desire to contribute to the common good. For example, if the needs of the burgeoning human population are to be met, it may be necessary for those with the highest standards of living to accept some modest reduction. But suppose this is accepted as the best policy; the fact will not of itself convince us to act accordingly. Perhaps we would prefer others to limit the size of their families. But this would be difficult in the face of conflicting religious beliefs and what many may regard as gross interference with their inalienable rights. Courteous attention to the prejudices of others and an awareness of our own will be necessary if we are to agree on and enact possible strategies.

In order to take responsibility for our knowledge and determine policies that will contribute to the well-being of the world we love, we must take advantage of what we know of the ways in which societies, groups, and communities function. How in fact are policies formed in the light of evidence? How will they best be expressed if they are to be successfully implemented and achieve maximum public benefit?

Understanding the physical world so as to devise policies that will tackle some of the environmental issues facing humankind is complex. Trying to understand society by the social sciences is, if anything, even more complex: since the researcher is a member of the community he or she is investigating, his or her capacity to be objective is in question. Peter Winch concluded that since inquiries about human nature, human relationships, and human society could not be objectively investigated "from the inside," the social sciences were not science at all but a disguised form of philosophy (Winch, 1958). He came to believe that the best one could do when studying a primitive society was to treat it as what Wittgenstein called a "language game" or a "form of life" (Glock, 1996). Even so, it is not valueless, because it could suggest useful critical comparisons with one's own society.

From the extremes of both positions, it is clear that with respect to the social sciences, it is even more essential than it is with the physical sciences, if that is imaginable, to work in conversation with scholars across many disciplines. A primary reason for this is not simply the problems associated with the collection and classification of data but the mutual exploration of the prejudice and underlying values of the many individuals involved in the description and analysis of a given culture or tribe. There are social scientists who believe that they are only able to speak from within the class, gender, race, or generation of which they are members; thus only a woman can understand the circumstances pertaining to being a woman, only a poor person the circumstances of those in poverty.

If true, this would leave one social scientist unable to understand the language of another social scientist talking about a different social group. However, recent work on the origins of *Homo sapiens* suggests that the human race, whatever its local differences and contrasting customs, is in fact one race, so a reasonably objective discussion of human nature can be developed. The confrontational dimension of social inquiry is not its essential nature. Rather, one can and should undertake social inquiry from the point of view of the well-being of humankind and indeed the well-being of the whole of creation, since humankind is a responsible aspect of what it means to be a creature (Agassi, 1974, pp. 305–16). Loving creation includes loving all humanity; justice without love will lack compassion.

The essential feature of the professional, whatever his or her discipline, is that he or she remains first and last a person—of course, a person with special responsibilities because of his or her position and experience. Hence the wise will recognize their dependence on others; be aware that potential prejudice requires open conversation with others, and integrity of judgment requires attention to clarity of language. Interestingly, Yves Congar, a *peritus* at Vatican II, in his discussion of the role of the laity in the Church, propounded an analogous view with regard to the clergy. He used the term "total ecclesiology" to cover all Christians, both laity and clergy, emphasizing the point that every believer, whatever his or her experience and responsibilities, remains a lay person (Congar, 1957, pp. xxvii–xxviii). All are called to live in the image of God and give themselves to the world's well-being; there is a public language in which Christians can converse with one another, whatever their position in the community.

The Glue of Language

A key ingredient of human identity is associated with the acquisition of language: with it, we hold things together. Without it, we would not be able to explore the world together or pass on what we learn to future generations. Yet the complexities of human interaction are apparent in the sheer number of languages that humankind employs. George Steiner points to the fact that linguistic structure embodies a way of life; translation is not simply dealing with words but trying to enter into another culture in order to "say" something in one's own culture. In fact, all communication involves translation: "A human being performs an act of translation, in the full sense of the word, when receiving a speech-message from any other human being" (Steiner, 1985, p. 47).

Jared Diamond reports that more than one thousand of the world's approximately seven thousand languages exist in New Guinea, but he draws attention to the fact that most tribal members are able to communicate in more than one language and that multilingualism has advantages.

The confusing multiplicity of languages is a problem for Old Testament thinking (Gen. 11:1–9). It seemed so contrary to common sense that some explanation had to be offered. One tradition in Genesis assumes that the children of Noah were, after the flood, intended to spread across the whole earth, whereas they settled down to build a city with a huge tower. Yahweh was displeased, and he frustrated their initiative by confusing their language. The story may simply be an etiological explanation of the puzzling existence of so many languages. But there is a possible alternative interpretation of the story, which seems more theologically consistent with God's creativity and his love of his world and his people.

Any attempt to settle down, to find security by resisting the inborn desire to explore, to experiment, to be curious, and to add to human knowledge and experience, was contrary to God's purposive vision for humanity. To retreat into a "safe place" is actually impossible: there is no such place. Christians believe to do so would be to try to withdraw from the reality of God's presence and live in sin. This theme is consistent with the Israelites' celebration of their liberation from the Pharaoh's Egypt. Their release from captivity was not to a place where they would be left alone to settle down and do nothing—they frequently had to be rescued from their lethargy, complacency, and indifference to God and his Law, even if that involved defeat and exile to a foreign land where they could regain their sense of their identity as God's Chosen People. Analogously, when faced with a new language, the business of translation creates the possibility of a new vision of life for which one can be grateful.

And when it comes down to it, translation is always possible: twentieth-century Anglo-Saxon philosophy was besotted with the question of language. Noam Chomsky was as impressed that human beings could understand one another as he was by the fact that there were many languages. His controversial proposal was that the possibility of translation—even of understanding what another said in one's own language—would be explained if there was hardwired into the human brain an inexpressible "ur-grammar" that underpinned all languages. This could account for the fact that even children can understand and create meaningful sentences that they had never heard before. The capacity to translate is a feature of all communication, even within a natural language, as well as between different languages: we have to interpret what each other means by what each other says. This accounts for technical languages, such as mathematics and chemistry, since they limit, to a degree, the ambiguity implicit in ordinary speech. In principle, it is therefore potentially possible to understand one another sufficiently to be cooperative (Chomsky, 1986).

The Christian tradition embodies this in the account of Pentecost. The vision here is congruent with Chomsky's speculation. Acknowledgment of God's presence affirms the essential unity of humanity, which hitherto had lacked full expression. By attending to one another's language and culture, every society and nation, whatever its traditions and history, can enter into the community of the one humankind (Acts 2:1–12).

Chomsky is often criticized for spreading his controversial linguistic perspective to political matters, but it seems a natural implication of his theory. If, as he believes, there is a common humanity and our linguistic facility bears witness to this fact, we have duties to one another as human beings. Conflict between races, nations, classes, generations, and so on was simply false to human nature. Therefore he was against the Vietnam War and aghast that he lived in a society in which a comatose citizen might be allowed to die because his or her health insurance could not be checked. Chomsky would agree with Erasmus, I believe, when he says,

> Now amidst all the good this world affords, what is more delightful to the heart of man, what more beneficial to society, than love and amity? Nothing, surely . . . Peace is at once the mother and the nurse of all that is good for man: War, on a sudden, and at one stroke, overwhelms, extinguishes, abolishes whatever is cheerful, whatever is happy and beautiful and pours a foul torrent of disasters on the life of mortals. Peace shines upon human affairs like the vernal sun. The fields are cultivated, the gardens bloom, the cattle are fed upon a thousand hills, new buildings arise, ancient edifices are repaired, riches flow, pleasures smile, laws retain their vigour, the discipline of the police prevails, religion glows with ardour, justice bears sway, humanity and charity increase, arts and manufactures feel the genial warmth of encouragement, the gains of the poor are more plentiful, the opulence of the rich displays itself with additional splendor, liberal studies flourish, the young are well educated, the old enjoy their ease, marriages are happy, good men thrive, and the bad are kept under control. (Erasmus quoted in Gittings, 2012, p. 104)

Our common humanity is hard-wired to want justice, to live peaceably, and to live humbly with God—and to want to know why when it does not happen. The common good is a perspective that is intelligible, hence the particular vocation of the professional to serve the public interest in his or her attention to the concerns of his or her client. Far from being self-interested, humankind might be better understood as *Homo empathicus* (Krznaric, 2014, pp. xiii–xvii, 2–12). Until we wholeheartedly try to live out the truth of this with gratitude, we shall never be at peace.

The Art of Living: Wholeness or Completeness?

If one is to express gratitude for the curiosity God has implanted in the human being, one must commit oneself to accepting the urge to inquire, which amounts implicitly to the desire to create. Thus, complementing and supporting the desire to engage in scientific inquiry, there is also the world of the imagination; the arts of poetry, painting, sculpture, architecture, and the novel are all dimensions of our exploration of the world as we experience it. It is a demand on the whole self to inquire into the wholeness of God's creation and into the nature of God himself, the Creator, who has committed himself to making a success of his world. The key is openness to all experience and to the desire to follow knowledge wherever it leads. At the root of this is the human puzzlement about not only what it means to be human but what it, *all* of it, means and how it all hangs together.

The practical implications of the sheer fact of the world's existence and its contingent nature have stimulated much reflection. Why is there something rather than nothing? What or who could have brought the world into existence? And we try to settle down with a conclusion by seeking certainty: we want to end the argument and come to a clear, indisputable position. But there is none available, for we are immediately faced with a diversity of religions and philosophical approaches. Jonathan Sacks, the former Chief Rabbi, offers hope: "The test of faith is whether I can make space for difference. Can I recognize God's image in someone who is not in my image, whose language, faith, ideals are different from mine? If I cannot, then I have made God in my image instead of allowing him to remake me in his" (Sacks, 2002, p. 201). Above all, in the search for meaning, we are dependent on the experience of others; prejudice, certainty, or indifference will otherwise cloud our minds and make us seek an irrelevant and intolerant utopia to impose on others.

But maybe there are shortcuts, proofs for the existence of God on which we can rely and to which we can commit ourselves wholeheartedly; some have thought so. In *Physics*, Aristotle bases his thinking on the all-embracing experience of motion, which he states must always be caused by prior movement. But what activated or activates the unending motion we observe? "Since there must always be motion without intermission, there must necessarily be something eternal, whether one or many, that first imparts motion, and this first mover must be unmoved" (Aristotle, 1984c, *Phys.*, 258b, 6). But what evidence do we have for this unmoved mover? He adopts a different approach in the *Nicomachean Ethics*: "If, then, there is some end of the things we do, which we desire for its own sake (everything else being desired for the sake of this), and if we do not choose everything for the sake of something else (for at that rate the process would go on to infinity, so that our desire would be empty and vain) clearly this must be the good and the chief good" (1984b, 1, 2). Aquinas seems to accept Aristotle's position in principle, but in his Five Ways (proofs of the existence of God), he recognizes that God cannot himself be within the temporal series as the first cause but must necessarily be outside the series as the one in whom there is the ultimate loving power, which is responsible for the world's existence (Aquinas, 2006, I, q. 2 a3). But what sort of a proof is this? In fact, as Kenny implies, the so-called proofs are better thought of as ways of thinking about the meaning of "God" (Kenny, 2004, pp. 12–14). As such, they are still potentially illuminating and worth thinking about. For example, the cosmological argument may not be good natural theology: God's existence cannot be deduced from observations of the natural world. On the other hand, if God's nature is considered necessary and not contingent, how can we understand the relationship between God and the world? In what sense, if any, can one talk about the activity of God in the world?

Theologians have approached this matter in different ways. Paul Tillich, for example, simply talks of the actuality of God's presence in correlation with human need: God's presence is in itself the living activity that encourages humankind to work toward the fulfillment of his true nature. God is the existential "Ground of Being," who is truly the ultimate concern for humanity. To embrace God is to become a "New Being" established on sure foundations (Tillich, 1953, pp. 261–79). If, however, we determine that our well-being depends on things that are not of ultimate concern, we are in despair. Tillich's own experience as a chaplain in the First World War and an anxious observer of the turmoil of the Second World War were strong influences on the development of his theology. MacIntyre, as we have seen previously, believes that the Divine Being is that ultimate source of truth and love at which we aim. Pailin talks of the Divine Being as actively luring humankind into a loving relationship with him and with his creation, thus freeing the world to desire to understand. Adams, influenced by Plato, grounds all value, both moral and nonmoral, in the Being of God, who is the Supreme Good and is excellent without qualification. Since every excellence is found in God, any attempt to achieve or move toward excellence in whatever context, when properly understood, is an attempt to shape one's humanity in the image of God (Adams, 1999, pp. 28–38).

The questions raised for theology by the fact of the world's existence remain unanswered; however, there is no end to the delight and nourishment that comes from inquiry. For this we can be thankful.

Conclusion

Gratitude toward the Creator implies respect not only for God but for his gifts—enjoyment of the creation and acceptance of the necessity of service, even self-sacrifice—if the real potential of our humanity is to be achieved. To be curious is to be human. Here, thank God, is no continuing city—only the worthwhile pursuit of truth and justice so that by becoming more response-able, we can be more responsible and gratefully accept our roles as cocreators with God in the perfecting of the world, God's creation. God will continually disturb our peace by stimulating our curiosity so that we will journey on in love and not "settle down."

One naturally thinks first of being grateful for the gift of creation, of which human being is an intriguingly complex dimension. But we are curious too about our human nature, our diverse societies, our powers of communication, and our desire to be responsibly courteous in our dealings with one another, with God, and with the creation. It is astonishing that we can; for this we are grateful. The sheer fact of existence stimulates questions and opportunities for experiment that enhance our understanding of God, the worlds of our experience, and therefore what it means to be human. Philosophers analyze the concepts we employ in shaping our experience. Psychologists explore the influence of our sense of gratitude on our well-being. Meanwhile, the theologian grounds our human experience, including every dimension of our understanding, in a vital framework that includes God, the Redemptive Creator.

It is an essential ingredient of Christian Faith to take delight in the complex nature of creation, the diversity of our human responses, and the ways in which they provoke our inquiry. Indeed to live lives in "the image of God" is to be open to new experiences, with all that means for the ways in which we express our understanding in systems, images, languages, and communities. It is to live gratefully with hope.

The life of the professional inherits these dimensions of human experience and he or she attempts to express them in his or her courteous attention to the needs of the client in order to serve the common good and the well-being of the creation.

If we take real delight in our human search for truth, we will want to be aware of where we stand in history; this goes for the professional both as a person and in his or her professional role. What is our inheritance, and what do we intend to be our legacy? Gratitude to God includes present, past, and future; they are continuously present for those who see themselves to be in God's presence and in God's image.

Chapter 5

Inheritance and Legacy
The Open Power of the Present

Introduction

Gratitude is not limited to what we immediately benefit from. Truly grateful people will set what they appreciate in the context of everything that they inherit. Indeed they will grow as they find their place in the wholeness of the created order as revealed in evolution. Our present human condition embodies the world's history, in a manner of speaking, and is the recipient of everything we enjoy through the sensitivities and inquiries of previous generations. If our curiosity and our gratitude are to be real, they must be all-embracing. In this chapter, I place who we are and what we know, believe, and practice in an evolutionary, historical context, which I believe is enlarged and deepened when grounded in the universal theological framework I have outlined. God's gracious relationship with his world is coterminous with its life.

If professionals are therefore to accept full responsibility for their practice, they will have to take up the conversation of the generations: they stand in a tradition of which they need to be aware. But it is not a limited tradition. To be fully aware of where they stand, they will, as we shall see, need to be liberally educated, which will be to their and their clients' benefit and will inform sound professional practice. Moreover, what we inherit and what we hope to leave for our successors impacts our sense of who we are and what it means to be human.

Our Evolved Inheritance

We humans are who we are because we are part of the evolutionary process; as persons alive in God's good creation, it behooves us to appreciate and be grateful for the millennia that have given rise to our present capacity to explore and enjoy our world. It is generally accepted that the theory of evolution provides an illuminating account of creation's overall development, including that of not only human life but life itself. The general theory is rarely seriously debated, though exactly how it should be interpreted is of great interest. It is true, however, that a survey carried out in the United States by the Pew Research Center indicated that 33 percent of the US population rejected the idea of evolution altogether (Pew Research Center for Religion and Public Life, 2013). The figure has remained steady since the last survey in 2009, but close analysis indicates political change: fewer Republicans now accept evolution, which fits perhaps with a more conservative attitude toward life in general and suspicion of political change. The US figure is in strong contrast to that in Britain, where a YouGov poll of 2,116 people was carried out by Dr. Amy Unsworth of the Faraday Institute of Science and Religion in 2014. The results suggested that only 3 percent of the British population rejected the idea that plants and animals had evolved from earlier life forms, while only 6.8 percent rejected the idea that humans had evolved from nonhuman life forms.

Daniel Dennett called Darwin's contribution to human understanding a dangerous idea. He claimed that it made all other explanations redundant or at any rate contextualized them to such a degree that no explanation could be significant that did not take full account of the theory of evolution (Dennett, 1995; 2013, pp. 203ff.). In particular, he believed that the theory undermined the claims of religion. However, in my opinion, far from being dangerous to religious belief, Christian theological inquiry is liberated when the evolutionary perspective is placed within the lively theological framework I have outlined. Indeed, without its insights, we would lack reasonable accounts of any dimension of our experience. The fact is that human nature did not spring fully formed from the mind of God. Now we can see that evolution places humankind in the context of the whole of life and allows for the possibility of development. Above all, it makes room for the emergence of consciousness, self-consciousness, and self-directed, responsible, deliberative action.

We are bound in the web of the creative process and will only find ourselves as we uncover and come to terms with our place within it. The fact that we humans have evolved to be the persons we are, with the character, opportunities, hopes, and ambitions we have, is something for which we can be profoundly grateful. Indeed it is the aspect of our lives for which we should be most profoundly grateful. It means that we are within a dynamic, lively community of sensitivity, which can increasingly grow into taking responsibility for itself and its future. But we should underline the fact that, as MacIntyre claims, we shall not find ourselves completely as long as we attempt to offer explanations of creation that lack awareness of God, Creator and Redeemer. The search for the knowledge of God and the wisdom that comes from it are what we call theology.

We humans are made in the image of God. It transpires that our place within the evolutionary pattern is unique; humans are the only creatures in which there have emerged minds, communicative skills associated with the acquisition of language, and self-conscious awareness of their place within nature. The consequence is that we can distinguish between what nature does to us and what we have done to the world of nature. We know something of the forces, powers, direction of events, and processes in the natural world and recognize the harm done by our ill-considered, unthinking behavior. We become alive to our human response-abilities and are reminded of God's invitation to accept responsibility with him. Compared with the immensities of the world's evolution in space-time, we cannot help but remark on the brevity of the period of time it has taken humankind to bring the world to its present challenging condition. By the same token, stimulated by our God-given curiosity, we are free, if we wish, to choose to take evolution in a wiser direction.

There is, of course, no such thing as complete freedom. But we know the impact we are having on our total environment, including our life opportunities; we can focus our minds on the issues we face and set about tackling them. The more we learn, the greater our potential freedom, the greater response-abilities. We can begin to take responsibility for our future evolution and profoundly influence the future direction of the evolution of nature.

Growth in knowledge has to be accompanied by imaginative thinking and, above all, good character if we are to manage our evolutionary future in the interests of human well-being. Human sensitivity to the needs of others has to sharpen. Our God-given curiosity to learn about the world, within which we are set, includes curiosity about ourselves, how we should best behave in relation to one another, and how we can direct our attention to bringing about a common focus on human well-being. We may, through ignorance and fear, think that we can do no better than to concentrate on our personal needs, but a moment's reflection will open our eyes to the fact that we are dependent on one another for our flourishing as persons, and on God, whose creative intention is that his creation should flourish.

A Sense of History

As we have seen, the virtue of gratitude both awakens and is awakened by our natural curiosity; it is the expression of the whole self in response to the desire to understand our world, the Creator, and what it means to be human. To appreciate fully what this means, we need to be open to the broad vision presented by our evolutionary inheritance, which will nourish and free us from the limit of the present. Alongside our emergence in evolution, however, we inherit a place in the history of humankind; our historical inheritance dynamically informs how we have become who we are and what we can aspire to leave for the benefit of future generations. This is true for us as persons and for all of professional practice.

Thus, for example, an excellent physicist will want to enter the conversation of the generations by learning to take account of the history of his discipline. This is not simply out of respect for the achievements of previous practitioners—though we do, as Einstein said, stand on the shoulders of giants—nor is it merely because we may incidentally pick up worthwhile ideas of which we were ignorant. That may happen; we are very likely to recover neglected or forgotten data and be inspired by imaginative flights of fancy and styles of thinking that positively inform our current perplexities. The fact is that by entering into the historical development of our discipline and its interactions with other disciplines, we are likely to reflect on the wholeness of our experience. In so doing, we will be encouraged to tell ourselves new stories and be pointed to new ways of thinking. Even more particularly, we shall be stimulated by the attitudes, dispositions, and virtues of the persons involved—by their characters in fact. Their courage, integrity, and intellectual honesty will inspire our gratitude, remotivate our curiosity, and offer us models of excellence.

It is true of every professional, whether a scientist, lawyer, accountant, teacher, or priest: he or she will need to find his or her place in the tradition(s) of legal, educational, or pastoral practice and take up the conversation of the generations. They will find themselves asking questions: Where does the tradition lead me? Where do I stand vis-à-vis my inheritance? How do I take up the responsibilities implicit in my inheritance? What is the language that enables me to make sense of my experience? On whom do I model myself? What are the virtues of my professional practice, and what habits do I cultivate in order not only to acquire them in the first place but to continue to practice them in the face of all the challenges with which I shall undoubtedly be presented in due course? Gratitude will encourage professionals to think positively and remove any temptation to believe that their most valuable achievements are their own and their generation's. They cannot, as we say, pull themselves up by their own bootstraps.

Gratitude is not an inwardly focused emotional response: it is open and inclusive. Its full expression includes an appreciation of the broad tradition in which a person's professional practice is set. It will remind lawyers that a good lawyer will be aware of the contributions of social scientists, psychologists, politicians, rhetoricians, philosophers, ethicists, theologians, and the other practical disciplines that inform his or her ability to make sense of the evidence and come to sound judgments. There is a wholeness to the world of experience on which professionals rely. The fact that the Christian tradition sees this response-ability to be God-given only enhances the depth of the sense of gratitude that is felt, which in turn illuminates the divinely delegated personal authority of human responsibility.

Gratitude is usually assumed to be backward-looking, but this is an incomplete understanding of the virtue that has a vital future perspective, especially when placed in a theological framework. I am grateful for and inspired by the lives and work of excellent lawyers of previous generations, but God graciously encourages and sustains a forward-looking, anticipatory perspective. We do not move forward facing backward, thanking God for past benefits. On the contrary, with gratitude for what we inherit, we are empowered to look to the future with hope. The present is a fulcrum of past energy and future ambition; when we recognize this, we know that there is no "steady state" but always opportunities for rethinking the past, reconfiguring it, and making changes in order to share with God in the creation of new futures. My housemaster used to say that if things were not getting better, they were getting worse. His point was that since circumstances were always changing, there was no value in thinking that we could prosper by merely repeating what we had previously done. One had better learn to think things through in the light of a new situation and move on.

Time does not stand still; it cannot be stopped, repeated, or undone. However, the past is reinterpretable in the light of new information to the extent that its direction can be influenced. The consequence is that the future that is anticipated at a particular time is open and not determined. The point is that the present moment is the only open, dynamic opportunity we have to accept the responsibility that flows from our growing response-ability. This opportunity for the professional is the moment of personal interaction with the client in the service of the common good. It depends for its fulfillment on the liberating sense of gratitude for all that is past and for all that is to come.

There may of course be dimensions of our inheritance of which we are ashamed, for which we must take responsibility. The Christian theological tradition has linguistic and moral resources from which we can usefully draw in coming to terms with these aspects of human experience, redirecting us from the tyranny of guilt and empowering us for a new future.

Historical Perspective

"History," Mr. Ford assures us, "is bunk" (Huxley, 1950, p. 89). This is not true, but certainly, economic and political decisions seem to be made without reference to the history that lies behind them. In fact, the number of pupils taking history as a major study is apparently in decline in the schools of England and Wales: the contemporary zeitgeist celebrates, as Ford would have it, the new, the innovatory. However, while history may not be regarded an essential element of the current school curriculum, it is a matter of personal interest to many, as the flourishing heritage industry illustrates. We like to be entertained by television programs and books on historical themes: we listen to stories about the past perhaps because we believe we enter a world where we make no difference. There is, for example, currently great interest in the results of archaeological digs; Roman history attracts television viewers as do programs on the history of art and the First World War. The sixteenth century in Britain is a special case. We take pride in it: the clothes were gorgeous, and it was a dramatic period of English success, economic, political, religious, and military. Or so we think. What is more, it had fine literature—notably, Shakespeare—which continues to stir the mind and inform the emotions. But a selective approach to history diminishes the perspective of our sense of gratitude, for while the motivation of our gratitude must include the past, it is not, as I have affirmed, merely backward-looking.

Not only is it misleading to regard history as no more than a source of entertainment by selecting "the best bits"; to do so undermines our awareness of what it means to be human. We need to feel the virtue of gratitude in its full historical context if we are to grow into becoming our full selves. It identifies the responsibilities we inherit in our personal and professional lives and encourages us to aspire to a future that we will be pleased to leave to future generations. Our interest in the past tends to be voyeuristic, whereas it should be participatory; it is something in which we literally take part.

Abraham Maslow (1908–70), the American psychologist, developed a theory for what he called a "hierarchy of needs," which moved from the satisfaction of the demands of our physiological nature to requirements for safety, affection, public esteem, and self-actualization, in which he included problem solving, moral sensitivity, and lack of prejudice. His approach was positive, always affirming the idea that it was possible for an individual to aspire to achieve the next level in the hierarchy. Maslow distinguished between what he called "Being cognition" (B-cognition) and "Deficiency cognition" (D-cognition; Maslow, 1968). Deficiency cognition concerns everyday life, its needs and concerns; Being cognition focuses on participation, a union of subject and object, and a sense of wholeness.

Almost any experience may stimulate a vivid B-cognition, Maslow affirmed. Robert Bellah tells of an occasion in which Maslow reported, in his presence, a B-experience that was important and revelatory to him when serving as the chair of the Psychology Department at Brandeis University:

> He was expected to attend the graduation ceremony in full academic regalia. He had avoided such events previously, considering them silly rituals. But, he said, as the procession began to move he suddenly "saw" it as an endless procession. Far, far, ahead, at the very beginning of the procession, was Socrates. Quite a way back but still well ahead of Maslow was Spinoza. Then just ahead of him was Freud followed by his own teachers and himself. Behind him stretching endlessly were his students and his students' students generation after generation as yet unborn. Maslow assured us that what he experienced was not a hallucination: rather it was a particular kind of insight, an example of B-cognition. (Bellah, 2011, pp. 8–9)

Robert Bellah goes on to say, "He was in a sense apprehending the 'real' basis of any actual university . . . [for] if the university does not have a fundamental symbolic reference point that transcends the pragmatic considerations of the world of working and is in tension with those considerations, then it has lost its raison d'être" (p. 9). Bellah's comments raise questions for the intellectual and moral environment of the modern university. Does a university education, as experienced by today's undergraduates, I wonder, confirm them in their inheritance and inspire them to want to leave a sound legacy for future generations?

But it is not only with higher education that we are concerned; I want to affirm the same view with regard to everyone and all professions. A profession that has lost its sense of being in a tradition, of the mutual dependence of the professional and the client, and of sensitivity to the wholeness of its purpose in relation to other professions has lost all sense of what it means to be a profession. Above all, as I shall suggest in the following section, when professionals fail to realize that they stand in a tradition, they have lost the essential dimension of vocation.

Responsible Historical Inquiry

Openness to the outcomes of historical inquiry is a necessary feature of an educated person's thinking. We may not be responsible for "what happened" (whatever that means), but we are responsible for how we interpret and respond to it. Historians, at a given time, write up what they believe to be "the facts" if we are to understand the past. But what are "the facts"? We have a duty to review them and, in the light of new information, rewrite the story. What we inherit is not an indelible, true, and unchangeable account of the events but a version of what happened looked at through the eyes of the historian, who in telling his or her version of the story brings his or her own perspectives to bear. In so doing, the historian is accepting responsibility; the past is a living tradition with which we must engage in conversation so as to develop it and reinterpret it.

Take, for example, the biblical tradition the books of 1 and 2 Kings and 1 and 2 Chronicles: they rewrite the same history. 1 and 2 Kings are included by scholars in what are known as "the Former Prophets," together with the books of Joshua, Judges, and 1 and 2 Samuel. They form a unity; indeed the division between Samuel and Kings varies in ancient manuscripts, and the division between 1 and 2 Kings varies even more so. They are the product of the Deuteronomic tradition of the seventh century BC and probably were not by one author or editor, though that remains a possibility. The choice of material is theologically directed to explain how God's Chosen People came to be in exile, notwithstanding the covenant Yahweh made with Moses at Sinai and the giving of the Law. The explanation developed was that the respective kings of both Judah and Israel were guilty of gross misdemeanor with respect to cultic fidelity.

The books of 1 and 2 Chronicles, on the other hand, were written around 200 or 400 BC (scholars disagree on the date) in a different historical situation and largely ignore God's covenant with Moses on Mount Sinai. These books confirm the genealogies of David and Solomon, underlining the importance of the covenant Yahweh made with them, which led to the building of the Temple in Jerusalem. This is presented as crucial to the history and tradition of the Chosen People.

These interpretations of Israel's history are different but not in conflict: the author(s) encourages respect for the Law focused upon the Temple. Faithful community life involves cultic purity, strict obedience to the Law, and the centrality of the Temple.

The biblical example I have taken could be replicated in every period of history. The history of Anglo-Saxon England is being rewritten in the light of new evidence, much of which is archaeological. The so-called Dark Ages in Europe, we discover, were not Dark Ages at all: they were illuminated by a passion for scholarship, artistic creativity, and personal ambition. The European conquest of Africa was not the opening up of the "Dark Continent." There were rich cultures and long-standing tribal vitalities that were destroyed; the imperial history of Britain is in the process of being rewritten to take this into account. Moreover, the history of Britain itself cannot be told as the emergence of a constitutional monarchy in a United Kingdom of parliamentary, democratic government. New historical interpretations take up the story of Britain not merely to continue it but to review it in the light of current challenges and living experience. By so doing, these interpretations influence the way that current decisions are made and shape the legacy left for future generations. There is no fixed point.

Take, for example, the current debate about the future of the welfare state in Britain. The Beveridge Report, published during the Second World War in 1942, identified five giants that Britain needed to slay. They were want, disease, ignorance, squalor, and idleness. Beveridge proposed a safety net to support those who fell on hard times so that they would be able to contribute to the public good when their circumstances improved. No one questions the relevance of these concerns, but subsequent demands on the public purse have ballooned and are judged to pose a moral problem. Ought the present generation to leave a legacy of debt that will hamper the prospects of future generations? Politicians, ethicists, social scientists, medical professionals, taxation experts, theologians, and economists are looking for new ways forward that take account (for example) of the changing balance of the generations, shifts in public expectation, fiscal challenges, and ethical considerations.

Disciplines of Inquiry

There is nothing new about human inquiry; it is a feature of all human life. What is of more recent origin is the way that our inquiry has been shaped in order to respond to needs that have become apparent. We want greater prosperity but recognize that prosperity is not defined by having cash in hand.

For ease of communication and consistency of focus, we organize our knowledge into the disciplines of history, physics, sociology, philosophy, and so on. This is a sensible thing to do, provided we do not fall prey to the illusion that each discipline is self-contained; instead, to be useful and to flourish, a discipline has to be open to influences from other disciplines and aware of the incompleteness of its own structures. For example, when I was first introduced to the study of science at school, the first paragraph of each section of the textbook (often in small print) would frequently provide a brief background account of the social context that led to the topic becoming a focus of intellectual interest and experiment.

The account would usually include reference to one or two of the key scientists (including the dates of their lives) who had contributed to the development in understanding of the topic. In the case of magnetism, for example, Maxwell and Hertz would be mentioned along with the names of specific theorems, perhaps a relevant formula, and some practical implications. It was explained to us that this was not simply a background introduction to the important scientific facts that followed in the rest of the chapter but was integral to the science that was being explained. Science was a process of discovery, not a set of independent facts integrated into a wholly independent system that explained everything; it was the product of the curiosity stimulated by personal interest and societal need. Scientific explanations of natural or social phenomena, together with their practical outcomes, were owned by authors whose ambition (and even vocation) was to contribute to the well-being of society. Thus Boyle's law stated what Boyle discovered about the expansion of gases, Faraday's law explained electromagnetic induction, and so on. We were told that we inherited their legacy; it was now up to us to make good use of it. It was made clear to us that this was not only a matter of applying to the best of our ability what they had taught us in tackling the problems society currently faced; our responsibility was to enter into the tradition, take up their conversation, and leave a legacy on which future generations could continue to build.

We can see the interaction of the social environment with personal needs and the stimulus of human ingenuity and imaginative intellectual inquiry in the case of energy. Every human needs the kinetic energy produced naturally in the body through the consumption of food. This leads to the use of energy to produce food through hunting, fishing, the cultivation of crops, and so on. Crop production requires water, which is what stimulated the adaptation of techniques to divert water, and to a lesser extent store it, for irrigation. But to be useful, food had to be transported. To begin with, no doubt, humans would have had to carry it, drag it, or move it on water. The growing demand for power, not only for transport but for manufacture, stimulated the development of other energy sources: wood, peat, coal, and oil.

Ideas also need to travel, a dimension that is underlined by the success of the World Wide Web, which offers almost instantaneous communication but also requires energy. The production of energy has moved through periods of water, steam, electricity, nuclear fission, and soon, it is hoped, nuclear fusion and green energy. Failure to appreciate the social, political and economic influences of and upon science and technology leads to a failure to grasp its human dimension.

Nothing that I have said denies the importance of what is often called "blue-skies science"—that is, the pursuit of knowledge for its own sake. This too is important for humankind as an expression of its true nature. We want to know; we are endowed by God with the natural disposition to inquire. And we want to put what we know to good use in the furtherance of human well-being and the healthy evolution of the world; for that we are grateful. But if we are to do this well, we need to know what is meant by "a good education."

The Openness of Inquiry: Education

If we are to accept the responsibilities implicit in these developments, we require an education *system*, for it is of critical importance in making us aware of the breadth and depth of what we inherit and in encouraging a desire to leave a worthwhile legacy for future generations. On January 8, 1826, in St. Clement's Church, Oxford, John Henry Newman preached a sermon in a series on "obedience to the law and the purpose of education" (the text is available in Arthur and Nicholls, 2007, pp. 205–13). Newman was an Anglican at the time, but his views on education were consistent throughout his lifetime.

"Education," Newman said, "if conducted on right principles, is an inestimable blessing—if it were not, why should Christ have set up the

Christian Church at all? for what is it [but] a school of education for the next life?" (quoted in Arthur and Nicholls, 2007, p. 207).

"The next life" for St. Paul (and indeed for Newman) was life after death, when the significance of the truth about human nature would be confirmed in the eternity of Christ's loving presence. But it may also be applied to the present life in the sense that if the responsibilities that are presented by one's inheritance are to be taken up, as they should be, it will be necessary to be educated into them.

Newman took as his text, "Knowledge puffeth up but charity edifieth" (1 Cor. 8:1). Any education that confines itself to mere knowledge, in the sense of factual information, will be destructive to fundamental human values unless illuminated by love or charity. Moreover, it will militate against the formation of a true view of human nature: "Learning implies personal formation as well as intellectual development. Therefore all genuine learning is active not passive. It involves the use of the mind, not just the memory, and it is essentially a process of discovery that stimulates both the imagination and the intellect"—and, one might add, the emotions. "For Newman the 'Enlargement of mind' is not the passive reception of facts" (Arthur and Nicholls, 2007, p. 201).

Drawing on Newman's *Idea of a University*, Arthur and Nichols underline the vital significance of "enlargement of mind" in the growth toward human maturity:

> For Newman enlargement of mind is, on the one hand, characteristically *energetic* acting "upon and towards and among those new ideas which are rushing in upon it . . . it is the locomotion, the movement onwards, of the mental centre, to which both what we know, and what we are learning . . . gravitates." Enlargement of mind must also include a *synthetic* power, as he puts it, of "viewing many things at once as one whole" a *formative* power "reducing to order and meaning the matter of our acquirements . . . making the objects of our knowledge subjectively our own" a *critical* and *discriminating* power of "referring [many things] severally to their true place in the universal system of understanding their respective values, and determining their mutual dependence." Newman says that "a truly great intellect . . . is one which takes a connected view of old and new, past and present, far and near, and which has an insight into the influence of all these one on another; without which there is no whole and no centre." (p. 127–28; quotations from Newman, 1990, p. 120)

The glory of this insight is that it is difficult and demanding but possible—but only if one keeps in mind the thought that no account of human experience that eliminates reflection upon the world's and our relationship with God can be complete or ultimately satisfying.

Therefore the confinement of a person's education to a limited area of knowledge through the practice of specialization currently prevalent in schools, especially in higher education, is dangerous. It threatens the formation of an honest, creative, and responsible professional mind. Understanding of the wholeness of what the world has to offer is essential if we are to be in a position to accept responsibility for any part of it. Without some knowledge of the history of mathematics, one is unlikely to be the best "mathematician," though one may have a thorough grasp of the techniques and processes necessary for the solution of complex expressions. To *be* a "mathematician," one needs to see where, how, and what one's mathematical skills can do for the well-being of humankind. Again, without some knowledge of reasons for the development of the study of consciousness, the philosopher will lack the overall experience necessary to continue to be puzzled about what he or she is inquiring. In all inquiry, it is clear that there is no such thing as a "discrete discipline," totally independent of all others.

The German concept of *Bildung* is informative here. Its root lies in Pietistic theology, which encouraged the Christian to regard all his or her talents, attitudes, and virtues as gifts of God and to develop them to be formed in God's image (Good, 2005). To strive to be formed in the image of God, as we have interpreted it in this study, means that we can live free of prejudice, ignorance, and fear to focus on the interests and well-beings of our total environment and other people. In so doing, I suggest, we become cocreators with God in the emerging wholeness of the world of his creation. The real possibility that this can occur is confirmed for the Christian in the life, teachings, and death of Jesus; the eternal reality of this possibility is underlined in his Resurrection and ascension. It was, as we can readily see, costly for him. It may be so for every Christian, even to the extent of self-sacrifice, if he or she is to show what it means to be formed in God's image.

It is questionable whether our current education system sufficiently takes into account the notion that education is a matter of character formation as well as knowledge acquisition or the totality of the interrelation and interaction among education, history, and philosophy. The point is clearly recognized by Hegel and more recently by Alistair MacIntyre. The wholeness of inquiry only emerges when it embraces a metaphysical dimension that assumes the reality of God. Only then is our knowledge of "what it is to be human" illuminated by holding together every dimension of human experience. Only when the mind and the heart are open to God can we love the world for God's sake and abandon ourselves wholeheartedly to pursue our God-given curiosity and desire for truth. MacIntyre avers, "Philosophy is a form of enquiry that is directed toward the discovery and formulation of timeless truths, of the universal principle, both theoretical and practical, of right reason, but such discovery always provokes new questions, so that philosophy perennially has to renew itself, in part by revisiting its history" (MacIntyre, 2009, p. 166).

MacIntyre is surely right. Anything less would be fragmentary, unfocused, misdirected, and in turn produce a broken sense of "what it is to be human," a view underlined in Hilary Putnam's 1989 Gifford Lectures, which he called "Renewing Philosophy" (Putnam, 1992).

Theological Inquiry

Of all the disciplines, perhaps theology is currently the most misunderstood. Many, especially those opposed to religious belief in principle, regard it as a set of statements to which they attribute literal truth. Unfortunately, there are still some who do claim this to be the case. Bertrand Russell believed that the universe did not exist as an object of reference and that therefore to ask about its cause, origin, or purpose would be meaningless. He was wrong. While we cannot get outside our experience, we can explore it with gratitude to God for what we enjoy with him in his creation.

Christian theology is in fact a set of systems of inquiry that draw on many traditions set in many different cultures and historical circumstances. It is concerned with what it means to be human, what it means to have faith in God, and what it means to live life as a grateful person. The traditions respond to what we are learning about the nature of the world, our self-understanding, the many ways in which we explore and describe our experience, and the countless ways in which we express it in philosophy, the arts, and the sciences. Like language, the structure of human society, and every other discipline of human inquiry, theology has a history with which it behooves us to come to terms. We develop by getting to know thinkers such as St. Augustine, St. Thomas, Barth, von Balthasar, and Lonergan; as we enter into their worlds of inquiry not only do we grow intellectually, but we also develop and begin to take responsibility as human beings.

Embodied within the Christian tradition are the interdependent activities of remembrance, celebration, and anticipation; the moment of these activities is expressed in the Eucharist. In this sacramental act of worship, Christians take up the conversation implicit in the tradition, speak it among themselves in the community, and set about the business of making a reality out of what they hope for in their thought, reflection, action, and enjoyment. And they know all the time that there is no end to this hoping because there is no end to the God whose nature, presence, and meaning they strive to make real.

A Professional Vocation Requires a Liberal Education

The concept of vocation may seem to have little purchase now on a person's choice of career; it was once associated primarily with a religious vocation to the priesthood within the Christian tradition. Nevertheless, the term still has resonance in the public mind, particularly with regard to the life of the professional—lawyer, priest, doctor, and so on—as it suggests the use of one's gifts for the greater public good. We could do well to recover the values it carries with it. Indeed the several recently reported scandals in the National Health Service, for example, have led many to call for "a more professional approach" from all involved: the Care Quality Commission, senior managers, civil servants in the Ministry of Health and Social Services, doctors, nurses, and other health professionals. "A more professional approach" means putting patients first for the sake of the common good. A more professional approach also implies an awareness of the tradition of service and understanding into which the professional has entered when taking up his or her career.

Currently, as I have noted, the term "profession" covers wider range of occupations than those traditionally associated with it. Harold Silver and John Brennan talk of liberal vocationalism and analyze the historical tradition and language of vocation in order to extend their application to other professions, such as engineering and business studies (Silver and Brennan, 1988). They suggest that if a person is to deliver his or her professional training effectively, he or she also needs to be liberally educated; without this personal education, they argue, the person will lack the range of knowledge and experience within which to place his or her technical knowledge and apply it with human concern. In particular, it is a liberal education that will inform a professional of his or her inheritance and of the human tradition in which, as a doctor or priest, the professional stands. Moreover, as Newman emphasized in a previous quotation, the Aristotelian notion of the virtuous person is relevant here: a good education must give attention to the character of the person as well as equip him or her with the competence and skill to practice professionally. The lawyer, doctor, accountant, engineer, or priest remains a person notwithstanding his or her professional vocation.

Liberal education is a long-standing tradition in the United States:

> A truly liberal education is one that prepares us to live responsible, productive, and creative lives in a dramatically changing world. It is an education that fosters a well-grounded intellectual resilience, a disposition toward life-long learning, and an acceptance of responsibility for the ethical consequences of our ideas and actions. Liberal education requires that we understand the foundations of knowledge and enquiry about nature, culture and society: that we master core skills of perception, the importance of historical and cultural context, and that we explore the connections among formal learning, citizenship, and service to our communities. (Board of Directors of the Association of American Colleges and Universities, 1998)

In later publications, the Association of American Colleges and Schools discussed programs of study whereby the professional could be liberally educated, but the general perception was that liberal education was at least as much a style of learning as it was concerned with curriculum content (*Peer Review*, 2012). There is openness to the opportunity to explore and inquire, and there is encouragement to reflect on what one discovers in conversation with others, with the consequence that one comes to embody what one knows. This is close to what Aristotle means when he talks of acquiring the habit of thinking and behaving with integrity.

Martha Nussbaum has frequently defended the importance of a liberal education for the sake of human well-being (Nussbaum, 2010). She is critical of the policies of government and professional bodies, which she argues have reduced education to the acquisition of facts and an attention to outcomes with a focus on value to the economy. As a result, the qualities and personal benefits of the humanities are neglected in the interest of courses in science and technology and preprofessional courses in subjects such as accountancy and international finance. "Getting things right" is what counts most toward becoming a good professional. Economic pressures have led, in any case, to increases in staff-student ratios and class sizes, meaning that vital opportunities for discussion in small seminars, in which ideas can be tested in conversation with others, are much reduced or absent altogether. MacIntyre is right when he says, "It is by having our reasoning put to the question by others, by being called to account for ourselves and our actions by others, that we learn how to scrutinize ourselves as they scrutinize us and how to understand ourselves as they understand us" (MacIntyre, 1999, p. 148).

In particular, the attraction of preprofessional courses at the undergraduate level challenges the opportunity of the undergraduate seeking to enter a profession to become a liberally educated person. The result is that the professional, when he or she takes up an appointment, has a limited range of experience on which to draw when dealing with a client; he or she will therefore be inclined to rely on his or her technical knowledge to see him or her through. One might say this professional lacks the practical wisdom that comes from experience, which Aristotle calls *phronesis*; it will not be acquired at a stroke, but if it is not identified in professional training, the professional will lack the consciousness of what it means and how to develop it. This practical wisdom is more than a matter of language, but learning the language is essential if it is to be practiced; it should, in time, become second nature. If one is to *be* a true professional, he or she will have in mind, first and foremost, his or her vocation to serve the interests of society. Without that, he or she will be more inclined through weakness of will to be satisfied that his or her duty is first to comply, second to serve the interests of the company, and third to build up personal resources. The lack of debate and conversation in the experience of education removes the grist by which the undergraduate comes to terms with new ideas and the challenge of the perspectives of others.

Richard Sennett emphasizes that working with others is an acquired skill that must be formed early through the acquisition of good habits (Sennett, 2012). Moreover, in our current society, in which traditional bonds are disappearing, we have to find new ways of building and practicing the art of cooperation. Nothing could be more important for professionals. If they are to win the confidence of their clients, they will have to do more than be a source of information and objective advice. Clients will want to be assured that professionals are interested in them and are focused on serving them personally and not merely their own financial interests or those of their companies. Professionals will not be able to do that if they are not in conversation with the tradition and aware of the fullness of the context within which that takes place. Both are essential if professionals are to grow as people and evince pleasure in cooperating with their clients. And to grow as a person, it is necessary to become aware of one's vulnerability, otherwise one will always tend to rely on external authorities, such as rules and regulations; one will be compliant rather than morally responsible to the detriment of a client's interests and one's own moral sensitivity.

The British Monarchy: Queen Elizabeth II

At the time of the Diamond Jubilee of Queen Elizabeth II, the British nation was reminded that at her coronation in 1953, she had committed herself to a lifetime of service to her people. To accept the role she had inherited with such an obvious sense of gratitude and awareness of the privilege is a sign of grace that we would do well to mark. There is no greater example of vocation that can be pointed to in the current experience of the British nation than sixty years of unstinting royal service. This is all the more remarkable because she can call on no constitutional authority of her own: her only authority is that which flows from tradition, her experience, and her obviously gracious and incontrovertible concern for the well-being of the British nation and all her people.

The Queen entered into her inheritance supported by the values of her mother and grandmother: love of God, love of family, love of nation. The oath she took at her coronation put these into public words, and she has been guided by them in all that she has done, to which she added her own profound sense of duty. She equipped herself by familiarizing herself with the nation's history, often, it seems, thereby fortifying herself with more knowledge than some of the 12 British Prime Ministers who have served under her. At the same time, her lifelong experience has enabled her to contribute, through conversation and courteous personal interest, to the development of sound government and just administration.

A key to understanding the role of the monarchy in general and Queen Elizabeth II in particular is the awareness that tradition is dynamic and the grounds for development. I say development, not change, because the principles and values that are embodied in the monarchy remain; the forms in which they are presented may change from time to time. The Queen has been aware of this throughout her reign, allowing herself right from the beginning to be influenced by events. Thus, although not at first in favor of it, she was persuaded to accept television cameras in Westminster Abbey for the coronation. It was an enormous success, and every opportunity has been taken since then to present on television the pageantry of national celebration on royal occasions such as the Opening of Parliament and the Trooping of the Colour, which focus the gratitude of the nation on the continuities of history.

In many ways, the Queen is truly a professional who embodies in her person the values of the British nation. She has given her life to creating of a legacy of gratitude for the past and the present, which will inform the future.

Conclusion

There is, in a sense, no conclusion possible; our human inheritance and our national inheritance are open-ended and indeterminable. For that, we can be grateful. What we inherit does limit what is possible, whether looked at from the point of view of evolution or from that of our human histories, but it does not take away our opportunities to contribute to the world's well-being. We have the freedom that arises from the results of our God-given curiosity, if only we are willing to accept the responsibility that flows from our increasing response-abilities. It boils down to what we want, which is largely determinable by an examination of what we are trying to do, as Elizabeth Anscombe remarked. If we are grateful for our opportunities, not only will we be focused on the well-being of the civilized world and the future of our evolution, but we will be concerned with the individual well-being of our professional clients, family, and personal friends. Insofar as we can, we are also focused on each person's ability to care for those who are close to him or her. As I have underlined earlier, we professionals are persons first and professionals second; that is the order of our sense of relationship. A key to understanding what this means raises the matter of compassion and its relationship to gratitude. To this I now turn.

Chapter 6

Compassion

Introduction

Grateful persons are compassionate: they want to give to others what they believe they enjoy themselves. Jesus lives his life in thankful awareness that God is with him and has compassion for those who fail to see the world as graced by God's presence. He does not blame them. He has compassion, for example, on the crowd that follows him into the desert in the mistaken belief that he was their longed-for political leader (Matt. 15:32). The father (perhaps representing God the Father), grieved by his son's waste of his inheritance, is full of compassion when he sees him returning (Lk. 15:20). The Eucharist, the central act of Christian worship, is a compassionate celebration of God's presence with his people: none is excluded. The Celebrant, Christ, thanks God for all God's gifts, which he shares with the disciples and in principle with all people in the form of bread and wine.

Jesus's compassion is not prompted by a casual meeting with an individual or a group; it arises from his belief that the world is characterized by the life-giving presence of God, who cares for all. In his person, he takes up themes found in the Old Testament. In the book of Psalms, God is compassionate and merciful in the face of Israel's failure to live out its calling. God, despite the Israelites' sin, never abandons them: "Their heart was not steadfast towards him; they were not true to his covenant. Yet he, being compassionate, forgave their iniquity, and did not destroy them; often he restrained his anger, and did not stir up all his wrath." "With upright heart he tended them, and guided them with skillful hand" (Ps. 78:37–8, 72).

Compassion is an integral ingredient of virtuous professional practice: it not only confirms the client in his or her relationship but nourishes the person who is acting in a professional capacity. I shall develop this theme first with regard to the relationship of the personal and the professional. Then, after an examination of the meaning of compassion, I shall explore the relationship of compassion, with equality, and pity; the role of reason and the question of whether compassion can be taught; and if so, how.

Persons and Professionals

The professional is first and last a person, with moral responsibilities, virtues, and vices; he or she enjoys a personal relationship with friends, family, and members of society at large before he or she can be a professional with the responsibilities that follow. As the professional remembers the qualities and virtues that make for good personal character, the public service of the professional life will flourish. These personal qualities and virtues focus on the individual client, the reputation of the profession, and the service of the community. It used to be called a "vocation." With this in mind, it behooves the professional to pay attention to the quality of his or her personal life.

Luciano Giubbilei is a distinguished garden designer who created the Laurent-Perrier Gardens for the 2009, 2011, and 2014 Royal Horticultural Society Chelsea Flower Shows. When asked by Helen Gazeley in a 2011 interview how he had come to design such peaceful, lively, and moving gardens (literally and emotionally), he replied that his gardens were the product of self-knowledge as much as study and professional skill (Giubbilei, 2011). Lord Adebowale, the chief executive of *Turning Point*, believes that leadership is a state of mind, not a set of characteristics. Success depends on the culture of personal relationships within an organization, for when properly developed, they lead to the distribution of leadership—a point of view that is counterintuitive to the Western mind. William Kendall, who revitalized the chocolate manufacturer Green and Black and the New Covent Garden Soup Company, says that success involves the chief executive falling in love with what he or she is doing (Frearson, 2014).

In other words, personal passion matters. It is certainly true that a student has little chance of making progress without love for the subject he or she is studying. These insights are universally applicable, whether one is thinking of an artist, a businessman, or a dentist: self-knowledge is fundamental to good practice. The professional is first and last a person who needs to be nourished if he or she is to succeed professionally.

When we accept with grace what we have received from the efforts of those in whose traditions we stand, we begin to understand that our responsibility is not simply to those for whose care we are immediately accountable but, through the legacy we leave, to the well-being of future generations. Put in this way, the responsibilities of every professional person are truly daunting. What is more, it underlines the fact that mere compliance is an inadequate conduit for a living tradition. Indeed it might be said to be impossible and, as Lord Denning averred, stultifying.

In the British Common Law tradition, a judge does not simply apply the law in determining the outcome of a case; he takes personal responsibility for interpreting the law *and* taking the offending person into account. Lord Denning, the Master of the Rolls, did this most publicly and controversially: "What is the argument on the other side? Only this, that no case has been found in which it has been done before. That argument does not appeal to me in the least. If we never do anything that has not been done before, we shall never get anywhere. The law will stand still while the rest of the world goes on; and that will be bad for both" (Denning, 1954, p. 15 at 22). In fact, even statute laws and regulations published by the Executive require intelligent understanding and thoughtful application within a tradition.

Wherever we stand in society, tradition confirms that we are not alone as persons or as professionals: our sense of self is that of a "self in relation." John Macmurray puts it like this: "We need one another to be ourselves" (Macmurray, 1961, p. 211). He develops this theme in his Gifford Lectures for 1952 and 1954: "The simplest expression I can find for the thesis I have tried to maintain is this: All meaningful knowledge is for the sake of action and all meaningful action for the sake of friendship" (Macmurray, 1991, pp. 14–15).

To be ourselves is to be aware of others and to want our friendship to make a difference to their lives. Hence, when we are grateful for what we inherit and for everything we enjoy—education, health, food and well-being—we cannot help but also be aware that there are others in our society who are less favored and in need one way or another, hence the particular emotion of compassion to which gratitude gives rise.

Compassion is a comprehensive, crucially significant dimension of human experience; the lack of it dehumanizes and separates persons whose real lives will only be realized in relationships. Donne's familiar lines express this perfectly:

> No man is an island,
> Entire of itself,
> Every man is a piece of the continent,
> A part of the main. (Donne, 1946, p. 538)

Many of us (especially in the West) lack gratitude for our inheritance and seem to believe that it is a virtue to strive to make ourselves self-sufficient. Emotionally, and therefore really, it is impossible; one simply loses touch with reality. Macmurray again says, "Individual independence is an illusion; and the independent individual, the isolated self, is a nonentity" (Macmurray, 1961, p. 211). Those who try to cut themselves off from their past experience an analogous fate. Without context, they are profoundly alone and are likely to flounder for lack of support and experience a consequent loss of selfhood.

COMPASSION

Compassion has a special place in the Christian tradition, but it has significant purchase on the thinking of many traditions East and West, both religious and secular. The Dalai Lama, for example, refers to compassion as "the supreme emotion." Moreover, "compassion" is the most frequently occurring word in the Qur'an; it occurs at the beginning of each of its 144 chapters except the ninth. Alain de Botton affirms tenderness to be a virtue of Christian spirituality, of which atheists should take full note (de Botton, 2012, pp. 166–77).

This emotion is complex. Martha Nussbaum presents her position thus: "To put it simply, compassion is a painful emotion occasioned by the awareness of another person's misfortune" (Nussbaum, 2001, p. 301). This essentially Aristotelian position is helpful as a starting point. However, Aristotle distinguishes between undeserved and deserved misfortune. For the former, compassion is an appropriate moral response, whereas for the latter, passionless pity is more in order. Nussbaum herself makes the point that the unfortunate person should not bear total responsibility for his or her misfortune. Montaigne agrees: his awareness of human imperfection (including his own) led him to commend toleration and compassion for one's fellow man. For the Christian who accepts that all humankind is "in the image of God," the distinction between deserved and undeserved misfortune is irrelevant to the appropriateness of compassion. According to empirical research carried out by Monroe, altruism, the unselfish and devoted care for the well-being of others, is dependent on a perspective adopted by altruists who see themselves "as bound to all mankind through a common humanity" (Monroe, 1996, p. 5). God's compassion, incarnate in Christ, is for all, not some, and so should that be of Christians.

Christians commonly say a grace before meals. Two in particular come to mind: "Bless, O Lord, this food to our use and us to your service, and make us ever mindful of the needs of others" and "Give us grace, O Lord, to be ever thankful for Thy providence, with hearts always ready to provide for the needs of others." It is as if the sheer gratitude that the family feels for the daily gift of food is associated with compassion for those less fortunate. This tends to confirm that, as I have argued previously, gratitude has a forward-looking perspective as well as the more familiar retrospective aspect.

Empirical research indicates that people with a grateful disposition will tend to feel grateful more frequently, for more aspects of their experience, and toward more people (present and past) and concomitantly be encouraged to behave well toward others (McCullough, Emmons, and Tsang, 2002, pp. 112–27). This suggests indeed that a grateful disposition is not only a "moral barometer" but also a "moral motivator." Therefore to limit our understanding of the emotion of gratitude to appreciation of past gifts and benefactors is to ignore the stimulus it provokes for present and future acceptance of responsibilities. Such an appreciation is essential, for we do not walk into the future backward; if we do, we may trip and injure ourselves. A grateful person is enriched by an emotional disposition to accept responsibility to work with others for humanity's, and therefore for creation's, well-being.

In a world that the Christian regards as the unmerited gift of God's grace, gratitude cannot be passive: it stimulates compassion, which is itself not a passive condition. If one says of oneself that one feels compassion, one is at the same time claiming that one wants to act compassionately; the emotion of compassion is a statement of intent, not a self-reference to one's state of mind. To put it clearly, one cannot feel compassion without being compassionate and setting about the business of undertaking concerned action with others to make things better. The image that comes to mind is that of a U-turn; we hold out our hands to grasp the hands of others as we walk into the future together.

The Christian claims that humankind bears the image of God, which means that humans are free to give of themselves for the well-being of others, to share in God's creative activity as he works to bring the world to perfection. It is in God's nature to be compassionate; it is not an addition to his self-understanding, which arose through experience. It is likewise a quality of human nature but one we often ignore or neglect to express, perhaps through fear of the demands that might be made of us and/or a lack of awareness of the presence of God's Spirit to sustain us, whatever the circumstances in which we find ourselves.

Our condition is rooted in linguistic convention—our uses of language, of which Wittgenstein points out there are very many (Wittgenstein, 1958, para. 23). Austin identifies a style of utterance he calls "illocution," which he roughly understands as the implicit meaning of a sentence; he distinguishes it from "perlocution," which refers to the utterance of a sentence as actually to do something (Austin, 1962, pp. 99–131). He offers the word "promising" as an illustration of a further term, "performative." When a person says, "I promise to meet you at the ski resort in Colorado on Friday, next week," it is more than spoken words, which have meaning: it is an enactment of intention, which the addressed person is justified in believing. Whether it is true depends on whether the promise, barring accidents, is kept.

Analogously, I suggest that when a person says, "I feel compassion for Mr. McMurdo, whose son was in the marines and lost his life in Iraq," the sentence is tantamount to being a performative. One is doing something here, not merely mouthing words; the truth, of course, depends on whether the one who expresses compassion does something about it. It may mean writing a letter of condolence, attending the memorial service, and/or sending a check to Help the Heroes. Of course, one may not know what is best to do, but if so, a person of compassionate disposition will take steps to explore how best to express his or her compassion. Gratitude and compassion both prospectively motivate one to do better, accept responsibility, and serve one's fellow human beings. Typically, one might say that gratitude expresses itself in compassion and compassion in active generosity.

For Whom Should One Feel Compassion?

How far should one's generosity extend? Jesus was asked this very question by a lawyer: "Who is my neighbour?" (Lk. 10:29–37). He wanted to know who was and who was not a member of God's Chosen People in order to be clear on who required his neighborly attention. Jesus's parable of the Good Samaritan makes it clear that the Christian should have compassion for all after the pattern of God's compassion for the creation and all humanity.

The road from Jerusalem to Jericho was a notoriously dangerous road on which, if one were sensible, one would travel in a group for safety (Jeremias, 1969, p. 52). So is Jesus implying that this lonely traveler was foolish and had only himself to blame for his misfortune? Perhaps he had no friends or was ignorant of the road's reputation. Whatever his circumstances, he was robbed and left for dead. But he was in luck: others were on the same journey. A priest and a Levite came across him but did not touch him for fear of defilement; their responsibilities would be fulfilled if they complied with the law. The Samaritan was a pariah; however, when he saw the injured man, he did what he could on the spot, placed him on his animal, brought him to a hostelry where he left money for attendants to care for him, and promised when he returned to make good any further expense that had accrued.

So who is the neighbor? The lawyer, it seems, could not even bring himself to name the Samaritan and simply said, "the one who showed mercy." "Go and do likewise," said Jesus. The point is that one does not classify people as those who deserve compassion and those who do not, since all are included within the purview of the compassion of God, the Creator, Redeemer, and Sustainer of all things and all people. The focus of human compassion is the needy person in whose presence one stands; compliance is no substitute for compassionate moral concern. I believe this applies to professional practice: each client is a person to be treated with compassion.

Nussbaum, in her general account of compassion quoted previously, uses the word "misfortune"; I understand why she would do so. When, for example, a candidate fails his or her final examination to become a doctor despite his or her best efforts, one naturally feels compassionate toward the candidate. This would be even more true if the candidate were involved in an accident and were precluded from continuing with the medical course by his or her injuries. The student would be disappointed in either case, for he or she would have to take his or her career in a new direction. The student needs compassion if he or she is to pick up the pieces and move on.

However, the term "misfortune" suggests that compassion begins with a consideration of criteria. Should I be compassionate in this case? This process from the Christian position is *in principle* irrelevant. As distinct from Aristotle, who might have pity, the Christian sees all fellow human beings as persons to be treated with compassion. St. Paul is clear about this: he holds all humanity together as one when he declares, "For there is no distinction, since all have sinned and fall short of the glory of God" (Rom. 3:22–23). To fall short of the glory of God is to fail to see the world as characterized by the presence of God and to treat it as being within one's own control. In principle, one denies one's true humanity and closes one's eyes to the opportunities that flow from realizing one's freedom in God's creation to live a life open to all. To be human is to be compassionate, to be actively focused on the needs of others for their sake and for God's sake. It is to follow Christ, who embodies God's presence in creation.

To discriminate between those who deserve to be treated compassionately and those who do not is to act sinfully because it denies God's gracious presence. Moreover, it is an error of theological understanding to associate the condition of being a sinner only with past misbehavior; it is also a consequent inability to appreciate what the future offers and get on with living it. Gratitude for God's forgiveness liberates us into the freedom of God's gracious presence, where we can become aware of the open possibilities of the future that we inherit. Of course, one's past behavior may again and again prejudice one's capacity to discern the creative opportunities with which one is blessed, which is why it is necessary to celebrate regularly the sacrament of penance. All stand equal before God in their need of the assurance of his forgiveness. We are all sinners because we are inclined to stand around wringing our hands instead of getting on with the job of being human for Christ's sake. Such equality is not simply a metaphysical recognition of equality before God but an integral part of our humanity.

Equality and Compassion

Equality—not egalitarianism—is an essential quality of human life from the Christian point of view. Genuine equality involves treating every person according to his or her circumstances; egalitarianism is concerned with treating each person identically, whatever his or her circumstances. The former assumes a personal relationship between each person such that each affirms the well-being of the other; the latter assumes a formulaic pattern for all relationships in which the reality of the person is ignored or denied.

None of us can justly thank God that he is better than others. A genuine feeling for the equality of all persons, in the deepest sense, is a condition of a proper understanding of compassion. The Pharisee in Jesus's parable does not understand this: he is utterly unaware of his *personal* relationship with the tax gatherer when both stand in the presence of God. The Pharisee, standing by himself, was praying thus: "God, I thank you that I am not like other people: thieves, rogues, adulterers, or even like this tax-collector" (Lk. 18:9–14). Of course, no one stands by oneself; one stands alongside all other people, sinners before God, every one of whom enjoys the freedom proclaimed by and instantiated in the self-giving of God in Christ. Gratitude for this fact is the mark of a genuinely human person. One is therefore not only the subject of God's gracious compassion in Christ but also freed by him to be compassionate to all others who are, as a matter of fact, in the same condition as oneself. When that happens, one is reminded how close one is to failure. As John Bradford (1510?—1555) is reputed to have said on seeing some criminals taken to execution, "But for the grace of God there goes John Bradford."

An important Christological point is implicit in this position. Christ is not only the revealed presence of the Father with his people—who are all people—but the embodiment of all humanity. Thus, when we attend to the needs of each individual who presents himself or herself to us as a client, we are witnessing to the wholeness of all humanity and, in our compassion, serving Christ. Justice is the universal recognition of this fact, as Jesus's parable of judgment makes plain. Those to his left ask, "When did I ever see you hungry, thirsty, naked or ill?" The Son of Man replies, "Truly I tell you, just as you did not do it to one of the least of these, you did not do it to me" (Matt. 25:31–46). One is reminded of Aquinas's remark that gratitude is a virtue annexed to justice, by which he implies that gratitude for God's good gifts stimulates compassion for the common good to be expressed in serving other persons for Christ's sake.

John Rawls confirms the intimate relationship between equality and justice. His general conception is based on the assumption that in a world that is beyond one's control, no one would choose to risk disadvantaging himself or herself if he or she had the confidence that no one else would choose to try to determine his or her own advantage. He expresses his general position as follows: "All social primary goods—liberty and opportunity, income and wealth, and the bases of self-respect—are to be distributed equally unless an unequal distribution of any or all of these goods is to the advantage of the least favoured" (Rawls, 1972, p. 303).

Rawls has been variously criticized by philosophers who think his view of human nature assumes a false and unargued metaphysics (Sandel, 1982); who wish to begin from another baseline that will, for example, guarantee property rights (Nozick, 1974); or who argue for a different relationship between welfare and resources (Dworkin, 1981a and 1981b).

The philosophical issues raised by his critics are certainly important. However, from the point of view of the Christian theologian, there is merit in the position Rawls adopts. Since we are all sinners, there is no advantage that one person can justly assume over another: all are equal. Moreover, since that is a matter of justice, it means that the fact of forgiveness must be grounded in justice if healing is to be accepted. As a Rwandan woman caught up in the genocide of 1994 is reported to have said about her own experience, "You can't heal without feeling justice has been done" (The Forgiveness Project, 2010). That is exactly what Christians believe, but from their perspective, justice has been done—by God. Humanity has been healed; the future is open for all humans to behave humanely and with compassion. Indeed that is the basis for the gratitude of Christians, which raises the question of the relation of compassion to pity.

Compassion and Pity

The difference between compassion and pity is, I believe, significant: "A leper came to him begging him, and kneeling he said to him, 'If you choose, you can make me clean.' Moved with pity, Jesus stretched out his hand and touched him and said to him, 'I do choose'" (Mk. 1:41). This is the translation of the Greek according to the New Revised Standard Version (NRSV), which uses the word "pity." The Authorized (King James) Version translates the word as "compassion," which seems to me to express better the relationship that Jesus assumes in his conversation with the leper.

Pity is, I believe, inappropriate here because it is best thought of as a passive emotion in contrast to compassion. Jesus could pity the leper without any intention of healing him. Aristotle defines pity as pain at another person's misfortune. He is right: an expression of pity is like saying that one is in pain. It implies no suggestion of commitment to ameliorate the position of the one who is suffering, though the recognition of another's misfortune may be an occasion to inquire objectively as to what might be helpful. However, if so, it will be a second stage of the experience and not integral to the actual expression of pity. Hence the sufferer may petition a potential benefactor to take pity on him or her, but as I understand it, there is no implication, let alone presumption, that assistance will necessarily be forthcoming, since an expression of pity is not performative. This is clear when one reflects on the expression "Poor you." A person may say, "You poor thing!" when informed that he or she has been made redundant, but there is no implication here of anything more than at most a personal expression of a general feeling of sympathy—"Tough luck, old boy!"

How do sympathy and empathy relate in this context? I suggest that when I express sympathy with another, I remain aware that we are two people; I express my feelings for him or her, but in so doing, we both remain ourselves, two independent persons: "*I* have sympathetic feeling for *you*." On the other hand, if I say that I empathize with you, I imply that I feel what you feel to the extent that we share a common emotion (Krznaric, 2014, pp. x, 11). I am of course still free to choose whether to help you or not, but to express empathy and not at least inquire as to what I could do to assist brings the assertion of empathy into question.

Shakespeare offers a range of responses to feelings of pity following the death of Caesar. Mark Anthony points to Brutus's ingratitude in stabbing Caesar to death, calling it "the most unkindest cut of all." He was, Mark Anthony says, "Caesar's angel" and calls upon the gods to witness "how dearly Caesar loved him." He notices how the crowd is driven to weeping:

> O now you weep, and I perceive you feel
> The dint of pity.

"Dint" is itself a revealing word. It usually signifies a blow brought about by an external cause. "The dint of pity" is the mark of a threat to which one reacts impulsively without much thought. It is not best understood as a feeling, or emotion. The response of the crowd is therefore a natural demand for revenge—an unlikely way to express one's compassion, one would think.

> *All:* Revenge!—About!—Seek!—Burn!—Fire!—Kill!—Slay!—Let not a traitor live. (Shakespeare, 1955, *Julius Caesar*, Act III, Sc. II, l. 170–207)

P. F. Strawson might well call this a "reactive response" insofar as it is an uncontrolled, instinctive response to a situation that is clearly unjust (Strawson, 2008, pp. 4–7). One cannot understand compassion in this way; there is something more considered, reasonable, and essentially human about being compassionate as opposed to pitying. Strawson does in fact suggest that gratitude comes into the same category of reactive response, but I think he is mistaken when gratitude is considered from a theological and psychological perspective. Humankind is not caused by God or by circumstances to express gratitude; it is free to be grateful or not. Strawson is discussing the many kinds of relationships we can have with other people "as sharers of a common interest." For the Christian, the most essential common interest flows from one's relationship with God and the human equality that is a consequence of that relationship.

Griswold points out that to say, "I pity you," may amount to no more than a refusal to recognize a person as worthy of consideration: "I find you a miserable and worthless person, regardless of how pleased you feel about yourself" (Griswold, 2007). In contrast, while someone calling on someone else to take pity on him or her may be a heartfelt request for mercy and healing, it may equally be no more than a self-pitying request for help by a person who has no sense of self-worth or is unwilling or unable to make any effort to help himself or herself. In the case of an appeal to God, it is to one whom the appellant believes has the authority, capacity, desire, and character to heal. Even here, however, there is an implicit misunderstanding.

God does not take pity on humankind; he is compassionate, utterly committed to loving his creation, and he can do nothing else, since that is his nature. Moreover, he does so in association with humankind, whom he has raised from the slavery of sin to full sonship as a member of the family. The position is dramatically presented in the person of Christ, in whom the Divine and the human are alive without compromise or confusion between his divine and human natures. God does not take pity on the human condition; he has compassion for it.

Compassion and Reason

"Sympathy" is a word often regarded as synonymous with "compassion"; it has an analogous derivation, but from Greek rather than Latin. While in many contexts, "compassion" and "sympathy" are used synonymously to indicate a harmonious sensitivity, sympathy does not go far enough to carry the performative vigor implied when, for example, God is declared to be "a compassionate God." A useful comparison can be made between the Christian understanding of empathy and the admirable traditions of Buddhist teaching, which emerged in India from Hinduism in the sixth and fifth centuries BC. Both talk of compassion, but in illuminatingly contrasting ways.

The Buddhist story has it that Prince Siddhartha Gautama lived in the sixth century BC on the borders of Nepal and India. He abandoned his family and friends to pursue a spiritual journey, which led him to enlightenment when he was awakened to the truth that all things and therefore all human experience are transient. In the face of this, he realized that suffering arose from trying to achieve an impossible permanence. There was, he taught, no soul, no god, and no truth beyond the realization that all suffering was illusory in the sense that one would be relieved of it once one recognized the truth. Suffering was a creation of the human mind, as it strove to achieve what was beyond reason. At first, he was disinclined to share the truth because he thought he would be ridiculed, but he was persuaded to do so by Brahma, the Hindu god of creation. Gautama focused the rest of his life on the task of introducing others to his liberating discovery, as a result of which he is known as "the Compassionate One."

Gautama is regarded as the Supreme Buddha; however, *Buddha* is in fact not a person but rather a state of mind experienced by the enlightened ones who are thereby released from all suffering. The Buddhist is comforted by the knowledge that suffering is an illusion. Undoubtedly, the vision of life Gautama achieved was one that, for him and for many Buddhists, removed any identifiable self. But while there was no self to take account of, he was far from indifferent to the actual suffering of those who were not yet enlightened. Concern for the well-being of all the world's creatures, not just humankind, is an explicit perspective of Buddhism. But while Buddhism may involve courteous attention to others as one seeks to teach them the truth and restraint from taking the life of any other living creature, it is not empathetic and therefore distinct from the Christian approach. The Buddhist cannot enter into the suffering of another person because, as an enlightened person, he or she knows that the suffering of every person is illusory. The Buddhist's task is therefore limited to an attempt to demonstrate the illusory nature of all suffering so as to encourage others in their spiritual journeys toward enlightenment.

At the center of the Christian Faith, on the other hand, is God, the Creator, Redeemer, and Sustainer, whose intention in creating is to share the life of the world to which he has committed himself so as to bring it to perfection. His empathy for humankind is theologically explored in the doctrine of the incarnation. This remarkable claim that God became man and took upon himself the suffering that is the continuous experience of all humans is at the heart of the Christian understanding of God's gift of himself, for which Christians are grateful. The gracious "revelation" of God in Christ (if "revelation" is the right term to use) is that the world in which we find ourselves as human beings is a world from which God has never separated himself. Thus, although human beings may be in sin (that is, they may fall short of the glory of God through not recognizing his presence), God's compassionate nature is an ever-present reality. Aquinas affirms this when he writes, "in no human does [sin] so rule that the whole good of nature is corrupted." He continues with confidence, "an inclination to do those things which are in accord with the eternal law remains" (Aquinas, 2006, I.II, q. 93.6 ad 2).

Calvin, on the other hand, believed that humankind was utterly depraved. Human beings could not do anything to enhance their understanding of their miserable position in the world or inform their understanding of their absolute dependence on God for life and in death. He claimed that a person's future, day to day and at the end of life, depended entirely on the unmerited grace of God in forgiving sins. He therefore confined freedom to God and argued that a person's future was predestined. But he was mistaken. While it may be true that the health of humankind depends on the forgiveness of God, God's forgiveness is unconditional, real, and absolute: mankind is in principle forgiven and free.

Aquinas was therefore right when, for very good reasons, he rejected the idea that mankind was utterly cut off from God by sin. How could it be? Humans had been endowed with reason by God, and while they may be tempted through fear, poor judgment, and what St. John of the Cross called "the dark night of the soul" to abandon their search for God, they could be assured by reason that God had not abandoned them. How could they otherwise have even entertained the thought of the reality of God and his gracious relationship with the world?

Aquinas, in complete contrast with Calvin, in complete contrast with Calvin and Barth, maintained that reason, the residual goodness of humankind created in the image of God, underpinned an irremovable and essential freedom to choose to be compassionate. Of course, however, in setting out to express one's concern for others, one may be dismayed by one's failures and lose hope. And honesty will compel us to acknowledge our weaknesses and shortcomings. We fear the consequences, as the demands on us may be unsustainable. But at the same time, we know not only that we can seek forgiveness but that we are forgiven.

THE COMPASSION OF FORGIVENESS: RECONCILIATION AND RESTITUTION

Archbishop Desmond Tutu chaired the Truth and Reconciliation Commission, established in 1995, in an attempt to "manage" the incipient conflict that he feared threatened the dramatic change of direction in South African politics. The accession to power of Nelson Mandela marked the end of apartheid, which Tutu believed had brutalized both victims *and* oppressors. If all could admit the truth about the past, perhaps resentment could be contained and mutual forgiveness could bring hope for a new society. Desmond Tutu held that everyone depended on their relationships with all others, if they were to become the fully human people God intended them to be. This assertion is an attempt to hold together both the individual integrity of personal relationships and the many relationships within and between communities. Thus Tutu wrote, "Forgiveness will follow confession and healing will happen, and so contribute to national unity and reconciliation" (Tutu, 1999, p. 120). Gratitude for one's inheritance is incomplete, unreal, unfulfilling, and ultimately untransformative unless it takes account of the injustices of the past: "It is ultimately in our best interest that we become forgiving, reconciling, and reconciled people because without forgiveness, without reconciliation, we have no future" (p. 165).

These dramatic statements illustrate the conditions for individual personal relationships, relationships within a society (between races, religions, classes, genders, generations), and relationships between nations, hence the depth, length, and breadth of gratitude Christians feel for the freedom they enjoy consequent upon their forgiveness by God—a freedom that includes the power to forgive and the eschewing of resentment.

Bernard Williams calls attention to the fact that forgiveness is an unfashionable topic in moral philosophy but a common experience in ordinary life. He writes, "To be forgiven is something we sometimes ask, and forgiving is something we sometimes say we do. To ask to be forgiven is in part to acknowledge that the attitude displayed in our actions was such as might properly be resented and in part to repudiate that attitude for the future (or at least for the immediate future); and to forgive is to accept the repudiation and to forswear the resentment" (Williams, 2008, p. 6).

Resentment has no place in the heart of God. Our behavior may require forgiveness, but even forgiveness can become a mere formality without feeling, sympathy, or even compassion for the circumstances of the person whom one is "forgiving." To forgive in such a way is not really to forgive, because the expression of forgiveness is a performative. "I forgive you" is a powerful expression that reestablishes a relationship of trust, courtesy, and care. In the sacrament of penance, this is exactly what the priest does: he affirms the truth of God's forgiveness of the penitent sinner. Assured thereby of the presence of God, the sinner is free to renew his or her humanity and recover his or her natural capacity to be compassionate.

"To know all is to make one tolerant," wrote Mme. de Stael (de Stael, 1807, lib. iv, ch. 3). This is most especially true of that knowledge of oneself that comes from knowing the forgiveness of God. It is in this context that the dimension of sacramentality is important. For it is not the priest who forgives in the confessional; rather, he is the one whose priestly ordination gives him the authority to declare God's forgiveness of sins. Of course, the sacrament of penance can itself lose its vitality, become devalued, and come to be no more than a transaction of compliance. But we know this. Freud taught us that the best can become the worst at the drop of a hat. To an extent, this is what the reformation was about: the reality of confession was too often replaced by institutional compliance, which was unsatisfying to both priest and penitent.

Can Compassion Be Taught?

It seems, however, unreasonable to assert that compassion is an obligation: one cannot be required to be compassionate. Compassion is the expression of an affectionate concern for another, which prompts action in support of him or her. Above all, it is an emotion of love, concomitant with its expression in action. Can it be taught?

Plato in the *Meno* discusses whether "excellence" can be taught. *Arete* is often translated as "virtue"; it is an attempt to put into one word whatever it is that makes something an excellent thing of its kind. So a knife, a bicycle, an essay, or a sculpture can have *arete* of its own kind. And so can a human being. The *arete* of the human being holds together wisdom, true opinion, knowledge, and moral respect for justice, which Socrates persuades Meno can only be grasped through giving attention to careful questioning until one recognizes the truth for oneself. But in order to recognize the truth in response to the questioning, one must have known the answer already. So Socrates suggests that while knowledge cannot be formally taught, it can be recollected. But this of course depends on a belief in the preexistence of the human soul, a view that we today find difficult to understand. However, the idea is illuminating for the Christian in one profound context: forgiveness.

The fact is that, as Christians see it, humankind is forgiven. Hence it is a matter not of literal forgiveness at this moment in time but of being regularly reminded of the state of one's true relationship with God such that one recovers one's true self and becomes compassionate. This forgiveness is bound into the life, death, Resurrection, and ascension of Christ. Moreover, the Creed further asserts that "he descended into hell." Those traditions that fail to affirm the wholeness of the Good News miss the significance of this dimension of Christ's work: he leaves, as we might say, no stone unturned in his determination to complete the task he has been given by his Father. No one, not even one who absolutely fears for his or her future, is excluded from the promise of forgiveness. Gratitude lies at the heart of human celebration.

There are three things to be said about the teaching of compassion. First, there is the matter of liturgical habit, which lies at the heart of the Christian's celebration of the Faith. Weekly Mass, the Eucharist, is not simply a remembering of something Christ did in the past; it involves the identification of oneself with him and the performative expression of one's intention to live in the image of God—that is, as a compassionate person. Knowing that one fails to do so, giving in to a feeling of pity for others, and even resenting the way one has been treated all make the regular acknowledgement of sin a vital part of one's life. It is easy to ridicule this or even to regard it with contempt. After all, all one has to do, so it is said, is turn up at the confessional and make one's confession, and forgiveness is automatic. This is not so, of course. But what is true is that nothing stands between oneself and the fulfillment of one's human life of compassion if one really wants that life. Assurance of this is expressed in the whole pattern of shared life covered by the priestly responsibility for "the cure of souls." The fact that a general confession is a dimension of Eucharistic celebration acknowledges the fact that God's forgiveness is for communities, within communities, and between persons.

Second, there is the prayer that Christ taught his disciples in which Jesus invites his disciples to join with him daily in praying to "our Father." The "our" includes all people proleptically, not just a local worshipping community, a particular denomination of the Christian Church, or even one religion. "Give us this day our daily bread" is therefore a petition prayed with Christ on behalf of all people—not only me, my family, or my nation, but all people. Daily bread is an ambiguous term, but one illuminating scholarly understanding suggests that it refers to the daily ration of the ordinary soldier. That may be the context in which one should begin one's exploration of its meaning; however, we also know that "man does not live by bread alone, but by every word that comes from the mouth of God" (Matt. 4:4). Humankind does not flourish *qua* human being simply by eating; there is required education, shelter, society, a spiritual life, and above all, the nourishment that comes from recognizing and being grateful for the presence of God. But let's take simply the basic plea of human being for food: if we are serious and realize that each Christian in his or her praying, and each Christian community in its praying, is praying on behalf of all humanity that each person may go to bed at night with a full stomach, there must come at one and the same time the knowledge not only that we are failing but that we could, if we so chose, do more. Prayer is a performative action, as is all genuine liturgical performance.

Hence the following petition in the prayer is for forgiveness, the request again being on behalf of all, with full knowledge that we will be forgiven as we forgive those who have deceived us by their promises. "Lead us not into temptation, but deliver us from evil" is a prayer that has confused many. How would the God in whom Christians believe, and whose nature is to be compassionate, possibly lead us into temptation and not deliver us from evil? But we need to be delivered from our fears. The point is that since we may deceive ourselves into believing that God and our circumstances conspire against us, we need to clear our minds of any thought that God would be against us. Hence the petition is followed by an affirmation. No, God would not lead us into temptation; he will deliver us from evil: "For thine is the kingdom, the power and the glory," the absolute expression of the fullest confidence in God, his presence, his purpose, and his nature. Understood as a genuine performative, it confirms what we believe and intend to act upon.

The third thing to mention about the teaching of compassion involves the common life we live with one another, informed by stories, experienced in action, and affirmed in the gifts we receive for which we are truly grateful. Community is not achieved unless it is first assumed and then worked out. "Membership" of the Church is no different; it is not made but recognized, explored, and lived out.

Conclusion

Compassion is an aspect of the *arete* of our humanity: it is part of our essential nature as persons made in the image of God. This is true of the professional who, whatever his or her professional training and experience, remains a human being in society. To pretend that virtuous professional practice can be reduced to compliance is to forget the personal vocation to be compassionate. The question is, does fulfillment of a *contractual* relationship express the *arete* of what it means to be human, let alone the wholeness of the life of the compassionate person? Relationships, both personal and professional, require compassionate delivery if the persons, both the professional and the client, are to flourish.

The Person and Work of Jesus Christ is at the heart of the Christian's life since he or she is called to fulfill his or her vocation as one who is made in the image of God; Christ shapes every relationship to which the human being is inclined. St. John says, "All things came into being through him, and without him not one thing came into being" (Jn. 1:3–4). Service as gift is the theme underpinning our historical experience of God in the world. Yet according to Nussbaum, "Compassion is a painful emotion," which raises the question of sacrificial giving as a key element of service.

The Christian theological framework is characterized by God's love and compassion. God loves his creation, to which he graciously gives himself in Christ, thus confirming its essential goodness and future well-being. He shares compassionately in its growth toward perfection. The Christian community of faith, the Body of Christ, takes into its life the world of creation, which includes all people, whose gratitude is proleptically expressed in the Eucharist. Made in the image of God, we have been given the authority and essential courtesy to follow Christ, to give of ourselves affectionately in service to the world, to other people, and to God. In so doing, we shall live a fulfilled life. So it is for the professional with regard to the manner of his or her practice.

Chapter 7

The Gift of Service

Introduction

To what extent does the client see professional service as a gift? Should he or she receive it as a gift, and if so, what difference would it make to the quality of professional practice? These questions are pertinent when we consider the tendency for compliance to grow and moral sensitivity to decline as features of the relationship between professional and client. Compliance is, as I have said, an essential ingredient of good practice for which the client should be grateful. However, it is not sufficient if the client and the professional are to have the sort of relationship that each recognizes to be personal and morally creative. The mark of a grateful person is that he or she both gives and receives graciously. The vocation of the professional is willing to give his or her services to the client for their mutual well-being and the overriding interests of society at large.

I have argued that the Christian tradition provides an encouraging theological framework in which to ground a creative understanding of gratitude. It offers a perspective on what it means to be human that illuminates our capacity to become response-able and therefore grow into responsible people. In order to take up our responsibilities appropriately, I suggested, we must enter gratefully into the conversation of generations of scholars and our professional predecessors in order to discover our inheritance and consider the legacy we hope to leave for the future. This led to a consideration of compassion: what it is, how it is informed, and how it holds together our personal and professional lives. I now turn to discuss the idea of service, most particularly, the idea of service as gift. It is an integral perspective on

God's relationship with his creation and, I suggest, has implications that can transform both our personal and professional relationships.

Gift and Giving

Pleasure at receiving a gift is an experience that is very likely to produce the response of gratitude. Most particularly, I believe this to be the case when the gift is a service rather than an object, as for example, when I am ill and delighted by a friend's visit or when a teacher spends extra time helping me with a mathematical example. The classical world knows about giving, receiving, and responding in the myth of the three Graces. They are associated in Homer—and in later texts—with Aphrodite, the goddess of love, and are celebrated as consummate benefactors who bestow beauty and charm, physical, intellectual, artistic, and moral. Giving and receiving particularly lie at the heart of the Christian tradition. The creation is God's gracious gift, unsolicited and unmerited. This is no impersonal act, for God gives himself in love to his creating and reveals himself in Christ so that humankind can "see" his loving, sacrificial presence and work with him toward the fulfillment of his purpose in creating. Christians celebrate God's gift of himself in the central act of Christian worship, the Eucharist (the Service of Thanksgiving). They identify themselves with his sacrifice and are sent out into the world in the power of the Holy Spirit (that is, in full knowledge of God's presence with them) to do his will in serving the physical environment and human society. This possibility is the result of the fact that God made humankind in his image, which means that humans have the Christlike capacity to give themselves in service of one another, not merely to do things for them. This may seem like strange talk in a professional context, but it should not be so. Many of us have appreciated the willingness of the doctor to research our health problem, the lawyer to explore issues raised by a contract, or the accountant to investigate the tax claim of the Revenue Service. To receive this work as a gift rather than, for example, the fulfillment of an obligation is liberating to both professional and client.

Our society seems uncomfortable with this thought. The idea that service is most revealingly understood when it is regarded as a gift may seem a throwback to a society long gone: it is hard to see how it can be relevant in our current situation. Our present society is dominated by the desire to "get ahead," which means financial reward and fulfillment of ambition for promotion and power. However, regret at the passing of a more generous tradition, with its courteous relationships, is far from new: it may well be a characteristic feature of human nature.

A scene from Shakespeare's *As You Like It* clearly shows that the anxiety we have about social trends was present in early-seventeenth-century culture too. Shakespeare sets the scene: Adam, Orlando's faithful servant, warns him that he must flee the country, since his jealous and dangerous brother, Oliver, is set upon his destruction. Orlando's personal popularity with the people leads Oliver to believe that he constitutes a threat to his authority. Orlando refuses Adam's advice, saying that he would rather subject himself to the malice of his brother than disgrace his father's name by begging. But Adam will hear none of it and offers to support him with all his savings: five hundred crowns acquired through frugal living. Orlando is astonished—and grateful:

> O good old man, how well in thee appears
> The constant service of the antique world,
> When service sweat for duty, not for need.
> Thou art not for the fashion of these times,
> Where none will sweat but for promotion,
> And having that do choke their service up
> Even with the having; it is not so with thee.
> But poor old man, thou prun'st a rotten tree,
> That cannot so much as a blossom yield,
> In lieu of all thy pains and husbandry.
> But come thy ways, we'll go along together,
> And ere we have thy youthful wages spent,
> We'll light upon some settled low content. (Shakespeare, 1975, *As You Like It*, Act II, Sc. III, ll. 56–68)

It was most natural for Adam to express his compassionate concern for his lord by freely offering his service. What is more, his offer of service rescues Orlando from a false view of himself and from a self-destructive vision of his future. And by so doing, Adam liberates himself; they proceed together in unity of purpose, shared affection, and mutual gratitude.

> Master go on, and I will follow thee
> To the last gasp with truth and loyalty.
> From seventeen years, till now almost fourscore
> Here lived I, but now live here no more.
> At seventeen years, many their fortunes seek

But at fourscore, it is too late a week;
Yet fortune cannot recompense me better
Than to die well, and not my master's debtor. (ll. 69–76)

To Serve: To Be a Servant

How does the idea of service as gift help us to get inside contemporary professional relationships? Clearly, the relationship I shall be exploring impacts all professional relationships. But the professional is paid for his or her services; surely that makes a difference. In fact, remuneration is a separate matter. Marx stated his principle of social justice thus: "From each according to his ability, to each according to his need" (Marx, 1875). The Russian Constitution of 1936 (the so-called Stalin Constitution) revised it as follows: "From each according to his ability, to each according to his work." The constitution guaranteed work for all but required it as a duty, thus raising the matter of those who did not or could not "do their duty."

Of course, fixing the rate for the job will always be a difficult and contentious matter, involving questions of fairness and justice for society at large, the purposes of a particular organization, the persons involved, and the resources available. However, in every case, we should take seriously the view of the writer of the first letter to Timothy, who straightforwardly says, "The labourer deserves to be paid" (1 Tim. 5:18b). Actually, the language of the Authorized (King James) Version seems to get the meaning more directly—"The labourer is worthy of his hire"—the point being that all citizens are laborers and should behave in such a way as to be worthy of their hire. We are talking of a relationship that is much more than merely financial. But above all, it needs to be made clear that the fact of remuneration does not undermine the appropriateness of characterizing the mutuality of the personal relationship between professional and client as one of service for which each can and should be grateful.

To serve another may involve something very simple, such as witnessing a signature on a legal document or holding an umbrella while someone puts on a raincoat. We are grateful for such services that are matters of simple courtesy. They are often anticipated, as when an observant person steps forward to assist with putting on a coat, but they may be the result of a request for help or advice, as when a car driver asks for directions to his or her destination. But "service," as Christians understand the term, means much more: it implies that a person is making himself or herself available to look after the interests of someone else in one or another regard. The Christian wants, as we might say, to *be* of service to the person, not merely to provide one like a machine.

If this is to happen usefully, the Christian must be so disposed as to be capable of discerning another's needs. It seems that in simple circumstances, this is natural, perhaps even instinctive, human behavior, but insightful discernment of another's needs will require self-conscious attention to one's dispositions and the cultivation of appropriate virtues quite apart from the intellectual achievements of knowledge, skill, and what one gains from experience. This is consistent with Aquinas's theory of a virtue. Aquinas was much influenced in his ethical thinking by Aristotle's *Nicomachean Ethics*. He followed Aristotle in arguing that the expression of a virtue was more than the product of "the perfecting of a power"; if it were so, it would not necessarily have a moral quality. For it to have such a quality, a person would have to be of a certain condition: "In the first place he must have knowledge, secondly he must choose the acts, and choose them for their own sakes, and thirdly his action must proceed from a firm and unchangeable character" (Aristotle, 1984b, *N.E.*, 1105a31–33). Therefore, Aristotle continues, "Actions, then, are called just and temperate when they are such as a just man would do; but it is not the man who does them who is just and temperate, but the man who does them *as* just and temperate men do them" (1105b5–7).

Just to act in conformity with justice does not mean that one is behaving virtuously; one must want to behave virtuously and be able to recognize and know what it feels like to so behave. Humankind may have, for example, an instinctive desire for justice, but without exercising rational discipline in our instinctive ideas, we may overlook another's implicit but perhaps unexpressed need for justice and misdirect our concern for him or her so as in fact to selfishly satisfy our own desires. We must also *want* to be of service.

Michael Pakaluk in a recent article puts this very clearly:

> If a virtue in a strict sense is a trait that does not merely make someone *apt* to act reasonably but also make him want, fixedly and resolutely, to act reasonably, then practical wisdom looks to be a virtue in that sense too, insofar as one can claim that someone with practical wisdom does not merely "know how to" figure out for instance, what is the dangerous or moderate thing to do under the circumstances, but also *wants* to figure this out effectively: he *wants* to reason well, and to do so practically: that is, not as remaining on the level of thought, but as actually executing what was thought out. (Pakaluk, 2013, p. 38)

Any such apparently compassionate concern will itself need to be rationally disciplined, or it will be intrusive when expressed without regard for the moral independence of an intended recipient of service. Gratitude is not worth the words with which it is expressed unless it is freely given by a morally independent subject. No person is his or her brother's keeper, though Christians will have a disposition that is open to offering ready support to others in times of trouble. So if Christians are to be open to the possibility that they may be called upon for service, they must learn practical wisdom, educate their emotions, be aware of other people, want to be of service, and be capable of meeting others' needs.

A key insight in this process is a person's awareness that offering service is not simply complying with what is needed in terms of action; it is a dimension of who he or she is as a person. As J. S. Mill wrote, "It really is of importance not only what men do, but what manner of men they are to do it." The act of *giving* service is not fulfilled by mere performance of duty; it demands the whole person. There is an analogy to be made with learning: to learn a subject is more than committing to memory some formulas (though it cannot be denied that this may be part of it); it involves committing oneself to getting inside the subject so that the learning is something one does. It is not enough to "sort of know"; it is necessary to know what it feels like to actually know something, which means one has to learn what it means to *give* attention. In order to become the master of a subject, we have to *give* our full attention to it, *give* ourselves to the task. When one does this effectively and wholly, it arouses a personal feeling of gratitude within oneself for what one is learning and awareness that the knowledge one is in process of acquiring will equip one to be of service and thereby enter into new relationships. To know something thoroughly is a product of the activity of the whole person; it is to be in possession of something to the extent that it becomes a part of who one is and more than a brain-trace detectable by an EEG.

Discerning what others require, what the world needs if it is to grow to its promised perfection, and to *want* to give oneself in service to others and to the world is to begin to understand what the Christian means when he or she thinks of humankind as being created in the image of God. Therefore it is of course also (for the Christian) to want to serve God. Serving God means learning to love him and learning to serve him in human society and in the care of creation with the disciplined authority that flows from recognizing the covenantal relationships God has established with his creation and with his people. God's covenant with the world is a mutual, wholehearted, personal relationship for which we can be grateful. It also has much to teach us when we examine our personal and professional involvements.

COVENANT AND CONTRACT

What analogy can we find that will inform our understanding of not only God's gift of himself to his world but also his continuing service to it through his concerned, loving presence? The God-given authority of the individual Christian and of the Church is grounded in God's commitment of himself to the perfecting of his creation and his establishment thereby of an unbreakable relationship between Creator and creation. God *wants* to perfect his world. There are several powerful biblical analogies for the implied intimacy of God's relationship with Israel, each of which is illuminating in its own way. They include marriage, parent and child, shepherd and flock, and even king and subject, though this latter relationship is also subject to the suspicion that an earthly king may attempt to usurp the spiritual authority of God. The relationship assumed in these cases is quite distinct from that of a contract drawn up by lawyers in the light of negotiation. Contemporary scholars now agree that a more illuminating analogy is that of a covenant relationship (Heb., *b'rith*) such as those found in the Hebrew Scriptures; it is an "oral" agreement, not a written record, based on the power of the spoken word.

The concept of covenant within the Jewish and Christian traditions has the remarkable character that flows from its God-given sense of an assumed equality. It is not that God and the world are "equal" per se (no egalitarianism here!) but that God, of his own gracious nature, is set upon treating the world as having an identity of its own such that he chooses not to impose his will. It may even be that God cannot *impose* his will if he is to act in conformity with his own divine nature.

As I have argued previously, our understanding of current relationships and opportunities stands in traditions with which it behooves us to come to terms if we are to take up for ourselves the conversations on which they depend. But one needs to keep looking at the traditions to see how far and to what extent they are relevant. Thus G. E. Mendenhall, for example, seems to me to be wrong when he argues that the covenant of God with Israel follows the pattern of a suzerainty treaty most commonly found among Hittite documents (Mendenhall, 1954, pp. 49–76). These treaties are plainly between unequal parties; they are imposed by a suzerain on a vassal and are better understood as contracts (Pritchard, 1969, pp. 201–6). It is true that they confirm the exclusivity of the relationship and provide for the expression of full confidence in the suzerain by the vassal. But as distinct from the notion of covenant, the terms of these treaties require the vassal to work in the interests of the suzerain—to maintain peace with the suzerain and with other vassals, to provide military assistance as required under threat of dire consequences in the event that he fails to fulfill all his obligations. Subservience is the primary feature of the relationship here—not so for God and his world or God in relation to humankind. Humankind is said, after all, to be made in the image of God and to be empowered by God to share with him in the perfecting of his world.

The Continuing Mutuality of the Covenant Relationship

The covenant between Yahweh and Israel is unique. It is not the consequence of conflict and certainly is not a reward for worthy service on the part of the people of Israel; its nature is dependent on God's free choice of the Israelites to be his people. It assumes mutual fidelity and absolute trust. The concept is taken up by St. Paul and the early Church Fathers and is fruitfully pursued in the Christian tradition of theological inquiry as it continues to develop (Exod. 20:22–23:33; Gal. 3:10–24). Scott Hahn's discussion of the covenant relationship is helpful for its inclusion of personal character (Hahn, 1998).

There is moreover a twin depth to the relationship between God and his creation.

Whereas the religions of the Near East, in which Judaism was set, identified the divine either with the natural world as a whole or with individual features of human experience of the natural world, such as thunder or erotic love, in the Hebrew Scriptures, God and nature are not to be confused. They give God an identity utterly independent of the creation for which nevertheless he has total response-ability and therefore can and does justly accept responsibility. God is not merely in an affectionate relationship with nature, but as Creator, with the natural world and with the history of its people. And it is an eternal, unbreakable relationship; it could be nothing else, given the nature of God as Christians understand him.

There are two accounts of creation in the book of Genesis. In the first, Yahweh is said to have completed his work of creation in six days and to have taken a rest on the seventh (Gen. 1). This almost implies that he felt as if he had done his work by bringing the world into being! A second "account" is more imaginatively dynamic and presents God as the originator of a creation with which he continues to involve himself (Gen. 2:4ff.). In this second account of creation, Chaos is not obliterated by God at a stroke but restrained and rendered powerless by the uninterrupted exercise of his redeeming love (cf. Ps. 89:10; Jb. 26:12). The result is a Hebrew tradition that embodies a living awareness of God's ever-present, loving kindness (Heb., *hesed*): God is acknowledged to be faithfully committed to the perfecting of his world, continuingly active in binding the forces of chaos. This second version of the creation story may illuminate the current debate between science and religion by bringing into a relationship the imaginative coherence of contemporary physics and the openness of God's relationship with creation.

But the Hebrew perception goes deeper than this. Jews would not know of God or therefore of his relationship with the creation had he not revealed himself to them. God as they responded to him was present not only in relation to the natural world of creation but in the world of their everyday experience, in history. Their experience of the covenantal relationship reveals the essential character of God's relationship with creation; it is the defining feature of his relationship with the Israelites, his Chosen People. Moreover, God's covenant with his people is not a simple one-way transaction. It is a mutual relationship to which God is eternally committed and, for its effective realization in creation and in history, requires the Israelites' active recognition of the mutuality between the covenant partners.

A covenant may be established between two individuals as a means of settling a dispute (Gen. 21:32), an alliance between two groups (Gen. 14:13), or an agreement to end war (2 Sam. 3:12–19). In each case, we are looking at an agreement between equals, even if the equality is something that is the outcome of conflict. In the case of God and Israel, there is not only a relationship between unequals (for the Divine is absolutely independent of his creation) but one that is initiated by the more powerful party with the weaker one in such a way as to endow the weaker party with an authority that it did not previously possess. In a profound sense, Israel is invited to meet with God and enter into conversation with him—even to debate with him. Thus Job, for example, is quite clear that despite all his suffering and the accusing attitudes of his false friends, if only he could get into the presence of Yahweh, he would be able to reason with him.

> O that I knew where I might find him,
>   that I might come even to his dwelling!
> I would lay my case before him,
>   and fill my mouth with arguments.

> I would learn what he would answer me,
>   and understand what he would say to me.
> Would he contend with me in the greatness of his power?
>   No: but he would give heed to me.
> There an upright person could reason with him,
>   And I should be acquitted for ever by my judge.
>   (Job 23:3–7)

Here is an individual believer whose whole demeanor assumes that he has an equality that enables him to argue with God. One might assume this from the Wisdom Tradition, but it is also present in the prophets in relation to all people of God. Thus Isaiah presumes that God invites his Chosen People to argue things out between them. Their sin may stand between them but it need not be so.

> Come now, let us argue it out,
>   says the Lord:
> though your sins are like scarlet,
>   they shall be like snow;
> though they are red like crimson,
>   they shall become like wool.
> If you are willing and obedient,
>   you shall eat the good of the land;
> But if you refuse and rebel,
>   you shall be devoured by the sword;
>   for the mouth of the Lord has spoken.
>   (Is. 1:18–20)

There is straightforwardness about the manner of Yahweh's address to his people, but it assumes a relationship in conversation that each is expected to understand and to which each is expected to respond.

The notion of covenant is also a feature of New Testament thought. St. Paul in his Letter to the Galatians declares that Christ sums up God's conversation with the world of humankind, for in Christ, the promises made to Abraham are fulfilled; the Law has been reinterpreted by the loving courtesies of faith and embodied in the liberty of family life: "But now that faith has come, we are no longer subject to a disciplinarian, for in Christ Jesus you are all children of God through faith. As many of you as were baptized into Christ have clothed yourselves with Christ. There is no longer Jew or Greek, there is no longer slave or free, there is no longer male and female; for all of you are one in Christ Jesus. And if you belong to Christ, then you are Abraham's offspring, heirs according to the promises" (Gal. 3:25–29). The family is precisely a community that holds together inequality and equality. This is what God asks of all people with regard to the covenant relationship he has established with them, hence the prayer that Jesus asks his disciples, and in principle all humankind, to join him in reciting: the *Our* Father.

The idea of service as gift is underpinned by the qualities implicit in a covenant relationship. God gives himself to his world and to his people (whom Christians take to include all people) in order that they may enjoy the full character of their humanity. Professionals must treat their clients as equals, engage them in conversation in order to place their concerns in context, and then bring to bear their professional knowledge in order to advise clients how best to proceed. The service may involve, indeed is likely to involve, parties who are unequal in the sense that one has more professional knowledge—or indeed has more power due to status or wealth—than the other. But in a significant sense, if they do not see one another also as equal persons, mutually dependent on one another, the relationship will be destructive to the personhood of both. Indeed, most particularly, the context will be one that undermines the possibility of the relationship of mutual gratitude.

This raises the question, what is the context of service? What is the environment in which service is given? How is it best perceived? And what are its consequences for behavior?

The Context of Service

God's covenantal relationship with the world opens up the wholeness of the context for service, which in theological terms is implicit in some important contemporary developments of the doctrine of the incarnation. Traditionally, the doctrine has been seen in historical terms in the person of Jesus Christ. However, as noted previously, St. John in his Gospel refers to Jesus as the Word through whom all things were made, thus associating God's presence with the whole of the created order and therefore with history (Jn. 1:1–4; cf. Col. 1:15–17). This too has been a fruitful line of inquiry in the debate between science and religion: it eliminates, for example, any question that God intervenes in the creation. God's commitment of himself to the well-being of the world is inclusive of the natural world and the world of human history; God's presence with his world is eternal (Knight, 2007).

The context in which service is set is not, therefore, confined to one particular dimension of human experience, such as political economy or economics. There is a wholeness about the sense of community within which an understanding of service must be interpreted. I begin by focusing on the Christian community of faith, the Church, and what is required of its members if it is to be sustained and flourish. According to St. Paul, the unity of the Christian community depends on each of its members seeking in faith to overcome evil with good; it is more than the mere avoidance of evil (Rom. 12:21). I say "in faith" because it identifies the intellectual, theological, and moral framework that makes sense of being empowered by God to live in his "image." Without the sensitivity aroused by an awareness of this divine dimension, one will lack the vision that comes from recognizing one's relationship with God, whose nature it is to be redemptively creative. It is this vision that not only inspires the moral insight with which Christians are called to live their lives but also confirms in them the reality that they are capable of so doing. A human being is indeed able, after the pattern of Christ's life, to give himself or herself in service to the community and to another person. Service is a fundamental dimension of virtue as Christians see it—most particularly, the concept of service as gift, which is an enlivening ingredient of any fully functioning society. And further, with others, through understanding the natural world by scientific inquiry, one is able to care for the whole of creation.

Right Judgment

There are further dimensions to be taken into account. St. Paul sets service in the context of right self-judgment with regard to one's relationship to the community. He asks that people not think of themselves more highly than they should but rather to think with sober judgment of themselves according to the measure of faith that God has assigned (Rom. 12:3–4). One cannot behave in a way that is beyond what is encouraged by one's faith because what a person is capable of achieving for the community is always strongly influenced, if not actually determined, by the measure of faith that God has assigned him or her. This illuminating insight points to the fact that one should never feel guilty about not living up to what one might have hoped to achieve, provided, of course, that one remains open to the possibility that one can always do more. It is a form of pride and potentially false shame to set one's ambitions beyond one's capacities and then blame oneself or others (or God) for failure.

Realistic judgment of one's abilities is very important because, of course, a person can become complacent, tolerate low achievement, and lazily settle into a pattern of living that allows him or her not only to do little but over time to be content to do less and less. My housemaster, who opined that if things were not getting better, they were undoubtedly getting worse, would demand that one *put oneself* into it, whether on the rugby field or when apparently flustered by some intellectual challenge. He was himself a living example of what it meant to "put oneself into it," as he concentrated upon sharing with us his enthusiasm for literature. Moral self-flagellation and self-pity is pointlessly debilitating; what is vital is to set about the task of working with God at increasing one's faith and thus enlarging one's vision of what one can achieve with him.

This means that all people must be humble in the sense that right judgment of themselves neither overestimates nor underestimates their capacity for affectionate concern and their authority to exercise power. True humility is the attitude of the person who rightly estimates his or her own abilities and potential influence. It is important to do this. Otherwise, he or she may overstep the mark and attempt to do things that others are better equipped for. Respect for the faith of others is an essential ingredient of personal humility and right judgment. We are all tempted to take over when we should hold back. To do so causes disputes and jealousies and can even incite a desire for revenge. Certainly, they are destructive of good relationships and threaten the well-being of both the individual and society.

St. Paul points to the coherence of a society in which each member fulfills his or her own vocation and is mutually supportive of all others: "We have gifts that differ according to the grace given to us: prophecy, in proportion to faith; ministry, in ministering; the teacher in teaching; the exhorter in exhortation; the giver in generosity: the leader, in diligence, the compassionate, in cheerfulness" (Rom. 12:6–8). It is not simply that we need to recognize that no person, and certainly no Christian, is omnicompetent, notwithstanding that he or she is affirmed in his or her faith by God's gracious presence. Rather, we are able, with gratitude, to recognize our dependence on the creation, other people, and God for our well-being *because* we are blessed by God's gracious presence. Moreover, the community at large is dependent for its well-being on each person playing his or her part. In a stained glass window at Kingswood School, Bath, founded by John Wesley in 1748, there are words that have inspired many a pupil: *Ad gloriam Dei optima, in usum ecclesiae et reipublicae* ("To the glory of God in the service of Church and State"). Something of these words is inherent in the notion of vocation.

The Church, the community of faith, may indeed fail to practice what it preaches. The standard it publicly displays is misleading of its true nature and evidence of the fact that it is both a human and a divine institution. However, the reason for this failure is partly that the Church draws attention to itself rather than to the God in whose presence it lives, moves, and has its being. By so doing, it assumes an authority it does not possess, a lively affection for others that it fails to express, and an omnicompetence that is clearly beyond its capacity. Notwithstanding this, the Church continues to celebrate the reality of God's presence with his world and with his people and remains always free to work with others in the long-term interests of the human race.

Refocusing on God in worship opens a person's mind to the length, depth, and breadth of God's love; deepens his or her faith; and raises hopes. Through the sharing of this common experience of Christians, the Church will find an appropriate self-awareness and right judgment and thus reveal its essential God-given authority.

Mutuality of Service in Sacrifice

The Christian doctrine of the Trinity is a fruitful, imaginative appreciation of the unity of God's nature, which illuminates his capacity to give himself to that which is other than himself. The Orthodox tradition of theological reflection explores this unity through a dynamic term, *perichoresis*, by which it expresses sensitively the interiority of the affectionate relationships of the Persons of the Trinity. The term is now widely discussed by Roman Catholic, Reformed, and Protestant theologians. The Father gives himself with thankfulness and in loving presence to the Son and to the Holy Spirit; the Son gives himself with thankfulness and in loving presence to the Father and to the Holy Spirit; the Holy Spirit gives himself with thankfulness and in loving presence to the Father and to the Son. The overflowing of their mutually affectionate coinherence frees God of his grace to give himself to and within creation without diminishing his own authority or threatening the freedom of the world he is making. The gratitude that the world, through humankind, offers to God for his gift of himself is expressed in worship and through the sacrificial service of both the natural world and fellow human beings.

Sarah Coakley, in her 2012 Gifford Lectures, *Sacrifice Regained: Evolution, Co-operation and God*, attacked the limited perspective on evolution that sees it in terms of selfishness. She argues instead for "what might be called an 'excess' in evolutionary cooperation and altruism—for those moments of an intensely sacrificial undertaking for others" that seem not to be constrainable to any current mathematical calculus of "payoffs" or "benefits." Such a sacrificial perspective on creativity we can see embodied in the divine incarnation of God in Christ and the continuing work of the Holy Spirit in creation.

The concept of service as gift is precisely implied in this perspective. God gives without thought of return but with the faith and in the hope that his nature of sacrificial giving will inspire the sacrificial giving of that to which he has given himself. The vocation implicit in every professional relationship is based on an analogous hope: the professional serves the interests of the client without thought of return but with the faith and the hope that his or her service will be received with gratitude. As I have argued, this relationship does not preclude remuneration, but when it is entered into merely for financial reward, the personal value of the relationship is lost, the notion of service demeaned, and feelings of gratitude undermined. You may ask where the sacrifice is, but a moment's reflection on the notion of vocation will make it plain. When I am determined to be a psychiatrist, for example, I will sacrifice myself to the business of "being with others for their sake" by means of continuous study, self-examination, attention to the personal circumstances of my clients, and the desire to serve their best interests. The process of learning, caring, and attending to the needs of others demands a genuine and continuous sacrifice if good is to be done rather than evil merely eschewed.

There are lessons here on which professionals can draw. They cannot rely on themselves or even exclusively on the expertise of their profession: if they are to give their service genuinely, they will have to be aware of how important it is to recognize that what they offer is an expression of the mutual concern and support of each profession for all other professions. The interdependence of the medical profession, with social services, education, philosophy, and theology, is increasingly clear as we struggle to keep our attention on the client and the professional as whole persons.

SHOULD CHARITABLE SERVICE BE REMUNERATED?

The emotion of compassion arouses a natural desire to offer service; surely, that is obvious. But does the fact that we have the freedom to offer service to others, with the quality associated with freely giving, mean that remuneration is not justifiable? Hardly! One could say that service is its own reward, and in an important sense, that may be so. But without remuneration, there would be no freedom to continue to offer service as a gift. That would be a deprivation that would undermine our human nature, for the offering of service to each other is a privilege of our humanity that all share. Indeed, when one thinks about it seriously, it is obvious that the privilege of service is not confined to the rich as poor Adam demonstrates in his behavior toward his lord, Orlando. It is an integral aspect of Christian Faith that we are all called to share gratefully in the service of one another.

But what about charities? Charities are voluntary bodies, publicly recognized legal entities established to support good causes. Members of the public are free to choose whether to give to charity, and if so, which charity they will support, whether it is the Children's Society, the Royal National Institute of Blind People, Oxfam, the local Church, or whatever. Charity law requires that all money raised be spent exclusively on the objects of the charity and that the costs of administration be kept to a minimum, consistent with compliance, effectiveness, efficiency, and good management. Recent changes in state welfare provision have, it is argued, led to the formation of new charities, such as food banks, as well as increased reliance on voluntary support for such basic things as good health care and the creation of work opportunities for young people, among many other services. In turn, this has led to a sharpened focus on those involved in the charitable world, the current performance of charities, their tax arrangements, and questions about their effectiveness and efficiency.

One concern in particular has provoked controversy: are the remuneration packages of the senior executives of some major charities reasonable, fair, and just? The press was apparently "scandalized" to discover that some were paid sums in excess of £100,000 per annum and that very few were rewarded with a salary of more than £200,000. The Unite Union took the matter up and publicly deplored the practice, accusing charities of associating themselves with the city pay culture of big business. It charged the charities with exploiting the generous gifts of pensioners and workers who make average or lower wages, thereby undermining public confidence and bringing the work of charities into disrepute: they were, by implication, misusing charitable funds to pay excessive salaries to their senior officers and chief executives. This criticism was taken to extraordinary lengths by some members of the public who registered shock that anyone who worked for a charity should receive any payment at all; charities should rely on the freely given, unremunerated service of volunteers. Of course, many small ones do.

It is likely that there will always be questions about the appropriate level of a chief executive's remuneration as determined by trustees in the charitable sector. The matters for consideration will be the same in the case of charities as in those that pertain to the public services, the private sector, or indeed the trade unions. In each context, it is the task of those who appoint the chief executive to serve the interests of all the stakeholders, not excluding the respective clients, by appointing the best person. If the responsibilities in each case are comparable, then it is reasonable to assume that the rewards will be comparable too. Actually, when considering the circumstances of a charity, it is the trustees who carry overall legal accountability and must ensure that their appointees are capable of carrying on the business of the charity responsibly. Nevertheless, one might reasonably hope, and it appears to be the case, that those appointed to direct charities would be willing to accept a remuneration package that is less than what they normally would receive were they employed in the private or indeed the public sector. The trustees are themselves, of course, not remunerated for the service they provide. Indeed they are precluded from the possibility of payment, apart from the repayment of out-of-pocket expenses. Their service is freely given.

Conclusion

Following the argument of Sarah Coakley, I suggest that when properly understood, an analogous vision lies behind the building of every community. Simply opposing evil by organizing constitutional arrangements and a legal system that will identify wrongdoing and determine the punishments that follow will be destructive to society if, at the same time, there is no practice prompted by a vision of what is good, acceptable, and of good report (Rom. 12:1–2).

Machiavelli explored this in his much-discussed and influential essay "Concerning Principalities," known posthumously by its more familiar title, *The Prince*. His cunning thesis is not, as frequently presented, that the only "good" comes from following the decisions of a political leader, whatever that leader determines, but that in order to secure the peaceful continuity of any "imperial" power over a long period of time, a constitution has to be established that can be defended against every challenge. The "evil" is whatever challenges the state, whose necessary authority transcends that of any individual citizen. But it will only be possible to defeat the "evil" if the constitution is established so as to seek and express the "good." Machiavelli writes, "Therefore a wise prince will seek means by which his subjects will always and in every possible condition of things have need of his government, and then they will always be faithful to him . . . It is the nature of men to be as much bound by the benefits they confer as by those they receive. From which it follows that, everything considered, a prudent prince will not find it difficult to uphold the courage of his subjects both at the commencement and at the close of siege, if he possess provisions and means to defend himself" (Machiavelli, 1935, pp. 48–49).

The provision of the necessities of life by the prince will require self-sacrifice and not merely the exercise of power if his authority is to ring true. What is more, the people must believe that he has the wherewithal, the self-confidence, and the desire to meet the demands that the situation places upon him and not simply to serve his own interests at their expense.

Every society and every professional relationship depends for its good on the giving of sacrificial service. God has what is required to meet the world's needs and the desire to offer it; the evidence of this is implicit in the created order and in the person of Christ, for here it is made clear that what is required for the redemptively creative order of the world is God himself. The gratitude of the Christian is directed toward the Trinitarian God for his gift of himself; only then is it possible to be grateful for whatever things God might also be said to have given. Gratitude should be first for the person, not for the gifts, for on that person's character will depend the value one puts on the gifts he or she has given.

I believe this to be the true character of professional relationships. They are concerned with persons—their characters and their capacity to accept responsibility and give themselves in service to others. They are not fulfilled by mere compliance with regulation determined by external authorities. The professional is concerned not merely to oppose evil but to promote the good. In order to take responsibility, it will be necessary always to want to give oneself in service to society at large—its well-being, prosperity, and happiness. In order to achieve this, the professional will have to have a true estimate of his or her own personal character because he or she first will have to learn to give attention to the person, his or her client, and not simply to the circumstances in which the client believes himself or herself to be embroiled or the rewards (i.e., gifts) with which the client will acknowledge his or her gratitude. This requires self-discipline and sensitivity if the professional is to know what it means to freely give attention. To this topic I turn in the following chapter.

Chapter 8

Learning to Give Attention

Introduction

Grateful people intent on being of service will be attentive to the needs of others and, as I have argued, compassionate and curious about the world. As people made in the image of God, they are free to give of themselves in service to others; indeed, when they do so, they reveal their true nature and bear witness to the self-giving presence of God in Christ. Hence nothing is more irritating than when I become aware that the person from whom I seek professional advice is not paying attention. There may be other important personal, professional, or business matters that are distracting him or her, but it does not matter; as far as I am concerned, I need his or her full attention.

It is always easy to pick up the signs; they are glancing through papers on the desk, not looking at me, failing to engage with the issues that I have raised, and asking questions I have already answered. But above all, there is the body language: they are unmistakably uninvolved. They are vivid demonstrations of the fact that attention is something one has in one's power to give, and this person is clearly not giving it to me. And that is the point: it is not simply a technical matter (is he or she attending to my problem?); it is fundamentally a matter of relationship, the personal relationship with me, the client.

In this chapter, my purpose is to look at the matter of giving attention in the context of the general Christian theological framework I have outlined. I shall examine the theological grounds of our attention-giving and explore what it implies for us—or perhaps better, offers us—with regard to the focus and manner of our giving attention. I shall also have something to say about how we might learn to improve our capacity to "give attention" and "pay attention." I shall explore its essential role in liberating the human being to live graciously with others in such a way as to know what he or she is doing and who he or she is. As we gain experience through giving ourselves in service to other persons and to God's creation, I shall argue that we become more aware of ourselves and truly find ourselves flourishing as persons. The process confirms us as persons and reveals us to ourselves as we learn to bear the responsibility of revealing ourselves to others. There can of course be a cost, which is why the language of *paying* attention is also informative. But first, I present some thoughts about the idea of attention.

Attention

Learning to give attention to the other person is a profound aspect of every relationship, including all successful professional relationships. It is easy when the person or the problem one is asked to deal with is attractive and interesting, but my concern here is with every client, every professional, and every problem with which we are presented. That may require a little more effort. Let us first put my discussion of attention in a brief historical context.

Locke regarded attention as a mode of thought hardly in need of special explanation: "When ideas float in our mind without any reflection or regard of the understanding, it is what the French call reverie; our language has scarce a name for it: when the ideas that offer themselves are taken notice of, and, as it were, registered in the memory, it is attention: when the mind with great earnestness, and of choice, fixes its view on any idea, considers it on all sides, and will not be called off by the ordinary solicitation of other ideas, it is that we call 'intention' or 'study'" (Locke, 1947, II, XIX, 1). There is a hint here that Locke sees attention as in some way linked to "intention"—that is, with a capacity to inform if not actually to influence behavior.

William James moves the discussion forward when he identifies two processes that occur in every attentive act: there is first an adjustment of sensory organs (e.g., turning the head); second, and most important, there is "the anticipatory preparation from within of the ideational centres concerned with the object to which attention is paid" (James, 1950, p. 411). James has the imagination in mind here. Giving attention involves intention to do something that in turn requires the use of, and therefore development of, the imagination.

Apart from a period in the mid-twentieth century when the behaviorism of B. F. Skinner swept all before it, the last hundred years has seen cognitive psychology emerge as the dominant influence in psychology. Attention has now become a major topic of interest to psychologists, though most of the focus has been on its mechanics, its neurophysiology. This direction of inquiry was in part stimulated by the insights of communications engineering. Broadbent, for example, was puzzled by the fact that despite the apparently confusing mass of information presented to human perception at any one time, it was possible for an individual to concentrate on particular ideas, experiences, and events, such that he or she could bring them together and work with them. This suggested to Broadbent that there was a capacity limit in the human brain that meant that most information was either not noticed or passed over (Broadbent, 1958). Broadbent associated attention with a bottleneck on the analogy of overload in information technology.

Such reductionist perspectives have been subjected to criticism by many, including Christopher Mole, who considered the concept of attention from a philosophical point of view. He proposes that attention is analogous to the performance of an orchestra (Mole, 2011). No one instrument or section of the orchestra can "perform" the whole work on its own; unison is a necessary condition. Analogously, Mole argues that attention involves the cognitive unison of all aspects of the human being, for attention can only be understood adverbially, Mole says. By this he means that attention implies agency; when people focus on what they are doing, they are acting attentively. We shall see that this is illuminating from the point of view of the professional relationship and finds an interesting echo in our theological framework.

Theological Context

The Christian theological framework within which we are free to act attentively for the world's well-being is God himself, God-in-Trinity. One might say, following Mole, that God's attentiveness to the world's well-being is the agent of his creative activity. In his commitment of himself to the world's well-being, God celebrates its beauty and delights in its freedom; in so doing, he shows himself to be uniquely capable of giving thanks for his creation, whatever the circumstances. To say of God that he is grateful is clearly anthropomorphic but is nevertheless, I believe, revealing of God's nature. It is a quality of God's attentiveness to be grateful for what he is attending to; he thoroughly enjoys it: "And God saw that it was good" (Gen. 1:10). His grateful attentiveness to the world's well-being is incarnate in Christ, who expresses God's freedom to focus on the world's flourishing and to give his whole attention to the fulfillment of his purpose in creating. God creates attentively. At the heart of the Faith, there lies the life-giving belief that God desires the well-being of everything he is making and is wholly focused on its flourishing: he loves it with all that he is.

This is why Aquinas in the *Summa Theologiae* places God at the heart of the very structure of this most profound of theologies, as Denys Turner illuminatingly points out (Turner, 2013, p. 101). In so doing, Aquinas embodies in his exposition an exploration of the distinctive Christian themes of grace, redemption, incarnation, and Trinity, which together constitute the essential dimensions of Christian theological inquiry. By working out what they mean theologically, not only is Aquinas writing an academic theological treatise; he is concerned to bring his students and the readers of his work into conversation with the God that these themes reveal, the God who is their source. In Aquinas's view, these themes are the living dimensions of God's relationship with his world and with humankind. There is common knowledge and reflexivity provoked by this joint attention (Campbell, 2005, pp. 287–97; Peacocke, 2005, pp. 298–324). Provoked by the gracious lure of God to engage in conversation with him, we gratefully recognize ourselves as redeemed persons living in the society of the wholeness of God-in-Trinity. We are liberated, as Christ himself was liberated, to learn to give attention to the world's needs and become open to the real possibility of sharing responsibility with God by giving ourselves wholeheartedly to its flourishing.

The Trinitarian God

But what do we mean when we refer to God, whose attention is focused on us, as God-in-Trinity? Let me first admit that, following Aquinas at this point, talk about God as Trinity is an example of where language comes to an end of its power. It is God who reveals himself in human experience to be a Trinitarian God; the doctrine is not a conclusion of rational inquiry, even though by the same token, it cannot be affirmed to be irrational. Language may come to the end of its authority, but recognizing this may liberate one into the very framework that informs what one grasps after. This is an important point made by Fronda in his intriguing exploration of Wittgenstein's approach to religious language (Fronda, 2010; cf., Putnam, 1992, pp. 134–57). The language of the Trinity grounds our experience of God and helps us to make sense of it, though it is of course nonempirical and launches us into further and deeper imaginative inquiry.

The Trinitarian God is understood in Christian theology to be the Creator who in creating does not simply engage in certain activities but gives himself to the world through Christ in concerned and courteous attention to its flourishing. God is a gracious, self-giving God, who in creating would deny his true nature if he were not himself involved in the profoundest relationship with that which he was making. Christians develop their theological understanding of this when they refer to God's commitment of himself as redemptively creative: God's creative presence in Christ literally characterizes the world he is making. It may "fall from grace"—that is, lose any sense of living in the presence of God—but it can never put itself beyond the God who is utterly focused on the world's flourishing, a fact that is contained within the notion of God as Holy Spirit. Any interpretation of the world of our experience that fails to take account of this fact is not simply incomplete, it is false.

But that is not all; for in coming to terms with what it means to be human, we have also to engage in some hard theological work if we are to understand the character of our humanity. The phrase with which we have to work, as we have seen previously, is that humankind is made in "the image of God." By this we mean that just as God gives himself once and for all to inform and enliven the world's life, so can the animals we know ourselves to be as human beings. But the character of these animals, these creatures made in God's image, will only be experienced as and when they give themselves attentively to the world's well-being. This means that the condition of being truly human is characterized by the willing ability not just to do things but to be someone who gives himself or herself to the world's flourishing. To live with any other focus for life is to live a lie. In Christian terms, it is to deny the image that is within us and to live in sin—that is, unaware of the truth that is within us.

However, if people are to know themselves redeemed by God's grace (as indeed they are) and discover what it means to give themselves in wholehearted service, it will be necessary for them to attend first to the Person of God and to learn to love him. An awareness of the relationship with God that God graciously has given us will nourish our capacity to be ourselves. The character of that relationship is friendship, which means the sharing of a common will, as Aquinas emphasizes frequently in his *Summa* and elsewhere (Schwarz, 2007, ch. 3–4). Friendship requires an assumed equality of persons in the relationship, which can only be the case for God and humankind because of God's gracious invitation, as recalled in the words of Jesus: "I do not call you servants any longer, because the servant does not know what the master is doing; but I have called you friends, because I have made known to you everything that I have heard from my Father" (Jn. 15:15). True friendship implies a common willing, hoping, and sharing of purpose, a genuine possibility, given God's gracious presence.

THE PERSON OF JESUS CHRIST

God is focused on the world's salvation in the Person of Jesus Christ. But gratitude for the conversation in which he involves us does not encompass the totality of theological inquiry about God-in-Trinity. Christology is concerned to understand the Person and Work of Christ so as to appreciate his role in salvation. This is clearly an important aspect of Christian theology, but when undertaken apart from the totality of the divine framework that makes sense of the world as God's creation, Christ tends to become a moral example, and the Faith itself little more than ethics. But Christ does not simply point to the presence of God: he is the presence of God. He shows in his own life and death that it is possible for the world to embody the Divine without compromising its own created nature or the character of the Creator. He is our humanity made "in God's image."

The worthy intention of some who focus on Christology is to make Christ intelligible within the limited perspective of most contemporary philosophical horizons for which religious language is contentious. But the very form of theological language illustrates how ordinary human discourse simply runs out of power when dealing with talk about God. I affirmed this when talking previously of the Christian understanding of God as Trinitarian: "talk about God as Trinity is an example of where language comes to an end of its power." The familiar final remark of Wittgenstein's Tractatus makes the point, "What we cannot speak about we must consign to silence" (Wittgenstein, 1961, p. 151). It is not, however, that there is nothing beyond language but that what is beyond language cannot be expressed in language. There is no reason to believe that the ineffable is unreal, as Aquinas confirms.

At the heart of what we are all about as Christians is learning to love *God*—something that we know is extremely difficult to put into words. Yet even very influential theologians, such as Karl Barth and von Balthasar, begin their theologizing with what to my mind is a thin theological perspective generated by focusing on Jesus. It is understandable, of course, because it seems that contemporary fundamental suspicions about matters ontological suggest talk about God should be avoided in favor of the easier, apparently more brotherly perspective stimulated by focusing on Jesus. He is, as it were, the intelligible "God with us" and "God for us."

Stanley Hauerwas, in my opinion, dilutes the truth inherent in Christian theology even more when he identifies the Church as a colony in an alien world (Hauerwas and Willimon, 1989). He points to what is essentially a Church-based ethics in the sense that the Church tells the story of God by making Christ's living presence visible in the lives of faithful believers who, with Christ, seek to heal the world's suffering. One hopes indeed that the lives of Christians within the community of faith will demonstrate what it means when the Church is referred to as "the Body of Christ," but Hauerwas is mistaken when he claims that Christian ethics is for the Church and not the world. All humans are created in the image of God with the same opportunities and potential. In fact, Christian theology is concerned with universal truth, not simply with the relevance of faith to practical outcomes considered from within the Christian enclave.

However, for this basic reason, we as Christians need to avoid any limitation of perspective and base our understanding of what it means to give attention to God on God himself and his giving of himself to the world's flourishing. We have to begin by entertaining the wholeness of the Godhead, the God-in-Trinity to whom Aquinas pointed; only thus will we be rooted in the truth. The Trinity is the model that Christians employ to explore what they mean by "the unity of God": there is but one God, who is wholly himself, undivided, eternally present, and eternally attentive. He is the God who gives his whole attention to the flourishing of the world, for which he accepts responsibility and for which he is wholly response-able.

While keeping in mind God's attentiveness to the needs of the world, let us now address the vital question of how difficult it is for us to learn to *give* attention.

Giving Attention

Moses reminds his liberated people on their way to the Promised Land of the covenant God had made with them. He addresses them in the following manner: "Hear, O Israel, the statutes and ordinances that I am addressing to you today; you shall learn them and observe them diligently" (Deut. 5:2). In other words, "*Pay* attention." The English expression is interesting because it expresses the important aspect that giving attention may be costly: it demands something of the person who is required to give attention. Christ's attention to his Father cost him his life. Christians, in their turn, are reminded of God's gracious presence and urged by Christ to deny themselves and take up their Cross and follow him: "For those who want to save their life will lose it, and those who lose their life for my sake will find it. For what will it profit them if they gain the whole world but forfeit their life? Or what will they give in return for their life?" (Matt. 16:24; Mk. 8:34). The point is that if a person focuses attention on himself or herself without regard for the world in which that person is set, he or she will atrophy and ultimately die. Those who "retire" from work without interest in or involvement with others are likely to suffer analogously: there is no life without others. "To deny oneself" is grossly misunderstood when it is taken to imply neglecting oneself or ignoring one's best interests. It is rather a matter of recognizing what exactly it means to act in one's best interests. Paradoxically, it is only by denying oneself and learning to focus on God, the creation, and the well-being of other persons that one can actually flourish.

Simone Weil understood this. Born into a Jewish family in Alsace-Lorraine in 1902, she had from an early age a passion for the poor and set herself to improve their lives. This took many forms but did not exclude seeking to inspire them through her enthusiasm for knowledge: she taught Plato to workers at the Renault factory during their lunch hours. She was attracted to Christianity and attended a Roman Catholic Church in Harlem in 1942 when she was briefly in America. However, she did not become a Christian because she would not separate herself from her people, especially when anti-Semitism was adopted as a policy by groups in France that were sympathetic with Nazism. When she came to Britain in 1943, she assumed the diet of the peasant in occupied France despite suffering from tuberculosis. She gave her whole attention, her whole self, to the well-being of the world: her physical body suffered (she died in 1943 at the age of 34), but as a person, she flourished.

Her notebooks and essays show the grounds of her commitments and the consequent breadth of her interests. She affirmed the faculty of attention to be the central aspect of genuine study: "Although people seem unaware of it today, the development of the faculty of attention forms the real object and almost the sole interest of studies" (Weil, 1951, p. 51). She makes plain that the faculty may or may not be developed, but if it is, it will require effort, as will any other faculty, such as hearing or listening. She goes on to say that if one is to cultivate the faculty of attention, there is no choice in the matter; one is not free to like mathematics and not to like history or literature: "All tasks which really call upon the power of attention are interesting for the same reason and to an almost equal degree. Moreover, intelligence will not be enhanced by will power which 'makes us set our teeth and endure suffering'" (p. 51). The lure of learning draws one to want to know; there is no compulsion, only the opportunity freely to express one's natural curiosity: "The intelligence can only be led by desire. For there to be desire, there must be pleasure and joy in the work. The intelligence only grows and bears fruit in joy. The joy of learning is as indispensable as breathing is in running" (p. 55). These sentiments influenced me to claim previously that God was full of gratitude for the world he was making; he must have been, or he would not be able to work attentively toward its perfection.

Weil's insight is worth pondering. Aquinas, following Aristotle, regards the soul to be the form of the body and, most particularly, to be intellectual and therefore rational: "Mind is the form of a man's body. Active things must have forms by which they act; only healthy bodies heal themselves, and only instructed minds know. Activity depends on actuality, and what makes things actual makes them active. Now the soul is what makes our body live; so the soul is the primary source of all those activities that differentiate levels of life: growth, sensation, movement, understanding. So whether we call our primary source of understanding mind or soul, it is the form of our body" (McDermott, 1989, p. 111).

The soul is therefore not a part of the body; it is the form of the human animal when understood as being intellectual—that is, as characterized by its essential capacity to be rational. Thus, when studying, as Weil says, what matters is not so much the casual interest that prompts one's desire to learn; what is vital is the wanting to know rooted in God's eternal desire to create humankind in his image. The inquiring, the paying attention, forms the soul—that is, everything that makes us human and enables us to take responsibility. Furthermore, as is implied by Anscombe's remarks about intention, for it to be true that one wants to know, one must be trying to learn (Anscombe, 1957, pp. 66–67). And for that to be possible is a matter of which way one is facing and on what one is focusing. Above all, attention is an attitude of the whole person, as Christopher Mole affirms, and not of some organ of the body such as the brain. It is I who know what I know, not my brain. But I must face the "target" of what I am striving for with all that I am, intellectually and emotionally.

It is one of the greatest gifts we possess as human beings for our attention to be something that is within our power to give or to withhold; it is a faculty that we are free to use or allow slowly to perish through lack of use. When we become aware of it as a divine gift, our gratitude directs us with pleasure and joy to seek to understand the world, ourselves, and above all, God, by engaging him in conversation. Of course, it takes time. There may likely be—indeed, there is—required, as the word "attention" implies, patience, waiting, and hard work.

The example of God informs our willingness to accept this. God does not, indeed cannot, compel us to respond to his invitation to engage in conversation with him or, therefore, require us to do his will by trying to live in his image. On the contrary, God can bear the pain of our disregard of him, which indeed is what is implied for him when we fail to hear, choose to ignore, or actually defy the inspiration he offers. But by the same token, we too can profitably learn to bear this pain when those we love act without regard to their relationship with us. Every parent has some idea of what is involved, for children (as a colleague once wrote on a pupil's Latin report) can be led to water but cannot be made to drink it. Drinking and clenching one's teeth are activities, like learning, that one has to do for oneself.

The professional person has to recognize an analogous dimension in every professional relationship. A doctor will advise any patient with emphysema to give up smoking, but the doctor cannot compel him or her to do so. An accountant may advise a client that certain benefits are benefits in kind and therefore taxable, but the accountant cannot force the client to accept his or her advice. A teacher may explain to a parent that if his or her child is to make a favorable grade in the forthcoming examination, the student should not stay up late playing online games. But the teacher cannot compel the parent to follow his or her advice. In every case, the professional has to bear the consequences while at the same time living in hope that the client may see the point and decide to take the advice. To overstep the mark would be fatal; one would lose one's reputation and all possible future influence. Bearing the pain of not being attended to when one is giving attention is personally demanding, but it can be done, as God shows in his relationship with the world. It makes it all the more important to realize that what one is called to give attention to is the person, not solely the situation.

Learning to Focus

Wittgenstein in his influential *Philosophical Investigations* explores the complex diversity of language use in relation to meaning. Where do we start? At the beginning of his work, he quotes Augustine's *Confessions* (1.8): "When they (my elders) named some object, and accordingly moved towards something, I saw this and I grasped that the thing was called by the sound they uttered when they meant to point it out . . . Thus, as I heard words repeatedly used in their proper places in various sentences, I gradually learnt to understand what objects they signified, and after I had trained my mouth to form these signs, I used them to express my own desires" (Wittgenstein, 1958, para. 1, ft. 1).

Wittgenstein enjoys demonstrating that traditional accounts of the acquisition of language, such as ostensive definition according to Augustine, are inadequate. When I point in a particular direction, for example, it is not clear to what exactly I am pointing, unless at the same time, I use sentences to focus your attention toward it. I may see a horse and rider in a race, but by pointing to it and saying, "Look," how does one know whether I am indicating that the rider's boot has come out of the stirrup, that the horse is an appaloosa, that I recognize the rider to be the new jockey in Paul Nicholls's stable, or that if the jockey continues to ride in the way he is at the moment, he will be unhorsed. Who knows? As Wittgenstein says, confusion arising from mistaken use of language may account for a large proportion of philosophical problems. After all, how do I *point* to my freedom? How do I *point* to the meaning of the conjunctions "and," "but," and "moreover," without which language would be unintelligible? Perhaps, as Wittgenstein says, I can *show* more than I can *say*. This is what I believe is the case with the Christian theological framework: it "grounds" more than we can say.

But it is not just a matter of language: even if we can clear up the difficulties with language learning, giving attention involves much more. For example, Michael Polanyi in his discussion of diagnosis points out that even when a doctor has what he or she regards as a clear picture of the basic evidence, consisting of his or her observations as a doctor together with what the patient tells him or her of the symptoms—to which must be added the pictures, numbers, and so on produced by the X-rays and CT scans—the true diagnosis is not a matter of putting everything together and making a simple deduction; it is crucially a matter of exercising personal judgment. And beyond this, in order to communicate successfully with the patient, the doctor must bring to bear the whole of himself or herself as a person into relation with the whole of the patient as a person: "The thought of truth implies a desire for it, and it is to that extent personal" (Polanyi, 1958, p. 308). The search for truth therefore requires personal commitment, which as Weil says, is a matter of pleasure and joy for which one is grateful.

Thus, as God in the incarnation graciously focused the whole of himself on the Person of Jesus Christ in order to "say" or "show" the truth about himself and the world he is continuously making, so must we human beings focus on the well-being of the other if we are to know the truth about ourselves and the world. In principle, this means that we have to do what we are free to do, to focus first on God-in-Trinity and take our nourishment from him.

Focusing on the person and his or her interests and needs is a complex matter, not a simple one. Yet that is what we expect from one another and, in particular, what we expect when we consult a professional. We recognize the difference when doctors relate to us as people rather than as sets of symptoms, even if we find it difficult to put it into words—and not just in our own case. That is obvious when we look at some of the reported unprofessional behavior of doctors and nurses.

Thus, after visiting a relative in hospital, we may say, "She is simply not being treated as a person! Basic needs may be met (though apparently not in every case), but she is not being encouraged to engage with her recovery." We may feel, after talking with the teacher of our child that he or she is not interested in the child; the teacher does no more than go through the motions. The child's work is marked and returned, but without comment, either written or oral. We might say, "She has no idea what it means to motivate a child and inspire his desire to learn." The auditor who does no more than look through the figures and declare that that they are compliant with the appropriate regulations may be doing what is demanded by the law. But more will be required if the client is to be satisfied. In each case, the information and its analysis are crucial, but what clients are looking for is the sort of personal engagement that recognizes that they are responsible people who can contribute to their own return to health, who can enhance their own desire to learn, and who can improve their own business performance.

What is essential to the process of giving attention is the relationship that enables each to see that he or she is facing in the same direction as and wanting the same things for the other—in other words, that they have, as Aquinas says, "a common will." Of course, such a relationship will require mutual honesty. The client must present accounts that are transparent, the parent must support the teacher with appropriate encouragement at home, and the patient must do his or her best to look after his or her own health. And on the professional's part, one must "tell it as it is," avoiding jargon and, when necessary, making it quite clear where risks are going to lead to serious consequences if they are not attended to. One may risk the loss of the other's attention, but that is consistent with maintaining one's own intention to focus on the well-being of the other. In the long run, it will also build up the trust that is in the interests of not only the parties directly involved but the flourishing of the whole of society.

What Do I Bring to Bear When I Give Attention?

The first thing I bring to bear when giving attention is my experience and what I explicitly and implicitly inherit from the traditions in which I sit. It is dangerous to identify a point at which this started as if there was a before and after. Thus, in the first instance, it may seem that my education as a professional started when I began my training as a doctor, priest, or lawyer. But a moment's reflection will show that this is a false assumption: there is an important sense in which there is no beginning and no end. It is obvious in the case of adult education. The good teacher will recognize that the student brings to the classroom an enormous body of knowledge and experience and that it is the teacher's task to release it into the river of the student's current learning. Actually, this is true at any stage of learning, formal and informal; wherever we are in life, we have something to bring to our learning. If not, we would paradoxically never be able to learn anything.

Moreover, it makes no sense to say that one has come to the end of what one needs to learn just because one has satisfied the examiners and become a qualified professional. There necessarily will be a continuing process of in-service education. This is not merely a matter of keeping up to date, important as that is; it concerns expanding one's imaginative sensitivity to the breadth and context of what one knows. Even more important is learning to pay attention to the practice of one's profession. The professional has to be what David Schön called a "reflective practitioner" who takes into account the experience he or she gains through working and turns it into practical knowledge (Schön, 1983).

In order to do this successfully, one will need to draw on more than professional training and experience; one's whole experience of life is available to be employed and will be required in order to fulfill one's responsibilities. A barrister, for example, can be faced with a case involving evidence from an unlimited range of knowledge. If the barrister is to deal with it successfully, he or she will have to be aware of the way language functions in the relevant contexts. Since he or she is unlikely to have all the necessary expertise, consulting the law reports for similar cases, calling upon the experience of colleagues, and where appropriate, calling upon the services of an expert witness will be necessary. Moreover, given the adversarial nature of the British legal system, he or she will also pay attention to the character of the opposing barrister and the social psychology of the jury in order to understand how the opponent is inclined to present evidence and argue his or her case. All this is required if the barrister is to act attentively.

An analogous situation arises in every professional relationship. The teacher is not merely passing on information but demonstrating how it can best be deployed in order to get to the truth. And above all, the teacher will want to engage students with him or her in the lifelong business of "wanting to know" and in the pleasure of knowing that they know. The doctor will not only give patients a diagnostic judgment but bring to bear his or her wider experience of life in order to engage patients with the implications for them and the ways in which they should conduct themselves in the future. The doctor will be concerned, however threatening and complicated the knowledge may be, to do his or her best to help the patient see it as liberating. This means that the professional must bring his *self* to bear in the client relationship, which is why it is rightly called a vocation and not a function. There is a personal dimension to the way in which every professional deals with a client, patient, or student.

Personal Reflection

There is a further perspective to grasp: being oneself and being in control of oneself is a necessary condition of being able to *give* attention. Being in relation to another person does not involve handing oneself over to them. To put it simply, in order to be oneself, one must keep one's distance. I think it is necessary to ground this in theological discussion.

I intimated previously that a theology beginning with Christ and with Christology is likely to be thin and one-dimensional in its interpretive power; I did not of course mean to imply by this that Christology was irrelevant to a full understanding of Christian theology. The best approach is to begin with the wholeness of God-in-Trinity and explore what it means to call him Creator, indeed Redemptive Creator, whose vital involvement with the world is eternal and real. The reality of God's commitment to the world's well-being is expressed in the doctrine of incarnation. God, Christians claim, has revealed himself in Christ, who is both human and divine. The materiality of the world and of the animal nature of our human lives is affirmed as

God's gift in the humanity of Christ; its spiritual, intellectual, and moral reality is affirmed by the divinity of Christ. When it confirms the divine and human nature of Christ, Christian Faith is declaring that God's "becoming incarnate" does not compromise his divinity. Each informs the other without confusing their natures or compromising their capacity for mutual relationship. Christ is one Person, human and divine.

There is something to be learned from this for professional practice. If I am as a priest to be free and able to listen to the concerns of a person who engages me in professional conversation, it is crucial that I do not allow myself to be overcome by his or her anxiety. I must not be taken over by this person but retain my freedom to be myself; if I do not, the possibility of a genuine personal relationship is prevented. Objective concern for the person's well-being is entirely consistent with my carefulness not to be emotionally influenced, though my professional concern to be of help must mean that I am emotionally sensitive to the issues with which the client is faced. I shall have compassion and sympathy with the client and indeed empathize with him or her. Maintaining myself as a person freely available for others requires that I take time to nourish my own self. It is easy to get sidetracked in this and to think that research on the condition of the client and his or her needs is what is important. It is, of course. Yet what I learn will only be of value to the client if and as I take steps to grow in self-knowledge and personal maturity and thus enhance my capacity for personal relationship. To learn to be available for others and to be able to assure them through my attitude, demeanor, and conversation that I am wholly attentive to them depends on attending to my own flourishing as a person.

But what does this involve? For the Christian, it begins with focusing one's attention on God and wanting to love him more, because by so doing, one becomes more and more aware of one's freedom to be oneself in taking responsibility for oneself and for the world. This means regular personal prayer, meeting with other Christians in public worship, and above all, celebrating God's presence in the Mass. Sarah Coakley has begun to develop a systematic theology that holds together in mutual interdependence the desire to pursue intellectual inquiry about God and the desire for a closer personal relationship with him (Coakley, 2013). To hold these aspects of human life in unity enables us, she argues, to begin to unpack the meaning of God's being in Trinity. God's desire to give himself utterly to the world's flourishing depends on the mutual society of the Trinity, not independently on the Father, the Son, or the Holy Spirit. Such an uncoupling of the

Persons of the Godhead is impossible—God is not to be thought of as simple. By definition, he cannot *be* alone; he is always in relationship, always with others, in order to be himself.

There is an analogy for us here. In order to nourish our *selves*, Christians believe that it is necessary that we focus on God. In so doing, we are already relating ourselves in community with the Father, the Son, and the Holy Spirit. But beyond that, there is the whole cultural, social, physical, moral, puzzlingly delightful human environment that we inherit and on which we can reflect. None of the dimensions summoned up in our imaginations is merely objectively interesting: each one is involved with all the others, hence Simone Weil's illuminating assertion that "studies" are not confineable to mathematics or history but involve all subjects inclusively. Thus to be "caught" by a Van Gogh painting of a corn field can transform my relationship with the natural world and listening to one of Beethoven's last quartets or Benjamin Britten's works for solo cello can illumine not just my world of sound but where I stand in relation to my sensitive appreciation of truth. When I have worked through a mathematical modeling of the Higgs boson particle (would that I could!), the chances are that my awareness of what we mean by "matter" will have been deepened far beyond anything I could have imagined "on my own." "Finding" myself will be a continuous process, yet at any time, I am nevertheless who I am and not another person. Just as God remains himself notwithstanding his giving of himself in attention to the world he is making, so can I as a professional remain myself while at the same time giving myself to the other.

Learning to Reflect

Learning to reflect is both an interior process and one that is involved with the whole world of human experience. It presumes an interior life, something that some believe is threatened by the rapid expansion of technical means of communication. Susan Greenfield, director of the Institute for the Science of the Mind, for example, fears that developments in the social media of iPads, iPhones, and so on could so absorb us such that the interior life that makes us who we are could atrophy (Greenfield, 2002). Her concern is not new. Karl Popper, in total ignorance of the communications revolution, wrote of the threats that could face us:

> We could conceive of a society in which men practically never meet face to face—in which all business is conducted by individuals in isolation

who communicate by typed letters or by telegrams, and who go about in closed motor cars. (Artificial insemination would even allow for propagation without a personal element.) Such a fictitious society might be called a "completely abstract or depersonalized society." The disturbing fact is that our modern society is beginning to resemble in some aspects just such a completely abstract society. Although we do not always drive alone in closed motor cars and may pass thousands of people in the street every day, we establish no personal relation with our fellow-pedestrians. Similarly, membership of a trade union may not mean more than the possession of a membership card and the payment of a subscription. There are many people living in a modern society who have no, or extremely few, intimate personal contacts, who live in anonymous isolation, and consequent unhappiness. For although society may become abstract, the biological make-up of man has not changed; men have social needs which they cannot satisfy in an abstract society. (Popper, 1957, pp. 174–75)

Such anxieties must be taken seriously. Notwithstanding this, we must never lose sight of the benefits that accrue. I have almost instant online access to masses of information that would have taken me weeks to gain were I searching in libraries. The temptation is to take this information for granted, not to check it, and to rely on the veracity of the evidence online as one unthinkingly used to trust the printed word. But we shall learn. It is possible to communicate with a doctor by voicemail, and possibly in the future by Skype, which will give a deceptive sense of being in face-to-face contact. Both are improvements on self-diagnosis on the basis of data online but are still no substitutes for face-to-face conversation. Listening, noticing, regarding, recognizing, intuiting, and learning to give attention are all dimensions of a relationship that will struggle to manifest itself apart from direct personal communication.

Being open to learning, to the other person, to the pleasures of knowing are necessary conditions of being in relationships; being open to the other person while at the same time remaining completely oneself is a necessary condition of every important professional relationship. A willing openness to this possibility is the ground of being a person who is grateful for the opportunity to behave attentively in relation to the other.

Conclusion

This brings us in conclusion to the matter of cooperation. Giving attention to the other is not one-way traffic; it is a mutual exercise. As

Christians see it, not even God could create a world on his own. That may seem questionable because surely Christians talk of God creating the world *ex nihilo*. True, but this is not a cosmological claim about the origin of the physical universe; it is a more personal perspective on the conditions under which the world exists and has its being. The point is not that God created the world in which we humans are set out of nothing but that nothing prevented God from pursuing his own pure intentions when, of his grace, without any inner compulsion or external constraint, he chose to create a world—a world to which he committed himself. His commitment of himself was not to take away the freedom of the world and to direct its future but to invite humankind to share in his purpose, which is why humankind is said by Jews and Christians to be made "in the image of God." We can share a common purpose with God and seek by all that we think and do to understand what the world's flourishing requires and how we can behave in such a way as to further it. We can wait on God and give our attention to the world's need without fear, in the light of the reason, which powers the observation that we enjoy and for which we are grateful.

Gratitude for our God-given curiosity and freedom to explore what it means to be made in God's image underpins our anticipation of what we can do and maintains our openness to God, to the world, and to one another. Gratitude liberates us to work with God by giving ourselves attentively to the needs of the other.

The professional relationship has a similar character. The world into which we are trying to bring the client, the patient, the student is not one that we as professionals can create by sheer will power. The effort is much more demanding: we are required to focus attentively, to give ourselves to the welfare of the client in the full, relevant knowledge of his or her situation. A generous sense of the importance of personal relationships is required if the professional is to free the client to take note of advice and take responsibility for himself or herself. What is required of the professional is a focus on the client and a broad understanding of his or her needs, which means an awareness of the totality of the environment in which they both stand and the desire to grow in understanding with the client so that both move forward together. If I just inform the patient that his or her symptoms are consistent with a diagnosis of dementia, I am far from fulfilling my responsibilities as a doctor. I need to empathize with my patients—to put myself in their shoes and, as a friend, do everything in my power to enable them to see the freedom that truth brings. Again, I shall fail in my professional responsibility if, as an auditor, I inform my clients that while their accounting practices are legal, they are unlikely to give them everything they need in order to avoid future threats to their businesses. We may well be surprised by the world that emerges, for we do not know the future, but whatever the world is, it will be one for which we can mutually become responsible and in which we shall continue to grow in response-ability.

In the following chapter, I shall explore the experience of sharing and learning to have a common will with God so as to build an open society.

Chapter 9

Sharing

Building Together

Introduction

Professionals with a vocation to serve the well-being of society at large know that they will not achieve this on their own: they will need to embrace a common purpose in order to share the work with others. As Scanlon points out, this means a mutual striving "to find terms of justification that others could not reasonably reject" (Scanlon, 1998, p. 361). For the Christian, the reasonable "terms of justification" are those that ground virtuous living in God and the theological framework that informs his or her life as a human being. A lively sense of personal gratitude for one's inheritance will open hidden futures, encourage compassion for others, and make one aware that service is a gift that requires one to learn to give attention to the other. Above all, gratitude is not only for the gift but for the giver, who is God, for his commitment, understanding, and empathy. He nourishes our best intentions with the expectation that we will serve with him in ensuring the well-being of creation.

In this chapter, I interpret the Christian theological framework in order to show God sharing his redemptive creativity with us, human beings made in his image. Gratitude is a key dimension of the professional relationship and virtuous professional practice: gratitude for what one inherits, for the professional community, and for the opportunity to share responsibility not only for and with the client but for the well-being of society at large. Professional relationships are essentially shared commitments to the common good.

Sharing implies an equality rooted in our materiality, the wholeness of what we are intent upon achieving, and the pursuit of meaning and truth in community.

Sharing with God

The idea of sharing is grounded in the Being of God as Trinity: it is fundamental to a Christian understanding of gratitude. The mutuality of the coinherent love between the Persons of the Trinity is the lively stimulus that grounds the openness of God's gracious creating. The Persons of the Trinity are coequal: they share their individuality in the unity of God—Father, Son, and Holy Spirit. What each Person is, is expressed by each and all Persons of the Trinity. The mutuality of the affirming love that confirms the wholeness of each Person of the Trinity *and* the identity of their lively unity is revealed in Jesus, the Christ. Out of the generosity of his Being, God shares himself with the world to which he gives his whole attention.

The revealing implication of the fact that humankind is made "in the image of God" is that they too can share themselves with the world if they so choose and thus, in the profoundest sense, be one with God in God's making of the world. The words "if they so choose" identify the key feature of our God-given human nature. Humans are free to become themselves through sharing themselves with creation; the invitation is demanding, daunting yet delightful. It will not be achieved in an instant; it will certainly require patience and may require sacrifice, as God reveals in the Person and Work of Christ. At the same time, it is encouraging, nourishing, and the root of our gratitude; it expresses itself in our care for one another and the world of creation and in our love of God.

The question of God's sharing of himself with humankind and the invitation to work with him raises questions of equality with regard to both the nature of God's relationship with humanity and interpersonal human relationships.

Sharing and the Question of Equality

The sharing of Being in God, which theologians explore in the doctrine of the Trinity, is a sharing among equals: the Persons of the Trinity are neither identical nor in a hierarchical relationship. Each Person of the Trinity—Father, Son and Holy Spirit—is free to enjoy a distinct relationship with the others, which enables God to be one in focusing his affectionate concern on the perfecting of the creation.

Let me take up again what I have mentioned earlier: the relation of authority to power. John Dunn distinguishes them broadly as follows: "Power, in one useful sense, is a relation between two or more human wills, in which one will can for some purposes effectively control the other will or set of wills" (Dunn, 2000, p. 75). Power assumes an actual or presumed loss of independence; more rarely, it can be exercised reasonably and benevolently. In theological terms, while God can be said to have power, he chooses not to exercise it because his purpose in creating is to confirm the independence of his creation and particularly of human beings. Were God to domineer, he would have no one with whom to *share* his Being; in effect, there would be no creation as we know it and no Creator to know.

Dunn's understanding of authority is in stark contrast: "Authority, in one useful sense, is a relation between specified human values, particular human understandings, and the wills guided or determined by those understandings" (p. 75). Authority depends for its legitimate exercise on the willing acceptance of the shared values that underpin a common ambition, which in political terms will take the form of social cooperation.

One may say analogously that God's authority in creating depends on the willing acceptance of common values and the commitment of human beings to align themselves with God in fulfilling his purposes for creation. In fact, in giving himself to the world, God is creating acts with an authority that has to be understood, interpreted, and appropriated if it is, in the light of experience, to be accepted and acted upon justly by humanity. Indeed God's authority only *really* exists when it is accepted as authoritative—that is, when in the light of experience, we find it valuable and informative, "worth accepting." God's nature is such that he is incapable of being himself *and* acting in an authoritarian manner. Dunn helpfully underlines the significance of values in what he says: "From the point of view of those subject to power or authority, the relation of power is an external relation between wills, and the relation of authority is an internal relation between a particular human understanding, the will which it guides, and the values to which it responds. It is the values which have authority; and any other human interpreter of these values who claims their sanctions is entitled to such authority only insofar as they do in fact speak for the values themselves: insofar as their interpretation is valid" (p. 75).

The Church is the interpreter of the Christian values implicit in Scripture and tradition (focused on the office of the Papacy and the magisterium in the case of Roman Catholicism); its authority is confirmed only "insofar as their interpretation is valid." It is evidently not the case that the perceived interpretation is always valid, but it is not fixed; there is conversation within the Church embodied in the development of a tradition that we can enter into, evaluate, and continue to reconfigure in the light of new circumstances.

Humankind is not equal to God, for God is in a category of his own. However, God's purpose in creating means that in exercising his authority, he *treats* us as equals by inviting us to share in his creative purpose. His affectionate concern confirms us as independent persons who are free to cooperate with him in the fulfillment of his purposes. Christ, who perfectly fulfilled God's purpose, invited us to pray with him that "God's will be done" and that his Kingdom be established. There has been much debate about the meaning of the expression "Kingdom of God." It is best understood as God's "activity in ruling" (Perrin, 1967, p. 55). Perrin later suggested that the expression is a "tensive symbol": it sums up the personal and social ambivalence implicit in the determined striving for something that is always both within and beyond one's reach (Perrin, 1976).

Human beings are clearly not equal to one another. On the other hand, just as God treats us as equals and invites us to become children rather than servants, so do we have the capacity to *treat* one another as equals albeit different. This is the mutual character of the professional relationship: professional and client are committed to the well-being of the other with the common purpose of serving the well-being of all persons.

The establishment of a relationship with the client, to which the professional is committed—one informed by values that both professional and client understand and can trust—is one that is both equal and different; it defines the essence of good practice. The professional must choose to treat the client as an equal partner in the relationship, for the client may not feel that he or she is so: it is not simply a fact that they are equal—though they are, as humans, exactly that.

Humanity Shares in the Materiality of Creation

Human beings are equal as products of evolution; their essential participation in worldly materiality is a form of God-given sharing in creation. We share with all other living things one genetic code, and it appears that we are moving with increasing confidence toward the view that "quantum mechanics is the bedrock of physical reality" (Al-Khalili and McFadden, 2014, p. 295). The happy consequence is therefore that we can support human health through drugs from plant material, test them, and develop surgical techniques by (contentiously) first experimenting on other animals. The point is that, as Aquinas following Aristotle affirms, far from being contrary to Christian Faith, we are properly understood to be bodies.

The assumptions and implications of this realization are much debated, but the reduction of our experience as human beings to explanations that are *merely* physical and "scientific" is a step too far. The thought that human being is *completely* describable in terms of neuroscience is mistaken. Of course we need the important insights that neuroscience offers if we are to understand what it means to be, as Christians say, a soul. An intriguing exposition drawing on neuroscience, theology, and psychology uses the term "embodied soulishness," which has something in common with Merleau-Ponty's "embodied subject" (Brown and Strawn, 2014). As human bodies, we also share with one another the search for meaning and truth in support of our desire for the world's well-being. Our intellectual inquiry includes an emotional response to the lure of God in the world's order and beauty. As persons called to share in God's work of creation, we are free to share with others in the light of a growing knowledge of the material world in order to build community. In so doing, we fulfill our human nature.

There are facts readily observable and enjoyed by every human being, for which we are grateful; they illuminate the fundamental nature of what we share as human beings. We actually share our physical being with the material of which the created world is constituted: we are made of the same material as the world—a fact we should never forget. St. Thomas is clear about this: "In short, for Thomas, a human being requires a living world structured ecologically, an ecology of which it is itself an integral, and interacting part" (Turner, 2013, p. 58).

As a matter of fact, we are so constituted that we cannot forget the fundamental nature of our relationship with our environment; death is an ever-present reminder of our mortality—the defining dimension of life when viewed in physical terms. Without the promise of death, there would be no reason to approach the world with curiosity and no opportunity to become responsible (Wilson, 2008, pp. 63–64). An endless race would be valueless.

As mortal persons, we have decisions to make within a time frame. Hence eternal life is not to be confused with being everlasting in time; rather, it expresses the essential continuity of a loving relationship with God. For the Christian, death opens the prospect of a redeemed and fulfilled life eternally shared with others. There is no such thing as an "individual" let alone a "private" heaven, but neither is there at this point in time any such thing as an individual person who is unrelated to creation, other people, and God. This insight is dependent on the fact, as Christians see it, that mere materiality, as commonly misunderstood in contemporary secular terms, does not totally define the nature of our human environment; rather, the world's materiality is imbued with the spiritual reality of the Divine and the consequent relationships and caring, of which our inner lives can become aware. By "imbued," I do not mean to imply that the soul is something different or separable from the material body: "The human soul just *is* the life of a body; it is how the body's life is human" (Turner, 2013, p. 72). God in Christ reveals this to be the essential nature of the creation that undergirds the wholeness of human life.

We may have to remind ourselves frequently that everything on earth, in heaven, and in hell is loved by God. The latter two are not, of course, "places" but rather central realities of experience that may be shared in any of the relationships of which every human being is aware. And it does not take much time; all can be shared in a day, as Wittgenstein remarked about hell: "The horrors of hell can be experienced in a single day; that is plenty of time" (Wittgenstein, 1980, p. 26e). Our moodiness is a psychological fact about ourselves at a particular time; it is never a discernment of the true condition of our relationship with God at any one time but a discernment of the variability of our sense that God is present at all times, hence the importance of the habit of giving thanks. In the case of the Eucharist, for example, even when there are no "feelings" on which we can rely, it reminds us of the fact of God's presence—hence also, the inherent value of learning to share with those who are of the Faith.

We can be grateful that in our materiality, there is focused the wholeness of our physical, spiritual, and moral experience but not of course the completeness that is yet to be achieved. The exercise of personal initiative makes us aware that successful inquiry involves choosing to share our knowledge, skills, and very selves if we are to be successful. Private "knowledge" about the world is no more possible than a private language, as Wittgenstein pointed out (Wittgenstein, 1958, paras. 243–315).

Our Shared Search for Meaning and Truth

Meaning is a cognitive and emotional sense of purpose and value. No aspiring search for meaning is possible as a lonely venture: it is a shared activity sensitive to all that we have inherited and is inspired by the intention to serve human well-being and the good of creation. We want to know and will therefore be "trying to understand," which means loving the world; in some respects, we may find this hard to do. In loving the world, we find that we need to draw on the enthusiasm of others and take into account their perspectives.

The fact that God loves the world and has given himself to it without holding back is an inspiration: he is attentive to the world's beauty and its inherent tendency to reveal its truth and goodness. God therefore, notwithstanding the squalor and misery of the world, commits himself to it, loves it, and seeks to redeem it; we as human beings made in God's image can aspire to do so too. God is not selective in his concern for the world; he is with it in every dimension of its life. The incarnation of Christ confirms the wholeness and intimacy of humans with the Divine but not of course their identity. Since in our search for meaning and truth, we share an environment informed by the gracious presence of God, on whom we can rely, we can with confidence explore it and enjoy the freedom to experiment.

God's sharing of himself with humankind demonstrates his understanding and respect for the nature of humanity and indeed of each person. Our perception that our curiosity about our environment, its sense and meaning, is God-given has an emotional aspect that is stimulating: God *wants* us to work with him toward the world's perfection. Without that curiosity, we would not attempt to find our place in the creation. Earlier, following Pailin, I mentioned that God in his creating lures us to take part in the life of the world in every dimension of its being. Are we mistaken if we think that God is *emotionally* involved with the world he is making so that the lure encouraged by the beauty and moral demand of the world we experience can be recognized as, or at least interpreted to be, divine activity?

We say that God "loves" the world, but to talk of an emotional commitment might suggest an anthropomorphism that threatens the absolute perfection of God's Being. For my own part, I accept that God is capable of suffering and that, in an important sense, he shares in the emotional life of his creation; this does not imply that God is subject to temptation or the likelihood of sinning. How could he be unaware of his presence with his creation? God is not unfeeling, but his aseity implies that his metaphysical nature is not changed or determined by his "experience." The lure of the world that we experience as we express our curiosity through inquiry may be quite properly construed as an expression of the divine purpose in creation, with which we can align ourselves if we so choose.

Robert C. Roberts has insights about the nature of emotion that are very helpful here. He talks of construals, by which he means sense perceptions that are not "pure" but depend for their understanding on what he calls "conceptual perception" (Roberts, 2013, pp. 39–48). These are not rare, for while there are, Roberts believes, "pure" sensory perceptions, most sensory impressions are "construals" in the sense that what we see is the consequence of what the percipient brings to bear on the data. He takes as an example the familiar figure of the duck-rabbit, which I may construe to be a duck or a rabbit according to the way I attend to my perception of the figure. Roberts goes on to suggest that the notion of a construal has particular interest in relation to the role of emotion in the moral life (pp. 46–48, 60–67). An emotion is a concern-based construal of a situation, which is open to interpretation. It may be something immediately demanding attention to which we instinctively respond, such as a child about to run across the road without looking, or something more long-term that requires serious consideration, such as global warming or population growth. In each case, the emotion is a concern-based construal of the sensory perception of the situation, which gives rise to moral reflection because we care about the outcomes. They demand our attention.

Not everyone is worried about the growth in population; some are more concerned about the imbalance between the generations brought about by increased longevity. Not everyone believes that something should be done about global warming, since there are normally fluctuations in climate patterns. Sensory perception in every case is far from pure because it seems to have evaluative properties whose interpretation will depend on which way one looks at them.

Roberts's felicitous insight illuminates the Christian perception of what it means to live in the world with faith and to share with God in the fulfilling of his purposes for the world. Christians believe that they live in a world infused with the reality of God's concerned presence. The lure of God's creation encourages us to be curious about our world and to set about the business of becoming more response-able, the consequence of which is the opportunity to live more responsibly. This feature of the human experience informs the relationship with clients that is aspired to by the good professional.

Attracted by the lure of a client's concerned commitment to resolving a problem, the professional sets about the business of giving full attention to the client and his or her situation. In so doing, the professional intends to become more response-able and therefore more in partnership with his or her client, more responsible. In inquiring, we experience emotions, aroused by sensory perceptions, of the circumstances in which we find ourselves; "our" circumstances as professionals will embrace the circumstances of our clients if we are, as we should be, empathetic. The God-given nature of our curiosity and the care that God evinces in his attention to the world's well-being leads us to see that the care we feel shares in God's care and encourages us to know that we are working with God for the world's well-being. This is the truth about our material world and the meaning we gratefully acknowledge in our experience of it.

Building Community: Emotion in Practice

A human being, it may be said, is made of stardust, energized by the sun and a particular expression of the genetic code that he or she shares with every living thing. These partly poetic and partly actual accounts of human nature are both necessary elements of any exploration of our place in the world: both stimulate further inquiry, including the exploration of our relationship with every other dimension of the world's being. When properly understood, they keep our feet on the ground.

More profoundly, as we have seen, humans are capable of choosing to commit to the world's well-being when they recognize the lure of creation as God's engagement with it and become coworkers with God in that creation. God's care is fundamental to the world's well-being; our concern is to discern God's will in our working in the world.

What is the world's well-being? It involves bringing out the unity in community that is enjoyed when the right relationships are revealed between all things, organic and inorganic, divine and human. Moreover, the world's well-being is not accounted for in any contemporary reductionist understanding of matter, for God's creating has a relational quality that is not expressible in reductionist terms. Such redemptive creating requires us to give attention to the world if we are to acquire genuine knowledge, skill, compassion, and justice, and above all, to recognize our natural curiosity as a desire to be one in love with God, with our fellow human beings, and with the creation. Our delight is the consequence of God's gracious presence, which lures us into giving it our attention. It is certainly a matter of reason and intellectual inquiry, as Aquinas rightly emphasizes, but as I have indicated previously, intellectual inquiry is more than mere ratiocination. "Wanting to know" requires intellectual commitment, aesthetic appreciation, moral insight, and emotional attention.

Robert C. Roberts suggests that emotions are perceptual constructs that are "experienced as a sensitivity to the situation" (Roberts, 2013, p. 86). Martha Nussbaum is equally persuasive about the informative nature of emotion. She writes, "Emotions shape the landscape of our mental and social lives." She adds later, "A lot is at stake in the decision to view emotions in this way, as intelligent responses to the perception of value" (Nussbaum, 2001, p. 1). There is certainly a lot at stake. Nussbaum explores their significance for the individual: "The value perceived in the object appears to be of a particular sort. It appears to make reference to the person's own flourishing. The object of the emotion is seen as *important* for some role it plays in the person's own life" (pp. 29–30).

Gratitude for what we receive of God and from God fills us with hope and points us toward the future. What we inherit and what we now enjoy through the services of others encourages us to want to contribute to the world's well-being. (Emmons's theory of gratitude as a moral barometer, moral reinforcer, and motivator emphasizes this point.) In turn, we are grateful when the service we give to others is appreciated: there is mutuality about the experience of gratitude. Serving others in such a way as to contribute personally to their well-being depends on learning to give attention to their circumstances, which is by no means a simple matter. Indeed it demands imagination, for to give attention to another person requires that we include the relationships that shape that person's experience.

It is unsurprising that a current aim of education, much emphasized in government guidelines and highly desired by employers, is the ability to work as a member of a team. There are things a team can do that a set of individuals working by themselves cannot achieve. To be a member of a team that works well together is a source of joy and satisfaction and something for which we can be very grateful. In the course of life, we are members of many teams, many associations; some will be permanent, some temporary, some voluntary, some required, and some inherited. Sharing is a creative experience that can, when engaged in with affectionate courtesy, increase our self-understanding and enhance the committed insight we bring to any enterprise. This experience is the product of learning to work *with* people rather than *for* people. As Christians understand this, the relationship with God is the inspirational relationship that underpins all others and gives them life.

What is the target that will satisfy our curiosity and ground our care in worthwhile activity? We shall only uncover the "target" we share *in via*. It is all "work in progress," the purpose(s) of which we unfold, criticize, and clarify as time goes on. A flourishing human society depends on shared ambition: learning what holds us together in community is a matter of discovering the purpose we share.

We are born into many "communities": the natural world, the human race, the nation, and so on. How we make sense of them and become response-able for them depends on our willingness to commit to their well-being. Our emotions have a key part to play in this, for as concern-based construals, we shall voluntarily respond to them personally and in communities. I began by setting the discussion in a theological context informed by love; a mutual concern for the well-being of all lies at the center of good relationships. It brings us together in such a way as to facilitate our mutual well-being and express our collaboration with God.

In sharing himself with the world he is creating, God surely knows what he wants to achieve and is willing to take the time to achieve it. However, a mark of our humanity is fear of the future, which leads us to want certainty and security. There is, of course, no such thing; it is an impossibility and contrary to the nature of the world and the God who is its redemptive Creator. Once again, our misconception is that God's power, knowledge, and love imply God's control of the world rather than of himself in relation to the world. God's purpose in creating is always in process, never completed.

There are, however, built into the Christian theological framework critical events that reveal the God who lies behind and within our daily experience of the world. These events and signs encourage an emotional response, a "concern-based construal," which stimulates interpretation. For example, the Person and Work of Jesus Christ, whose birth, teaching, Crucifixion, death, Resurrection, and ascension are events in which his disciples came to "recognize" Jesus as the Messiah and ultimately the Son of God. They reveal the Real Presence of God. The truth and the meaning implicit in them is discerned when God's invitation, implicit in creation, to pay attention and learn to inquire is gratefully accepted. We enter into the freedom of God's Kingdom when we begin to explore the nature of God's purpose in creation. Humanity copes with anxiety not by falsely assuming a security that is foreign to human nature but by taking up the challenge of sharing God's loving purpose in Christ for the world.

God's purpose cannot be *deduced* from Biblical texts; scholarly care is required not only to interpret the text but to reinterpret it in new circumstances. Human nature may not change, but our understanding of it does, as do the political, social, economic, and cultural situations in which it expresses itself. Some Christians continue to affirm a literalist position. Moreover, some militant atheists, such as Dawkins (Dawkins, 2006), are inclined to argue that any development of Christian theology is intellectually dishonest. Hart has responded, in turn, attacking Dawkins and Grayling for what he regards as their gross theological ignorance, blind assertion of scientific "fact," and amazing lack of intellectual curiosity (Hart, 2013, pp. 20–22). (There are, of course, positive arguments for atheism, which in the hubbub are ignored to the detriment of any stimulus they offer to serious theological inquiry.) Biblical texts are not ends in themselves but starting points for a conversation in which we are lively participants. If we fail to take up the conversation and refuse responsibility for sharing with God the exploration of the purpose(s) of his creating, we may be said to share in sin—to fall short of the glory of God.

James Mackey, the first Roman Catholic scholar to hold a chair of theology at the University of Edinburgh was stirred by the intentions of Pope John XXIII when he called the Second Vatican Council in 1962. MacKey says the Pope called for "some increasing openness and relevance to the cultures and condition of the present and the impending future" (MacKey, 2006, p. 3). In other words, the Pope wanted the Church in Christ's name to facilitate the world's conversation with God. In the light of this, Mackey grounds his theological exploration in a God whose eternal activity is to be found in evolving creation.

In relation to our contemporary culture and current understanding of the world in which we are set and whose physical nature we share, what sense can we now make of the following questions: What is God's purpose in creating? What is God's target for his creation? Is there a "fixed" goal to which everything inevitably tends, and if so, in what sense? It is for sure not a purpose in the sense that (if I may be permitted anthropomorphic language) God had in mind a particular physical "end" or a political, economic, or social structure. If that had been his purpose, then why did he not effect a perfect world *ab initio*? It was surely open to him to do so, since there were neither internal nor external constraints on what he might have chosen to do—a point of view implicit in the claim that God created the world *ex nihilo*. One must therefore assume that this was not consistent with his purpose or indeed his divine nature. So what is his purpose?

The fundamental gift, for which we are grateful, is life—and life in its most vital, creative form, love. What God offers is not a finished world in which we simply take our place and perform as we have been predetermined to behave; on the contrary, what we are grateful for is the liberty to appreciate the values and virtues that will enable life to flourish. Our gratitude is not simply for human life but for all life and all creation. As St. Paul wrote, "The whole creation has been groaning in labour pains until now, and not only the creation, but we ourselves, who have the first fruits of the Spirit, groan inwardly while we wait for adoption, the redemption of our bodies"(Rom. 8:22–23). There is, in other words, a divinely given "natural" process inherent in the world as we experience it in which we have a role to play—a world we can tease into shape. We have moreover some freedom as to how we shape it. Subject to the values that are inherent in the world, conditioned by the character of God himself, we are free to share in God's creating because we are made in his image. The political constitution, the economic system, or the social structure may be whatever it is, but if it is to flourish and contribute to human well-being and nourish the world as it is, there are values that will necessarily condition our choices and signs that will be necessary for us to pick up on and learn from when things go wrong.

Sharing in Community

"You have been told, O man, what is good and what Yahweh asks of you, simply this: to act justly, love tenderly, and to walk humbly with your God" (Mic. 6:8). "To act justly" is, in New Testament terms, to behave in such a way as you would like others to behave with regard to you. "To love tenderly" is to go beyond what is legally or even socially required so that the person for whom we are caring knows that we are focused on his or her health and not on the reputation we shall garner by looking after him or her well. "To walk humbly with your God" is to behave in conformity with your human nature and not to assume that the world can be taken in any direction you choose just because you want to do so.

The notion of vocation, as traditionally understood, points to an acceptance of a professional role that assumes personal responsibility for standards of behavior that are in the public interest, not simply one's own interest, that of one's company, or even that of one's profession. To walk humbly with your God is the basis of being able to act justly and to love tenderly.

The sheer beauty of the world entices our interest and provokes our courteous attention not only toward it but toward the Creator, whose acceptance of responsibility for it we are privileged and invited to share: "The order and harmony of the created world results from the diversity of beings and from the relationships which exist among them. Man discovers them progressively as the laws of nature. They call forth the admiration of scholars. The beauty of creation reflects the infinite beauty of the Creator and ought to inspire the respect and submission of man's intellect and will" (Catholic Church, 1994, para. 341).

The laws of nature are, of course, only rough and ready approximations of how the world is: always subject to development and/or change in the light of experience. Even the most generally accepted patterns of understanding, such as evolution, are incomplete. They may be true in a general sense, but what is implied by the claim is regularly updated because of new discoveries, the search for which we share in.

We share responsibility in the many relationships and forms of association through which we work with God for the natural world and for human prosperity. The fact that these relationships and associations are multiple is critical to the success of any one of them. Opportunities, challenges, and implications arise within political and socioeconomic structures, voluntary communities, and the intimacies of personal family life.

We share our human nature with the totality of the material world; we share our mortal lives with the rest of humanity. For our personal well-being, we therefore rely on sharing in the care of the natural world and depend on accepting our responsibility for all humanity. This demands that we give attention to political, economic, and social relationships in order to build what John Rawls calls "a well-ordered society" based on justice construed as fairness. The stability of such a society depends, he argues, on an overlapping consensus of reasonable and rational persons whose moral motivation will be based on principles informed by a philosophical (not psychological) conception of the good, a sense of justice, and a love of mankind (Rawls, 1972, pp. 470–96). Rawls implies that the stability of a well-ordered society relies on more than the application of technical skill: it involves a love of mankind.

Martha Nussbaum shares much of Rawls's perspective but regards his reference to a principled "love of mankind" as passionless and without emotional content; it misses the point: "We might say that a liberal state asks citizens who have different overall conceptions of the meaning and purpose of life to overlap and agree in a shared political space, the space of fundamental principles and constitutional ideals. But then, if those principles are to be efficacious, the state must also encourage love and devotion to those ideals" (Nussbaum, 2013, p. 7). She suggests that in fact, his view of the role of emotion is far too limited, particularly with regard to the role of love, which should not be limited to mankind but include everything that sustains humanity: "I shall argue that all of the core emotions that sustain a decent society have their roots in or are forms of love—by which I mean an intense attachment to things outside the control of our will" (p. 15). Without love, justice would be no more than compliance and lack a public concern for truth. I would add that love in its most creative expression is the product of gratitude for all that one knows and has received.

Nussbaum's focus, as is Rawls's, is on the democratic nation-state. This constitutes certainly one of the communities for which one might be grateful and have creative love. The political structure of a government under which people live may of course be one of very many kinds: tribal, feudal, monarchical, absolutist, imperial, military, religious, plutocratic, democratic, bureaucratic, or dictatorial to name only some. None of them is necessarily destructive to the possibility of "the good life," though all may become so, depending on the quality of its leadership and the manner of its exercise of authority. There is certainly much to commend democracy because it promises public debate as the means of establishing a "reasonable consensus" on which to build a "well-ordered state," yet cynicism about the quality of leadership and suspicion on the part of the general public about the motives of many in power are deemed by many to threaten its future. Democracy, as Winston Churchill is reputed to have said, is the worst political system apart from all the rest.

We may say that we want "the good life," but what that means is a matter of debate in which every citizen has a right to share. One may trace this to the Greek *polis*, in which every citizen had a right and a duty to share in the making and the executing of public policy. This in turn raises the question of citizenship, for it was not everyone whose life was affected by the decisions of the state as to who was a citizen and who therefore had the right to participate in the debate and any subsequent vote. For example, neither women nor slaves had political rights, and they were excluded from voting in councils and assemblies and from taking part in any judicial matters. A woman's duty was to produce legitimate children; any political role she might have exercised came through the influence she may have had on her husband, father, or other authorities. A primary concern of democratic political enterprise in a state is that every citizen shares in one community and therefore has an opportunity to live responsibly with others.

Professional Practice and the Common Good

For the Christian, the community is wider than the nation-state: "the good life" for which one strives is not confined by its limits. There is one creation, one human race, and one Redemptive Creator in whose image we live and move and have our being. God treats all people as citizens of his Kingdom in the world, which is the object of his love; all are invited in principle to share in the conversation with him about the future. Christians are not stimulated simply to build a stable, well-ordered state but a stable, well-ordered world. The word for this is "community," for which the New Testament word is *koinonia*. *Koinonia* is the common life of the community of faith, which implies a deep sense of responsibility for one another that is enjoined by their common response to the Good News of God's presence in Christ. This is not the consequence of claiming to believe in Jesus; it has a moral quality that is wider and more redemptively creative, which needs to be set in the context of our gratitude for God's gracious love in creation, covering all things and all people. In principle, *koinonia* exists already in creation, in human societies, in families because of God's gracious presence; it is our human responsibility to work at the business of making it a reality. Sarah Bachelard suggests that it is the Resurrection that, when properly understood, opens worlds of possibility that nourish the moral imagination: the emotional construal we bring to our ordinary experience in the light of the Resurrection transforms our world.

The moral imagination, inspired by the Resurrection, is more than a successful economy, more than friendship, more than basic service. It involves the willing acceptance of a common life, which means giving attention to the well-being of others, caring for the creation, and living out human life as it was made in the image of God. In a powerful sense, this is implicit in just and effective professional relationships. The professional and the client are sharing in the building of a well-ordered world in whose values they share. The relationship between the professional and the client is both equal and different; it is shaped by intellectual, emotional, and moral dimensions. In the first instance, it is important that the professional and the client each respect the independence of the other. If the needs of the client and the service of the professional are to be brought together, it will only be by means of an honest respect that each has for the interests of the other. There are, after all, things I have to do for myself that only I can do: clenching my teeth is one. But more revealingly in this context, the professional offers advice that the client must consider, and the client must do that for himself or herself.

Thus clients must be as clear as they can in their own minds as to what it is they are seeking from professionals, and professionals must be wary of promising to do more than is within their power to do. Clients and professionals have to engage with one another if clarity is to emerge through participation in genuine conversation. I take the example of the education profession and the teacher-student relationship, but the same or analogous features will figure in every professional relationship. The teacher's relationship with the student should not be one *de haut en bas*, for the teacher should never think of himself or herself as condescending; on the contrary, the teacher should invite the student to share his or her enthusiasm for the subject so that by empathy with the student's position, the teacher can inspire him or her to want to learn for himself or herself.

A first requisite for the teacher is to assist the student in bringing to mind what in fact he or she already knows, to help the student recognize its relevance so that he or she can build on it. Only then will the teacher know what next to bring to the attention of the student and begin to form a strategy for getting across new material. At each stage of the pedagogical process, the student has to believe that the teacher wants him or her to learn, and the teacher has to believe that the student is trying to learn. The implicit relationship is one of love—love of the subject and love of the student. The term has unfortunate overtones because it has gathered around it a set of mushy, sentimental, and reductionist associations that limit its reference. Love, in the useful sense appropriate here, means genuine concern for one's well-being—in this case, the educational progress of the student—but not only that: the concern of the good teacher is for the total well-being, intellectual, emotional and moral, of the student because without this general affection for him or her, the personal quality of the relationship on which both rely will dissipate over time in the light of experience. There is implicit here a sharing of the self analogous to that which God has with the world. The teacher cannot "teach" the student in the sense of "causing the student to have learned" something. On the contrary, the student is free to learn if he or she so chooses, but he or she has to choose to do so and put in the time, concentrated attention, and purposefulness that is necessary. It requires patience on both their parts, and from time to time, there may arise a condition that one can only describe as suffering. Learning to bear the "pain" in order to want to go on trying to teach and trying to learn makes fundamental demands on the relationship, which reveals its true quality. In this case, the values are shared.

The relationships between the teacher and the student; the doctor and the patient; the lawyer or accountant and the client; the police officer and the member of the public; the military and the "enemy," which it respects; the journalist and the public; the public relations manager and the media will all share the same values if they are to be true to their purposes. There is actually a sense in which each professional is involved in a performance akin to that of a musician. The pianist practices to enhance his or her technical competence, studies the history of music in order to gain insight into the traditions in which the composition is set, explores the composer's life experience, and experiments with the musicality of his or her playing and the possible interpretations of the piece; there are many other aspects of the music, the instrument, the acoustics in the hall, and so on to take into account. The musician may have all this in place but without the committed attention of the listener on whom he or she depends, his or her playing will be empty. Performance is a shared experience of something beyond the immediate activity of performer or listener: it introduces both to a new awareness of the wholeness of things, it grasps for the wholeness of beauty and may surprise both by what is revealed. The professional may have the knowledge, experience, technique, and intention to perform well, but without the full attention and goodwill of the client, the professional's advice or performance will fall empty from his or her hands.

Conclusion

God shares himself with the world: humankind, created "in the image of God," can choose to follow Christ and gratefully share with the world. The human being does in fact share in the materiality of God's creation because the body is made of the same material as the world. He or she shares with fellow humans across the ages in their search for meaning and purpose in the world. In so doing, intellectually, morally, and emotionally, they respond to the lure of the world, which they interpret as an expression of God's presence in the world. More profoundly, as we have seen, all people are capable, in the light of this concern-based perception, of committing themselves. In so doing, we begin to discern the purpose of God in creating and embracing, as far as we can, the values implicit within the world; we become coworkers with God in creation. Such redemptive creating is expressed in political, economic, and social structures for which we are entirely accountable. To be effective, we require knowledge, skill, compassion, justice, and above all, a desire to be one in love with God, with our fellow human beings, and with the world of creation. The professional focuses concern on a person in a particular personal context, inviting him or her to share a common set of values in order that they may together build a future that each desires and that both regard as in their common interest.

There is a wholeness implicit in the gratitude we express to God, to our fellow human beings, and to the world of which we are a part. I shall turn to consideration of this in the following chapter in a discussion of beauty and its relationship with justice. Fundamentally, it concerns celebration and focuses on the Eucharist—a work the community offers, always anticipatory but proleptically complete on each occasion. "The beauty of holiness" is an explicitly Christian theological expression, but it states the perfection of God's sharing of himself with the world and our grateful sharing with one another in the service of God and the world.

Chapter 10

The Beauty of Holiness

Introduction

Our inclination is to focus on immediate matters. However, perspective is important; from time to time, we need to stand back and try to see things whole. The professional relationship, I have argued, has a personal perspective that involves the whole of the self. We need to be reminded of this from time to time. My thought is that the experience of beauty can reveal the depth and breadth of truth and present us with a sense of wholeness. I shall explore this in relation to professional practice and the constant need to be aroused to the moral dimension, which takes us through and beyond compliance. There is an analogy here with Jesus's attitude toward the law as expressed in the Sermon on the Mount: "Do not think that I have come to abolish the law or the prophets; I have come not to abolish but to fulfill" (Matt. 5:17). In other words, we must be compliant but put compliance in a larger framework.

Beauty is something for which everyone is grateful; it is something we want to attend to, to share, to enjoy. When I contemplate *Supper at Emmaus* by Caravaggio, read a sonnet by Donne, or share in a performance of *King Lear*, I find myself drawn into another world that I immediately want to talk about and share with others. I have mentioned that the Resurrection can make an analogous impact (Bachelard, 2014). I am emotionally moved and intellectually stimulated. In fact, I not only experience the particular but have my perspective broadened and deepened to the extent that I may be called to reconsider my humanity, my philosophy of life, and my place in the world.

There is, moreover, a moral perspective to beauty, but we need a language with which to talk about it. There is truth to be grasped—a real world that, when discerned from within the Christian theological framework, has the reality of the loving presence of God in Christ.

Plato and Jesus on Beauty

The Greek *to kalon* is frequently translated as "beauty" and the adjective *kalos* as "beautiful." However, there is more to it than is covered by the terms "attractive" or "pleasant." For Plato, *to kalon* has a moral depth, which suggests that "virtue" or "virtuous" would be a better translation (Plato, 1963, p. 537, *Symp.* 183e). What is beautiful attracts the good person and reveals to him or her the moral value that underlies it. "The beautiful," "the good," and "the just" are three mutually supportive aspects of truth. The key to seeking truth, which every human being desires above everything else, is to adopt a balanced position that holds all three in a reasoned relationship with one another. A balanced judgment is vital, for as Hare points out, no fanatic is susceptible to reason (Hare, 1963, pp. 159–85).

Much of the same, but with an added dimension, is true of the New Testament's use of the term. Jesus, for example, urges his hearers in the Sermon on the Mount, "Let your light shine before others, so that they may see your good works and give glory to your Father in heaven" (Matt. 5:16). Three features of this passage are particularly significant. First and very importantly, Jesus's words are not addressed to his disciples exclusively but to all those present: "the crowds were astounded at his teaching, for he taught them as one having authority, and not as their scribes" (Matt. 5:1–2; 7:28–29). Everyone is called to do good works. Second, the beauty of people's good works (Gk., *kala erga*) reveals their moral worth, but moreover, third, it "gives glory to the Father in heaven." Here is the added depth of the Divine, for "giving *glory*" implies the revelation of God's presence.

Since all humankind is made in God's image, every human being is open to the experience of beauty, which can stimulate a renewed moral concern that implies equality of treatment and justice for all. Moreover, I shall argue, beauty opens a perspective on the Divine by bearing witness to the presence of God with his creation. Our true human happiness is fulfilled as we try to make a reality of the possibilities implicit in the fact of God's presence. Ultimately, Karl Rahner says this is experienced in "the Beatific Vision," the happiness that comes to every person who shares in the life of the Glorified Lord (Rahner, 1975).

The Relevance of Beauty

Professional life involves both careful attention to the needs of the client and an awareness of the many complex circumstances in which the client's needs are set. Moreover, the professional has a responsibility to secure the reputation of his profession, to fulfill his or her vocation to serve the common good and the natural world on whose well-being society depends. Maintaining an appropriate balance between them all is an art, not a science; it requires *phronesis*, practical wisdom. Aristotle offers the following account of the "man of practical wisdom":

> Now it is thought to be a mark of a man of practical wisdom to be able to deliberate well about what is good and expedient for himself, not in some particular respect, e.g. about what sorts of things conduce to health or to strength but about what sorts of things conduce to the good life in general. This is shown by the fact that we credit men with practical wisdom in some particular respect when they have calculated well with a view to some good end which is one of these that are not the object of any art. Thus in general the man who is capable of deliberating has practical wisdom. (Aristotle, 1984b, *N.E.*, 1140a)

The practically wise person will calculate effectively in the light of his or her knowledge and, in addition, identify the situations that require deliberation and the exercise of calm judgment.

To do this successfully, at least two things will be necessary: regular reflection on past experience and openness to promptings emerging from new stimuli. The former should be a major aspect of initial education, whereas the latter is acquired through a lifetime's development of the capacity to learn from and test experience. A major reason for this is the accidental and unpredictable nature of events that challenge trained assumptions and bring about changes in attitude that have a consequent impact on virtuous behavior.

Beauty can surprise us and, in so doing, revivify a sense of vocation; it can bring us into touch with dimensions of the world of which we are ignorant or ones that we are inclined, consciously or unconsciously, to put aside because we are absorbed with more immediate matters. The moral aspect of the experience of beauty reminds us that generous human relationships are rooted in love and justice. An affirming gratitude flowing from the experience of the mysterious beauty of a flower, a poem, or a person can have life-changing results. Einstein said, "The most beautiful thing we can experience is the mysterious. It is the source of all true art and all science. They to whom this emotion is a stranger, who can no longer pause to wonder and stand rapt in awe, are as good as dead: their eyes are closed." The result might be a welcome change in attitude and lead to significant developments in our use of language, which can be revelatory. For example, when Jeremy Hunt, secretary for health in the United Kingdom, said recently that doctors "must stop thinking of patients as 'bodies harbouring a pathology' . . . and instead recognize them as people," he pointed, as an example, to the importance of addressing a patient by name. In so doing, the doctor identifies, and points to, the mystery of the person for whose health the doctor and the patient are mutually responsible.

There are dynamic theological roots that illuminate the vitality of this personal experience, which I shall develop later. They are linked, I believe, to our "ordinary" delight in beauty and inspire our sense of the mystery of *living* human being, as Einstein felt. The beauty of God revealed in Christ informs our personhood, which is made in the image of God.

Eileen Scarry has an intriguing approach to the subject: she draws attention to four aspects of beauty. Beauty is sacred, unprecedented, and lifesaving; moreover, it encourages deliberation (Scarry, 2000, pp. 23–24, 28). Her use of the latter term suggests a relationship with Aristotle's practical wisdom; beauty stimulates the desire to deliberate, to question who one is and what one should do. Beauty is revelatory, without parallel, life-giving, and meaningful in the sense that it promises the benefits that flow from contemplating its significance. It is never passively content with itself; rather, it is always demanding, stimulating, and encouraging. Scarry goes on to claim that "beauty is a starting point for education" (p. 31), a point emphasized by Caldecott (Caldecott, 2012).

So where does beauty figure in the debate about what constitutes good, just, and coherent professional practice? Good professional practice, as we have seen, requires not only that we give attention to the individual client but that in order to do so effectively, we call to mind as fully as we can the general circumstances that give rise to the particular case and pertain to the advice we offer. Precisely how this can be done is a serious question, given that the research demands presented by a client's problem may be all-consuming. Moreover, there will very likely be external pressures on the professional to meet, for example, income targets set by the employer or time pressures in the case of the medical practitioner, which will further serve to distract.

How can we revivify our vision, come to terms with the inherent tension present in all ethical behavior, and keep in mind the depth and range of the perspectives specifically involved in professional life? Can we come to terms with the fact that we are responsible to society at large and to the individual client? I suggest that beauty offers an experience that can liberate the professional and assist in keeping things in perspective precisely because it is instantiated in the particular, and at the same time, draws attention to the mysterious.

THE LANGUAGE OF BEAUTY

Beauty is difficult to discuss: it hardly emerges in critical inquiry, as Denis Donoghue found when he was a student at University College, Dublin. He read Latin and English and was introduced to the works of Shakespeare, Milton, and Horace, but the matter of their beauty was not raised. He found the same to be true when he studied classical singing at the Royal Irish Academy of Music, where, he comments, the focus of Brian Boydell's tuition was on breathing: beauty was taken for granted and never discussed. Yet he would have been informed and inspired, he believes, if he had been introduced in context to beauty. It would have opened his mind and heart to a new depth of meaning. The matter of the particular music and literature would have been deepened and widened for him through arousing awareness of its relation to other dimensions. Then, in turn, an enhanced sensitivity and insight would have assisted not just his "aesthetic appreciation" but what he could aspire to achieve in physical performance. Moreover, there are wider implications. Donoghue goes on to say, "If I did not think about beauty in those years, it follows that I never heard of its social and political implications" (Donoghue, 2003, p. 5), and, I would have to add, its moral interest.

The loss of the word "beauty" in context is not a small matter. Sociologists of language have shown how profoundly language can impact the attitudes, feelings, motives, and behaviors of society and of groups (such as the professions). The importance of language teaching and language acquisition can, therefore, hardly be overemphasized. The fact that "beauty" was not a word that turned up in critical conversation meant for Donoghue that the dimension of the beautiful was absent from his critical armory. Even if beauty is intuitively experienced, the fact that we cannot name it will diminish our capacity to appreciate it; certainly it will make it impossible for us to deepen our understanding of it by engaging in conversation with others about it.

Mari Ruti notes the active power of language in shaping "new" worlds: "Among other things, [language] is a versatile medium for introducing new values, ideals, meanings, and patterns of appreciation into the world. In addition, even creative endeavors that do not rely on language, such as painting, sculpture, photography, garden design and dance, can be enriched by an encounter with language. In other words, the reward we get from a painting (to take just one example) can be multiplied by our ability to attribute various meanings to it, so that as much pleasure has arisen from our efforts to decipher Mona Lisa's smile as from the smile itself" (Ruti, 2013, pp. 57–58). Ruti's introduction of the concept of meaning is critical here. Conversation about beautiful things is an ingredient of "the good life," which may take us by surprise and keep alive our awareness of the truth deep in the heart of things—and their meaning.

The Revival of Interest

After a period of neglect, beauty has once again become a subject of interest for philosophers, especially Iris Murdoch (1977), Anthony Saville (1982), Eva Schaper (1983), and the theologians von Balthasar (1965–91), Gesa Theissen (2004), and David Hart (2004). Neglect of the topic by philosophers was the product of the desiccation that some logical positivists brought to the subject: linguistic analysis contributed much to our understanding but only "at ground level." Lifting our eyes to take in the experience of beauty can open our minds to the wholeness of things while at the same time drawing attention to and taking life from the delightful or the disturbing, particularity of a situation, person, work of art, mathematical expression, or flower. Moreover, since the experience can take one by surprise, it is not something that one can guard oneself against; it can stimulate hard thinking about meaning that can be personally transformative. Kant puts it this way: when one's attention is caught by a beautiful picture or the vastness of the heavens on a clear night sky, its aesthetic appreciation involves disinterested contemplation if the underlying form is to be realized and its true beauty discovered (Kant, 1952, p. 118).

Schopenhauer believed this to be the case too. For him, it is the sublime and the beautiful that liberate human beings from subjection to the suffering caused by their *willing* of the world to be—the endless desire for self-perpetuation: "Aesthetic pleasure in the beautiful consists, to a large extent, in the fact that, when we enter the state of pure contemplation, we are raised for the moment above all willing, above all desires and cares, we are, so to speak, rid of ourselves" (Schopenhauer, 1969, p. 390). It opens up the world of the mystical, from which he does not exclude the possibility that the thing-in-itself may be apprehended "through the paths of ethics, aesthetics and asceticism" (Mannion, 2003, p. 245).

However, Schopenhauer's thought that the experience of the beautiful may enable us to be "rid of ourselves" can easily be misconstrued. What Schopenhauer has in mind is that when contemplating a beautiful object, we may have our breaths taken away. We may, in this sense, be transported. But the self is not eliminated. On the contrary, the beautiful, as Donoghue avers, opens the self to deeper experience and connects a beautiful object with other related beautiful things. The self is *transformed* by the aspiration to know beauty from both an intellectual and moral perspective. The implication is that the person will be stirred to aspire to moral insight and just behavior. Beauty, on this account, is therefore both beyond and within our ordinary experience.

It was Wittgenstein who cryptically stated that "the sense of the world must lie outside the world. In the world everything is as it is, and everything happens as it does happen: *in* it no value exists—and if it did, it would have no value. If there is any value that does have value, it must lie outside the whole sphere of what happens and is the case" (Wittgenstein, 1961, para. 6.41). By this, Wittgenstein means that neither aesthetics nor ethics are values that can be pointed to or empirically identified per se. But he did not, of course, wish to imply that beauty was uninstantiatable without value or beyond experience. He appreciated art, but he was also clear that he could not describe what appreciation was: "It is not only difficult to describe what appreciation is, but impossible. To describe what it consists in we would have to describe the whole environment." Indeed, he goes further, "What belongs to a language-game is a whole culture" (Wittgenstein, 1966, pp. 7–8).

Mark A. McIntosh points to the experience of Dora in visiting the National Gallery as described by Iris Murdoch in her early novel *The Bell*: "Her heart was filled with love for the pictures, their authority, their marvelous generosity, their splendour . . . The pictures were something real outside herself, which spoke to her in kindly yet in sovereign tones, something superior and good whose presence destroyed the dreary trance-like solipsism of her earlier mood. When the world had seemed to be subjective it had seemed to be without interest or value. But now there was something else in it after all" (Murdoch, 1962, pp. 191). McIntosh comments, "The real world and the good are found in the same place, and Dora's practice of attention to beauty has made possible her liberation from her 'dreary trance-like solipsism'—long enough at least for the reality of the good to gain a purchase in her life again" (McIntosh, 2004, pp. 202–3). Dora loved the pictures, and for this she is grateful. It seems that being in the presence of a beautiful object, person, or story evokes the virtue of gratitude and the desire for the good.

The Power of Beauty

The power of beauty stems from the fact that when we come across something that is beautiful, it can, as I have said, take us by surprise—it attracts us and makes a difference to us. Scarry is aware of what seems to her to be the dynamic quality of beauty and its role as stimulus for the desire for truth. She claims that beauty and truth are allied but not identical: "It is not that a poem or a painting or a palm tree or a person is 'true,' but rather that it ignites the desire for truth . . . It creates, without itself fulfilling, the aspiration for enduring certitude. It comes to us, with no work of our own; then leaves us prepared to undergo a giant labor" (Scarry, 2011, pp. 52–53). It demands to be copied, to be brought into relationship with all other experiences of beauty, and to be made real in ordinary life. Yet its ultimate reembodiment in another particular is beyond anyone to achieve completely. Above all, attention to a beautiful object evokes the virtue of gratitude, which in turn stimulates the desire to share the experience.

Beauty is not something we can possess; it cannot be privatized. Indeed there is something obscene, even sacrilegious, when a work of art is hidden in a bank vault: such behavior violates the public world of shared experience and amounts to criminal trespass—even theft. Beauty has to be shared. In pointing to a painting, reading a poem aloud, or introducing a student to a new field of mathematics, I open myself to a new conversation in which I hold together the public and the private experience. I thus confirm the personal (not individual) nature of all experience that only comes to life when shared: "An understanding of beauty and an enthusiasm for it are one and the same thing" (von Ebner-Eschenbach, 1994, p. 24). Not wanting to share beauty is to refuse to be grateful for it and therefore to be denied the depth of experience that is an integral part of it.

The language we use to discuss our response to beauty is important, for with it, we share ourselves with others in the search for meaning. We recognize the difference between mere description and evaluation, which puts matters into not just one context but many. It is likely that the number of contexts in which we find ourselves will be increased by conversation with each person, since no two situations from which beauty is perceived will be the same. But above all, our attention will be drawn to the objective nature of the beautiful, and beauty's permanence though it will be impossible to define beauty or ultimately describe it. It will be important for us to come to terms with this and respond to its stimulus.

Permanence is a vital aspect of beauty, but the permanence is not unchanging. C. S. Lewis talked of recognizing a piece of literature as a "classic," by which he meant that it was possible to return to it again and again, to discuss it with others, and always to find something new. It is, in one sense, always contemporary. Von Ebner-Eschenbach said, "People who read only the classics are sure to remain up-to-date" (p. 31). Anthony Saville talks of a work having "stature," by which he meant that it stands the test of time.

Beauty and the Desire for Truth

Scarry's remarks that "beauty ignites the desire for truth" and that it is "a starting point for education" are analogous to the experience Roberts refers to when he says that emotions are "concern-based construals" (Roberts, 2013, pp. 9–48). Beauty arouses the desire to protect it, to share it, to replicate it, which is a concern-based perceptual construal of the experience of beauty. Beauty is an essential feature of human life: its loss would undermine the worthwhileness of life and threaten the search for meaning.

Fortunately, beauty appears to be not a matter of human construction but something that actively reveals itself as the object, whether it be the poem, the novel, the garden, or the pot that takes shape through the liberating, skilled hands of the potter. Henry Moore talked about his sculpting as an attempt to reveal what was locked within the material before him. Hence Moore's choice of the piece of stone he would use was a matter of very careful consideration: it was at least as important as the skill with which he addressed it. He had no sense of being able to impose his will upon unwilling material. Thus one of his major problems was knowing when he had finished; it was a matter of recognizing when the object he was looking for appeared in front of him. The "truth" is not made but recognized.

The novelist has an analogous experience when setting out to write. He or she will have a story in mind when sitting down in front of the computer, but as the writer progresses, he or she is likely to find that the characters have their own lives that prevent him or her from bending them in the way he or she had intended. On the contrary, the novelist discovers that the story, as it develops, is a partnership between the author and the characters with whom he or she is journeying; their experiences and relationships have a profound influence on the direction the novel takes. The search for "truth," in each case, takes over; it is never complete but has simply to be brought to an end. If and when the artist is satisfied with what has been produced, he or she will be grateful. And then the reader will take over in a new partnership; his or her reading will reveal new dimensions of the story and new aspects of the characters, and if the novel becomes a classic, such as Tolstoy's *Anna Karenina*, the process will continue forever. The dynamic character of beauty is permanently revelatory. As Italo Calvino said, "A classic is a book that has never finished what it has to say."

Roberts's point is that "emotions function as a kind of perception in which situations are presented to the subject in their evaluative aspect" (Roberts, 2013, p. 53). My suggestion is that the perception of beauty presents an evaluative aspect of the whole of life to the percipient for which he or she is grateful and that, as Scarry says, "ignites the desire for truth"—and justice. The evaluative aspects implicit within beauty are its life-giving and its distributive qualities.

The professional cannot control the client or determine on his or her own the outcome of the matter on which he or she is being consulted. The professional must work in partnership with the client, moreover, not to "force" an outcome, but to come to one in conversation, in the light of all the evidence and in full knowledge of the circumstances, to "reveal the truth within." The appreciation of beauty inherent in an object or in the natural world will open an analogous awareness that the truth is present and justice can be done.

Beauty, Justice, and Equality

But what do we mean by justice, and what is its connection with professional practice? Rawls, let us recall, bases social justice on an assumed veil of ignorance. His view is that since the result of life choices is a lottery, we would rationally choose equality. Rawls advances two principles that he believes will define a just society. "First," he says, "each person is to have an equal right to the most extensive basic liberty compatible with a similar liberty for others. Second, social and economic inequalities are to be arranged so that they are both (a) reasonably expected to be to everybody's advantage, and (b) attached to positions and offices open to all" (Rawls, 1972, p. 60).

Thus, he argues, it will only be just for A to be advantaged, if this person's advantage also benefits the least advantaged. For example, if it can be shown that disproportionate financial benefit or an extended period of education is required to recruit for an essential profession, which in turn serves society's most disadvantaged members, a member of that profession may justly be so rewarded. Indeed Rawls believes that such an understanding of justice "is continuous with the love of mankind"; when conceived of in this way, justice is fairness.

Scarry notes that traditionally, the quality of symmetry has been a characteristic feature of the aesthetic discussion of a beautiful object; what one looks for when comparing two beautiful objects is their relative symmetry. Personal judgment is involved because we are talking of symmetry, not identity. But symmetry too is what we look for when judging the quality of personal relationships, which means that we can see an analogous relationship between the appreciation of beauty and the recognition of just personal relationships. Kant makes the point that "[beauty] must please apart from all interest" (Kant, 1952, p. 118). This is tantamount to saying that to be in the presence of a beautiful object is to be aware of its beauty. This is not intuitive; it is rationally apprehended and therefore open to discussion. When I see something that is beautiful, my first thought is to share it, which I do by pointing to it and wanting to engage someone else in conversation about it. That is the impact that it makes upon me.

This provokes the reminder that the essential vocation of the professional is to share his or her knowledge and experience as he or she acts in the interests of society at large when attending intently to the particular concern of an individual client. The call to be just—and thus to act fairly—lies at the heart of all good professional practice, yet immersion in the concerns of an individual client may so absorb my attention as to threaten my capacity to take into account the general context in which it is set. The experience of Beauty prompts a reminder of what one knows one must take into account if one is to act justly. It can occur in many ways. Beauty may strike one through the shock of a challenging perspective presented by a composer whose music is new or be provoked by a reminder of the revelatory nature of a treasured classic—either may provoke a new awareness of the moral depth of the issues with which I am in fact dealing as a professional, for as I remarked at the beginning of the chapter, beauty, the good, and the just are mutually apparent and mutually informative. Moreover, as we have seen previously, no one can protect against its possibility because it takes people unawares and makes them aware of things that they might have forgotten or tried to put out of mind. As Scarry points out, "Through its beauty, the world continually recommits us to a rigorous standard of perceptual care: if we do not seek it out, it comes and finds us" (Scarry, 1999, p. 81).

Both beauty and justice are fair and attractive: we are lured by what is both fair and attractive; we want to give attention to it and share it.

To apprehend beauty is to want to look for other examples, even to copy it as nearly as we can. There is a distinctive quality to the experience connected with the fact that it is inherent in human nature to want to be just and to want to be treated justly. Scarry puts it like this: "There is a continuity between the thing pursued and the attributes of the pursuer" (p. 87). A person who pursues the good hopes to become good; a person who pursues truth hopes to become knowledgeable, and in due course wise. Yet what of the people who pursue beauty? They hardly expect to become beautiful themselves. What, in fact, they can become is more just. The symmetry one finds in the consideration of beauty is replicated in the circumstances of individual persons, which implies the importance of treating them justly and therefore equally and fairly.

Beauty is lifesaving, and above all, possesses an essential distributive quality that places upon the beholder the desire to share. At that point, the matter of fairness is presented. To be in the presence of beauty is to discern the fairness that is available to all; when attending to the concern of a particular client, one is reminded of the symmetry of the circumstances in which all clients stand in relation to the professional and the absolutely vital importance of treating them equally if one is to act justly. Aquinas's perception of justice assumes not only the equivalence of things exchanged but the equality of the persons who do the exchange.

In *Thinking in an Emergency*, Scarry further reminds us of what we sometimes seem to have forgotten: we have both the responsibility *and the ability* to protect one another, both within the boundaries of our own nations and across national boundaries (Scarry, 2011). The particular circumstances that Scarry has in mind are those that have come to the fore in the nuclear age. The dramatically limited time in which a decision to act must be taken in the event of a nuclear threat is such that power is in the possession of very few people: in the United States, the nuclear button is in the hands of the president. The pressure to make decisions quickly has been much more general since the development of the World Wide Web with its capacity for virtually instantaneous communication. The sender of an email tends to expect an answer to a query within minutes, thus reducing the time for careful consideration to almost zero.

This means that we professionals may lose sight of the fact that we have both the responsibility and the ability to protect one another by acting justly with regard to clients and our professions and in the interests of society at large. There is always time to get things right, to act justly. Not to recognize this is to behave without true regard for our human nature. In this context, beauty, with its timeless significance and revelatory power, can revivify our living humanity by reminding us of its generosity, compassion, and fairness—in both senses. We know beauty and have the capacity to act justly if we want to. For this reason, we can gratefully accept our creation in the image of God and be responsible in the ways in which we maintain and build our environment.

THE REVELATORY AUTHORITY OF BEAUTY

The wholeness of what is available to human experience is nowhere more revealing than in the way in which we discuss and take account of health. What is it to be a healthy person? Health and health promotion are key dimensions of a just society, for which balanced judgment and appreciation of pattern are integral. Moreover, if proper judgment is to be exercised, we will have to take account of more than the physical condition of an individual patient. The World Health Organization issued an important statement after the first International Conference on Health Promotion in Ottawa in 1986:

> Health promotion is the process of enabling people to increase control over, and to improve their health. To reach a state of complete physical, mental, and social well-being an individual or group must be able to identify and to realize aspirations, to satisfy needs, and to change or cope with the environment. Health is, therefore, seen as a resource for everyday life, not the objective of living. Health is a positive concept emphasizing social and personal resources, as well as physical capacities. Therefore health promotion is not just the responsibility of the health sector but goes beyond healthy lifestyles to well-being. (World Health Organization, 1986, p. 1)

The statement goes on to list eight fundamental conditions and resources for health promotion. These are peace, shelter, education, food, income, a stable ecosystem, sustainable resources, social justice, and equity. The cultural environment is embraced as a dimension of the environment that requires attention too. Appreciation of health is a language game that involves, as Wittgenstein said, a whole culture.

One can take issue with some of the language used in this statement: what, for example, does "complete" mean in conjunction with physical, mental, and social well-being? But it is not meaningless: one might best take it to imply that when considering health and health promotion, nothing is excluded, nothing irrelevant. This is where the revelatory authority of beauty is crucially relevant: mere functionality is inadequate.

There is more to good health than a body that is "fit"; it must also be "fit for purpose," which raises a great number of other questions. Beauty opens human being to that which demands attention, is beyond our grasp and yet paradoxically within reach in the sense that we want to copy it. Bernard Lonergan has this in mind when he discusses the aesthetic pattern of all experience:

> The aesthetic and artistic are symbolic. Free experience and free creation are prone to justify themselves by an ulterior purpose or significance. Art, then, becomes symbolic, but what is symbolized is obscure. It is an expression of the human subject outside the limits of adequate intellectual formulation or appraisal. It seeks to mean, to convey, to impart something that is to be reached, not through science or philosophy, but through a participation and, in some fashion, a reenactment of the artist's inspiration and intention. Pre-scientific and pre-philosophic, it may strain for truth and value without defining them. Post-biological, it may reflect the psychological depths yet, by that very fact it will go beyond them. (Lonergan, 1958, p. 185)

Beauty is increasingly appreciated as being of practical relevance in professional practice—for example, in health care. Paintings find a place in hospital corridors, and poetry pamphlets appear in doctors' surgeries. Kenneth Calman, former chief medical officer of England and Wales, recommended literature to his fellow medical practitioners because "stories assist in the development of emotional knowledge" (Calman, 2001, p. 227). The design of hospitals and general practitioners' practices, both externally and internally, have a major impact on the welfare of all who work in hospitals and their patients. Good design actually encourages speedier return to health and therefore reduces costs, but that is not the point. Beauty brings into the professional relationship the depth and breadth of the whole environment in which we live, work, and enjoy our lively humanity. It motivates staff at all levels and encourages the patient to promote his or her own health. This was well known in the past. St. Bartholomew's Hospital, for example, which was founded in 1123 by the Augustinian monk Rahere was built with a courtyard planted with trees and fountains, into which patients were wheeled in fine weather. Moreover, the recognition that art, especially painting, might be integral to good health is not new: William Hogarth had painted a large mural for St. Bartholomew's in 1735.

The appreciation of beauty in health care and medical education continues to grow. The charity Paintings in Hospitals was founded in the United Kingdom as long ago as 1959 by Sheridan Russell, who with help from the Nuffield Foundation, established an art collection that could be drawn upon by hospitals and Nursing Homes. The journal *Medical Humanities* was launched in 1980 and the Association of Medical Humanities in 2002; they are concerned with health care, research, and education. The Glasgow Conference of 2008, titled "Creative Space—Arts Humanities and Healthcare," covered topics including medical curricula, clinical practice; literature and medicine, architecture, and the healing environment. A former patient has given Yale University and University College London money to sponsor a prize for an original poem exploring our common experience as human beings.

I have chosen to focus on the medical profession, but engineers, lawyers, accountants, and so on have a growing interest in the arts as a means of extending and deepening their insight into the nature of professional practice. However, in looking through the official statements and evident enthusiasm of many doctors and managers to improve the environment, I have not found mention of the word "beauty." The critical perspective that is brought to bear is often exciting and certainly intelligent, but it will be important that the language of beauty is brought into the conversation, or we shall miss, as Lonergan implies, a fundamental dimension of the world, attention to which is a transforming characteristic of being human.

THE THEOLOGICAL FRAMEWORK

Beauty reminds us of the theological depth that lies within, behind, and beyond our experience of a beautiful object. It is not simple and steady but intriguingly attractive; it does not leave us alone but stimulates experiment and exploration. Philosophers, as we have noted, paid little attention to it until relatively recently. It cannot be said that theologians have been blind to it, but only comparatively recently has it has again become a focus of theological inquiry. St. Augustine, Aquinas, Luther, Kierkegaard, and Barth took beauty seriously, but it is von Balthasar who centered upon it in his *Theological Aesthetics*. He claims that beauty is the central feature of the Christian insight into the nature of God; it lies at the root of love and gratitude in human life. Indeed, so vital is beauty to the human realization of God's presence that Breandan Leahy can go so far as to say in a succinct essay that without it, good and truth would lose their authority: "If beauty were to be bracketed out, then the good and truth, lose their evidence and are no longer binding" (Leahy, 1994, p. 34).

Beauty is the face of the good and true that we can know in our human experience: it makes them attractive and welcoming. Solzhenitsyn argued this in his acceptance speech for the 1970 Nobel Prize for Literature:

> And so perhaps that old trinity of Truth and Good and Beauty is not just the formal outworn formula it used to seem to us during our heady, materialistic youth. If the crests of these three trees join together, as the investigators and explorers used to affirm, and if the too obvious, too straight branches of Truth and Good are crushed or amputated and cannot reach the light—yet perhaps the whimsical, unpredictable, unexpected branches of Beauty will make their way through and soar up *to that very place* and in this way perform the work of all three. (Solzhenitsyn, 1970)

Good professional practice requires that attention be paid to the concerns of the client in the context of care for the well-being of society at large. This is our vocation. It is a demanding responsibility, yet one that we know in our hearts we can fulfill. What we choose to do will, of course, always be experimental: we shall have to learn from experience if we are to make progress in the effecting of our vocation. The Christian claim is that this professional relationship is analogous to and rooted in that which God enjoys with his creation. We call God "Redeemer" precisely because we believe that in creating, God takes overall responsibility for the world: he has committed himself to the business of bringing to perfection what he has put his hand to. God does not hold himself back because his intention in creating is to manifest his love. The basic character of God's care for his creation holds together the particular and the general: his universal, loving presence is manifest in the particularity of the Person of Christ.

For the Christian, the fundamental reality that is beyond and within the world in which he or she exists is found in Christ, for it is he who instantiates and expresses the glory of God, which is God's presence. St. John calls him "the Word" and declares that through him, all things are spoken into being: there is nothing excluded from conversation with God. Hence to love Christ is to love God. But to love God, who is the Creator, is necessarily to love the world that he is making and to accept his invitation to share with him in the work of bringing it to perfection. And we can do so because, as human beings, we are made in the image of God: we are actually free to respond to the invitation of Christ to follow him. He loved God, and so can we; he loved the world of people and the natural world of which we are a dimension, and so can we.

What we love has a vital influence on what we want, and what we want is fundamentally revealed by what we are actually trying to get. If we love worthless things based on false values, we shall self-destruct, because what we will be trying to bring about takes no account of the reality of God's presence in Christ. In essence, we shall be living a lie, for our world *is* a world of God's making in which he is present in Christ. Hence St. Paul urges the Church in Philippi to set their hearts and minds on worthwhile things: "Finally, beloved, whatever is true, whatever is honourable, whatever is just, whatever is pure, whatever is lovely, whatever is gracious, if there is any excellence, if there is anything worthy of praise, think about these things" (Phil. 4:8). There is more to what Paul is pointing to than moral endeavor. The Philippian Church is to contemplate not only what is true and honorable but what is lovely. The Greek word is *prosphiles*, which implies beauty, attractiveness, even allure, and (in classical Greek at any rate) whatever evokes gratitude. We can see that beauty evokes a response: a desire to copy it, to share it, to be party to its equal distribution, to be just.

Von Balthasar focuses on the idea of form in his exposition of theological aesthetics. Assuming the intelligibility of the world, von Balthasar argues that the lively "model" that lies within and behind it is the form that is present in Christ. The beauty that is discerned in him reveals the beauty of God, whose presence enlivens the world and his people. The attraction of his person can convince us of the beauty inherent in the world and lure us to want to understand the world we share with him, to share it with others, and thus to contribute to establishing a just society in which all share. Breandan Leahy says, "In his emphasis on form throughout the theological aesthetics he maintains an approach that tries to marry not only the objective structures of beauty such as the three elements outlined in Thomas Aquinas, form, harmony and radiance, but also the subjective structures in perception so prominent since the Kantian turning point in the concept of transcendentiality" (Leahy, 1994, p. 30).

The splendor of the form in Christ is, as Leahy says, "the archetype of beauty. The splendor or radiance of the Christ-form has an attractive power because in Christ we see what God's glory is but also how God's glory is, in Irenaean terms, man fully alive" (p. 30). Christ's form informs our world and our humanity so that we are inspired to want to live in the image of God.

Beauty, which we enjoy, presents to us the reality of Being, which lies within and beyond the world in which we find it. It encourages us to love God, to love the world, and to realize that we can share with God in his life and in his work. We regularly remind ourselves of this fact when we celebrate the Real Presence of God in Christ in the Eucharist. The beauty of the Eucharist is in the event, the liturgy, and the authority with which all present are sent out to live in the image of God in the real world that God is creating with us.

Conclusion

Professional practice is an exceedingly complex matter if it is to be undertaken effectively, courteously, and justly. It involves both careful attention to the particulars of a client's circumstances and sensitivity to the well-being of society and of the creation in which the client's concern is set. In focusing on the circumstances of an individual person, one may forget or ignore the context in which it is set. One needs to be reminded of that general context and of the real opportunity that one has to behave well with regard to both the individual and society. Beauty can bring to mind the breadth and depth of the world in which it has life and therefore present to the professional the real context in which he or she must act, which includes the general as well as the particular. In fact, as Scarry has argued, beauty attracts our attention and motivates us to want to share our vision, to distribute it fairly, and to instantiate it as and when we find it possible to do so. Beauty is dynamic in its impact and reminds us of the good and true, which we can attempt to make real in the individual situation by sharing with the client. It is not usual, in our contemporary society, to talk of a professional relationship as expressing love, yet that is what it amounts to when it is inspired by a concern to be just and to act justly.

The language of beauty is crucial. Without the language, we shall be unaware of beauty, lack the facility to talk about it, and explore its meaning, let alone instantiate it in practice. Beauty will be confused with decoration, which is no more than a matter of taste. I have suggested, following von Balthasar, that beauty lies at the core of the world's life in the Being of God, the form of which is incarnate in the Person of Christ and is expressed in the world that we enjoy. What the professional does in acting professionally is express the fundamental reality of the relationship that gives life to the world.

But of course, we may from time to time fail. We may be unable to get alongside our client and empathize with him or her; we may be tempted to favor the interests of our profession, our bank account;

we may come to believe that we are attempting the impossible and give up. Our desire to be fair may be overwhelmed by all manner of influences. Can we recover the vision we have lost and reestablish the real presence of hope and love? I turn to this question in the next chapter.

Chapter 11

Picking up the Pieces

Introduction

No one will get everything right every time: it is not humanly possible. Ronald Dworkin remarks that the enormity of our human responsibilities is such that none of us is likely to fulfill them, even to our own satisfaction. Try as he or she might, the professional will make mistakes. Notwithstanding diligent attention to detail, he or she will from time to time let down the client, betray the profession, and/or fail the employer. And this is quite apart from the vocation to freely serve the well-being of society at large. Most professionals find themselves in these predicaments as a result of what they have or have not done. So what are they to do?

Knowing What to Do

Of course, one could always try to argue it out and hope to persuade the client that one was right, but it would be unwise to do so. Perhaps we could try to be indifferent to the consequences, simply shrug our shoulders, and say to ourselves, "These things happen!" There are such people, but not many, and in any case, it doesn't work.

In fact, upon realizing what he or she has done, the true professional will be mortified, knowing that he or she could and should have done better. Moreover, this is not simply because of the damage that may accrue to the client's interests but because of what we might have done to the reputation of our profession, our *amour propre*, and the well-being of society at large. We will feel ashamed and want to do something about it. That is the point: the professional will recognize that it is not simply that "things" have gone wrong; there is more to it. We know we are in error and that we are willing—and want—to take responsibility for it. Therefore, if we are serious, we will be trying to do something to put things right by reestablishing a good relationship with the client and our conscience.

Constant sniping in the media makes this difficult in the face of incontestable malpractice on the part of some professionals. Some professional organizations (for example, Financial Services, the police, and the National Health Service of the United Kingdom) have acknowledged the problem and taken steps in an attempt to restore public confidence. Yet public opinion surveys suggest mistrust is growing, though that is easily exaggerated. Any failure is a disaster for those who suffer the consequences, but the implication that most professionals are incompetent, self-serving, or indifferent to their vocation is simply untrue. Hence, when asked for our personal experience, we are inclined to agree that we trust our general practitioner and our child's teacher.

So what is the professional person to do? Many ways have been tried: I shall examine rules and regulation, apology, resorting to law, confession, and reconciliation all in the context of the theological framework with which, by now, we have become familiar.

Keep to the Rules

One option is to fall back upon compliance with external standards. To this end, businesses, professional and voluntary bodies, and even government departments publish codes of conduct. The codes conform to legal frameworks and frequently have statutory authority. Some are couched in terms that make it clear that more is demanded than mere technical efficiency and superficial compliance. They may, for example, implicitly assume the fundamental importance of honesty and courtesy.

Complete satisfaction of the demands of compliance is, however, virtually impossible. Not only may I fail to put in place every jot and tittle required by the system, but no rule-based system can cover all cases and remove the necessity for personal judgment. And we know it is self-defeating to demand the impossible of oneself; every football referee will affirm this. Those who are responsible for drafting Acts of Parliament know this only too well: not even the most subtle drafting can prevent an ingenious lawyer from identifying legally defensible exceptions to the legislation. Tax law is a conspicuous case in point.

Notwithstanding that we know no system can remove personal responsibility, it is still tempting for the professional to seek satisfaction by complying with external rules. But it does not work; it is *personally* unsatisfying. Therefore, while I may fulfill to the maximum extent possible the requirements of my profession as defined by "the system," I may still feel personally dissatisfied, and so may my client. Technical efficiency is a necessary condition of good practice but is rarely, if ever, sufficient. Satisfaction of the law may be a virtue, but it does not make a person virtuous.

If compliance is ultimately impossible and personally unsatisfying, another route to fulfilling my professional responsibilities would be to set my own personal standards of excellence and to try to fulfill them. But there is no end to this process, which would be personally debilitating. To be seduced by the illusion that I could, if I tried harder, fulfill all my responsibilities would likely give rise to scrupulosity, a psychological disorder arising from a pathological sense of guilt about supposed moral failings or religious malpractice, which will threaten my sense of self. Nurses are particularly prone to scrupulosity and the personal stress that can undermine their confidence.

However, while the questions raised may be testing, if I believe myself to have harmed another by not taking responsibility when, on reflection, I should and could have done so, I must find reasonable and commonsensical ways of coming to terms with my failings and at least learn to pick up the pieces so as to recover a positive working relationship with the person I have failed. Public and personal perspectives figure in my moral situation. A personal apology may offer a way forward, and I examine this approach later. But first, what am *I* responsible for?

Being Responsible

Professionals want to act responsibly: we want to show that we are virtuous persons. But what are my responsibilities? The fact is that I am at one and the same time responsible for ensuring compliance insofar as it is possible and also responsible for the moral quality of the relationship I have as a professional with my client. In so doing, I lay myself open to the depth of moral concern required for the personal well-being of the client and his or her interests—and not only the client's interests but mine too. We know that there is more to being a virtuous professional practitioner than accepting an obligation for responsible *professional* practice: we want not only to act responsibly but to be ethically responsible persons and to be recognized as such. But can I know what I am responsible for? In the last resort, our responsibilities are likely to be unending and ultimately indefinable, but at least we can begin to think them through.

I am, for example, responsible for what I do and for the consequences. But "what I do" is too vague. Certainly, I am responsible for my behavior, but the vagueness of the reference may tempt me to define it and thereby limit the range of that for which I am accountable. This can lead to a culture of compliance, which we know is ultimately unsatisfactory and unsatisfying. However, there is a dimension to codes of practice for which our moral perception can encourage us to share responsibility: we can set about understanding what underpins the regulations and contribute to improvements. The process is ongoing at the moment in the regulation of banking and financial services: personal dissatisfaction with the system gives us a sense of where we want to be, but we are unclear about how to get there.

More important, I am also responsible for who I am, my emotional temper, my attitudes, and my character. Emotions are an important aspect of our moral lives and clearly a subject of increasing interest to both philosophers and psychologists, since they are not without cognitive content. They will not be entirely under my control at all times, but they are influenced by relationships, particularly those with parents and teachers, and have a role in the formation of character and the self that is lifelong. My emotions will be shaped through unpredictable experience: this is inevitable because the future and the consequences of past choices are beyond my control.

Our emotions are, as Roberts says, perceptual construals, nonempirical but related to empirical data: they show us to ourselves in virtue of what we value as worth doing. Bernard Lonergan, in one of his last writings, states boldly that "feelings reveal values to us. They dispose us to commitment. But they do not bring commitment about. For commitment is a personal act, a free and responsible act, a very open-eyed act in which we would settle what we are to become. It is open-eyed in the sense that it is consciously a decision about future decisions, aware that the best of plans cannot control the future, even aware that one's present commitment however firm cannot suspend the freedom that will be exercised in its future execution" (Lonergan, 1985, p. 169f.). Hence my feelings influence my habits, my interests, and above all, therefore, who I am—my character. None of these is completely in my hands, but I can, through choosing some experiences rather than others, have some influence upon them. I can, for example, choose my friends and what I read, both of which are likely to be influential.

I will also benefit from advice. As a member of many communities, societies, voluntary organizations, and professional bodies with a shared concern for the public good, I will have friends and colleagues on whom I can call for honest advice. Friends may criticize my behavior, attitudes, or feelings, but if offered compassionately, I shall listen to what they say. I may also enter imaginatively into the experience of others and be caused to think by reading novels or poems. These are ways in which I can influence my emotional life, discipline my habits, and improve my character. Recognition of failure in any of these dimensions of my life may stir my conscience and prompt a desire to do better—more particularly, to be a better person—in order to be a better professional. And that is the point: the personal character of the professional is of central importance to his or her professional practice. Happily, there always remains the possibility of moral reform, personal renewal, and therefore the restoration of integrity in professional practice.

We cannot, of course, be responsible for the circumstances of our births: we may simply have inherited social disadvantage, lack of educational opportunity, and poor health. Yet in each case, we can work hard to *take responsibility* for them. It may be very demanding because of political and socioeconomic factors, not to mention the inhibitions with which some religious traditions handicap their followers. But it is possible at least to improve the circumstances in which one finds oneself by working with others to stimulate change for the better; we would be morally irresponsible if we chose not to.

Our Responsibilities: Dworkin

The fact is that responsibility is not only a key dimension of professional practice but, more generally, an aspect of personal life. Ronald Dworkin remarks, "Responsibility is an indispensable concept across our intellectual life" (Dworkin, 2011, p. 102f.). No aspect of life is excluded: our reasoning, intellectual life, acceptance of public duty, interpersonal relationships, or professional practice. This was absolutely clear to Dworkin. In his opinion, the US Constitution, the basic framework of American life, must be interpreted through consistent moral principles, including justice and fairness. Ronald Dworkin's point is that without a clear sense of public and personal moral responsibility, there can be no reasonable account of justice and human rights. As he says, without such an approach, we would not "take rights seriously" (Dworkin, 1977).

Moreover, he argues in his book on the theory and practice of equality that since each person's life has equal importance to every other person's life, each person "has a moral obligation always to act with as much concern for the fate of everyone else in the world as for their own fate or that of their family and friends." Two principles, he argues, are widely accepted in Western democracies: "The first of these principles holds that once a human life has begun, it is of great and objective importance that it be successful rather than wasted, and that this is of equal importance in the case of each human life. The second holds that the person whose life it is has primary and nondelegable responsibility for that success" (Dworkin, 2000, p. 240).

Each person is free, within reason, to choose the kind of life he or she lives. Moreover, what one does influences the way one will behave on future occasions, for one's actions confirm or challenge one's habits. What is more, to act responsibly clearly involves accepting that choices affect everyone: professional behavior impacts not only the client but the reputation of his or her profession and, more broadly, the integrity of public life. The fact that some bankers treated client money as if it were their own has led to the loss of respect for all bankers. Not only that, but it has undermined the trust that citizens have in the moral character of society per se. This is consistent with Jesus's teaching: "Treat others as you would wish them to treat you" (Lk. 6:31).

Dworkin usefully distinguishes between responsibility as a virtue and responsibility as a relation. Responsibility in the virtue sense implies that a person acted responsibly or irresponsibly in a particular circumstance or that he or she behaved in an uncharacteristic way when failing to behave responsibly. Responsibility in a relational sense implies that a person was or was not responsible for the financial failure of his or her company or a road accident. In the latter case, a conclusive answer to the question of responsibility is possible. Thus investigation of the car accident in which one was involved may establish the causes. The driver may have been driving carelessly or failed to maintain the vehicle. The investigations concern compliance. However, while legal responsibility would be determined by empirical inquiry, the investigation would impinge upon the driver as a person. Is he or she to be regarded as a responsible person?

Responsibility as a relation is important, but my concern is focused on responsibility as a virtue. A responsible person will take all reasonable steps to become response-able in order to act responsibly and be a responsible person (see Chapter 4). I am an irresponsible driver if I fail to undertake due maintenance of my vehicle according to the manufacturer's recommendations. The doctor is irresponsible if he or she prescribes drugs before checking the patient's medical record; the civil engineer is irresponsible if he or she neglects to check that the contractor is using the appropriate quality of steel and concrete in building a bridge. In all these cases, the "errors" of judgment are linked with failures to become response-able that imply deficiencies in the character of the agent; he or she is an irresponsible person. So how can those in error come to terms with failures that are not simply errors of fact but personal failures of their moral character? Interestingly, as I have mentioned, Dworkin remarks that "responsibility so understood is impossible to achieve fully." I agree with him. But we could apologize. Would that be sufficient?

Apology

An apology may seem to be the most natural way to begin: if it leads to genuine forgiveness and brings the matter to an end, so much the better. However, an apology is not always quite so simple: circumstances can undermine the possibility of reconciliation, even when an apology is offered and apparently accepted. For example, suppose I discover that that you deliberately defrauded me of ten thousand pounds; whereas you had apologized for an accounting error, I may, not unreasonably, reject your apology.

An apology acknowledges accountability on our part when we say, "It was my fault," but not necessarily blameworthiness, which would require something like, "I was wrong." Even this, of course, may not imply moral blameworthiness. Nevertheless, both would express an attempt to renew a threatened or broken relationship. "I apologize," however, is not like "I promise": it is not a performative in the sense understood by J. L. Austin; it is a relational term and needs to be accepted in order to be real. The language we commonly use is interesting: we talk about "offering" an apology, and rightly so, because notwithstanding the fact that my apology may be sincerely offered, it may be refused. An apology may be rejected for many reasons: through resentment, through disbelief in one's sincerity, or because more is expected—compensation, for example.

Apologies come in all shapes and sizes. I may accidentally tread on your toe as we bump into one another running to catch a train. "Sorry" may be an adequate expression of regret in such cases as we both move swiftly on about our business. It is a helpful thing to do, but it hardly amounts to an apology—more like a *façon de parler*; there is no moral dimension to such a common experience, only sensible courtesy. On the other hand, if I were outrageously pushy in my attempt to get on the train, that would be different. Such behavior is morally reprehensible: I should feel guilty and *at least* apologize. If I knocked somebody over in my rush, then my apology should involve assisting him or her. A shouted "Sorry" as I dash on will hardly be seen as a genuine apology.

Of course, I may believe that I have a valid excuse for my apparently inconsiderate behavior and offer an explanation: maybe I was dashing to the hospital where my son was critically ill after a car accident. Acceptance of the excuse will be conditioned by the perceived attitude with which it is given, not merely the spoken words. And of course, the willingness of the injured party to accept it when offered will depend on his or her judgment of the circumstances that gave rise to the offence. Should I have left earlier, given the weather conditions? Moreover, even if accepted at the time, new facts about the incident may become apparent to the offended person later that alter his or her perception of my character and therefore the seriousness with which he or she regards my apology. They may lead him or her to ignore my apology.

The same is true in the professional context. If I lose a major proportion of my investment as a result of poor advice from my financial consultant or find myself in the hospital with a heart attack because of the failure of my general practitioner to recognize my "indigestion" as a heart condition, I shall want an explanation that amounts to more than an excuse!

An apology may indeed be a good place to start; it is a natural way in which to try to reestablish a relationship. Apologies can be helpful when sincerely offered and genuinely accepted. But they are far from simple, as Nick Smith outlines. He suggests that what he calls a "categorical apology" consists of 11 elements (Smith, 2008, pp. 28–107). These include the corroboration of the facts, the acknowledgement of responsibility and acceptance of blame, the mutual recognition and acceptance of the moral principles underlying the case, and perhaps above all, the treatment of the victim as a moral interlocutor. The elements are stringent and draw attention to the essentially moral nature of the professional relationship.

Factual agreement about the circumstances is necessary before any further conversation can proceed. Having established the facts, we are in a position to identify the moral fault and attribute blame. Thus I may try to excuse myself and say as your financial advisor, "My IT system crashed, and I had no back-up." But more explanation would be necessary because if I were delaying the servicing of my IT system in an attempt to control my cash flow at the end of the month, I would have failed you and would be morally to blame. The facts are clear, I accept responsibility, and we should be able to agree on the moral principles involved. As a result, I should do my best to recompense you where possible and undertake to act more responsibly in the future. Above all, I should always treat you, my client, as a moral interlocutor and not as a problem to be resolved or a nuisance to be coped with.

In such serious cases, a sincere apology given with genuine regret for the outcome can nevertheless lead positively to forgiveness and reconciliation. When that happens, both parties are grateful to one another: The client is grateful that the professional has acknowledged his or her responsibility and expressed the intention to do all in his or her power to put things right and, above all, not to make the same mistake again. The professional is grateful to the client for his or her forgiveness, which includes an appreciation that the client will do what he or she can to reestablish a relationship so that they can continue to work together. Not in every case can the compensation be proportionate: I can repay cash you have lost, but I cannot undo your heart attack.

But even genuine apologies, as we know, are likely in many contexts to promise more than they can deliver, and what is more, they can be overdone. For one thing, there may be aspects of the situation that only emerge as time goes on, and when that happens, suspicion may once more arise for the person wronged. Was the apology genuine? Was the financial adviser honest? Was he or she simply looking for a way out in order to salve his or her conscience? Is he or she a virtuous person?

Moreover, there is a deeper dimension, as G. K. Chesteron opined, "A stiff apology is a second insult . . . the injured party does not want to be compensated because he has been wronged; he wants to be healed because he has been wronged." I shall return to the important matter of healing later. But we must first look at the complication for the understanding of apology that follows from the fact that it can be drawn into a legal framework.

Resort to Law: Settlement in Court

A resort to law can provide the possibility of resolution of conflict, especially when there is no agreement as to the facts and therefore no recognition of blameworthiness or acceptance of responsibility. But it seems to me that even when the process is effective in determining the legal situation and thereby upholding justice, the outcome is more a matter of compliance than an occasion of the essential restoration of trust and the reestablishment of good professional relationships. This is clear from an exploration of the way in which an apology may impact the legal context.

I may instinctively wish to apologize but find the lawyer advising me to be against it, since to offer an apology could be construed as an admission of guilt (Cohen, 2002). In certain US states (for example, California and Florida), some expressions of sympathy are excluded from admissibility as evidence; thus, after injury through poor medical treatment in a hospital, a doctor may say, "I am sorry you are hurt" with impunity but not "I'm sorry that I injured you." On the other hand, a lawyer, in certain circumstances, may advise the client in the course of the court hearing to offer an apology in an attempt to reduce the penalty in the event of a guilty verdict.

Marlynn Wei, in an interesting essay, suggests that the reasons that may inhibit a doctor from apologizing are inherent in the norms of the profession (Wei, 2006). They include a fear of litigation, the tradition of self-regulation, the mask of infallibility, a fear of the loss of trust, and an assumed asymmetry in the relationship between doctor and patient. She suggests that these norms are cultural and beyond the scope of the law. That may well be so, but they underline, once more, the importance of recognizing the moral quality of the doctor-patient relationship, a quality that is characteristic of every relationship between the professional and the client. Nick Smith mentioned that one of the elements of a categorical apology is that each party should treat the other as a moral interlocutor, and as I noted previously, Ronald Dworkin insists that each person who exists is equal to each other person and therefore entitled to be treated with justice and fairness.

There is another general human condition that relates to the urge to apologize, which merits further consideration. An apology and the desire for forgiveness may be stimulated by conscience and the consequent recognition of one's personal responsibility for the harm one has done. I shall develop this fundamental perspective later on, since it puts into a more significant context the offer of an apology—namely, confession—and rescues it from the constricted flavor of a legal process.

The Theological Framework

A creative perspective on responsible professional practice is opened up, I believe, when it is placed within the lively organic structure of the Christian theological framework. It reveals the wholeness of the reality that lies behind and beneath our experience and illumines the personal moral character of the professional relationship. I do not, of course, wish to imply that there can be no moral professional practice apart from an awareness of a theological underpinning. Indeed philosophy is helpfully tackling such concepts as conscience, shame, and forgiveness (Williams, 1993, pp. 75–102, 219–23). Psychology, once the domain of the dark side of life, has now opened a positive focus on ways in which we can make ourselves happier and better willing and able to accept responsibility. But while we can therefore now talk positively of self-creation (Glover, 1983), the theological framework puts self-creation in an ontological context that provides a more complete picture. It offers an invigorating interpretative layer that gives rise to rich insights. It transforms shame into positive energy. It shows that generous relationships are real.

The world is, according to our theological framework, actually made so that we can know ourselves, serve one another, and work with God to reveal his, the world's, and our true nature. It is the nature of God to give himself to the establishment of an effective relationship with his creation and to do so without fear or anxiety: his whole attention is focused on the world's and humankind's well-being. The fellow-feeling of God with his creation, his empathy with humankind, is declared in the Person of Jesus Christ. Theological exploration of the meaning of this for human being suggests that what God is for us can be expressed—and therefore lived out—in human experience. God is, in Christ, inviting human beings to share in his life of self-giving love. The claim that human beings are made in the image of God implies that they too can establish relationships based on mutual understanding, affection, and self-giving. Through recognizing not only the desirability of this pattern of life but also its reasonableness and feasibility, the professional will contribute to the world's well-being and thus serve the personal interest of the client and the common good. Despite the well-directed remark of Dworkin, it is possible for us to be responsible people, even if we must also accept that we cannot absolutely fulfill all our responsibilities every time.

Furthermore, the theological framework sets the ideas of confession, forgiveness, and absolution in the world of the Divine Presence, a context that is transforming, nourishing, and sustaining. Our conscience witnesses to the truth, the possibility of justice, and the courtesy of reconciliation.

Conscience

So what about conscience? What role does that have to play? Interestingly, most of the concern with conscience seems to focus on bad conscience, whereas it is also important to remember that there is such a thing as a good conscience. However, it is true that even my good conscience can accuse me of bad practice, make me aware of the harm I have done, and above all, accuse me of my failure to live up to the best that I know. In effect, I may not have failed to be compliant, but I may realize that I have been no more than compliant and have failed to be a person in relationship with my client—failed indeed to recognize him or her as an equal moral interlocutor. Above all, there is raised in my mind my own status as a moral interlocutor: in what sense am I a "self," a responsible virtuous person? What is involved here?

My conscience may be stirred as the import of what I have done dawns on me. In this case, my sense of guilt may inhibit my ability to apologize; it may even make clear to me that in any case, an apology is hardly adequate. I will want to be forgiven as a practical matter and therefore apologize with a view to regaining public recognition of my desire to accept my responsibilities. But while this is all to the good, it may not go far enough; it may simply be an expression of my intention to comply with public expectation regarding good manners. What is more, the acceptance by the wronged person of my apology and my gratitude for his or her forgiveness may still leave me hurt or ashamed or both. My confidence to do better in the future needs to be supported.

What Aquinas has to say is helpful here: he draws an illuminating distinction between synteresis and conscience, which he regards as two aspects of the practical reason (McDermott, 1989, pp. 123–24). Synteresis is a natural, God-given habit of the human mind whereby we may know that the basic principles of moral behavior are inexpungible, even as the result of human sin: they are not the result of inquiry but habits of thought that underpin an implicit confidence that we know that we are free to practice the good and eschew the bad. The saying "Behave to others as you would wish them to behave toward you" is thus a natural insight of the practical reason.

Our conscience applies our knowledge by means of reason to these innate first principles, which cannot themselves be in error, in order to guide what we choose to do in specific circumstances. When the conscience argues clearly in the light of these first principles of moral behavior, the resulting decision will be good and further confirm the desired habit of acting well. But conscience may reason wrongly and in error lead us to choose evil rather than good. We may fail to notice a full range of the choices open to us, neglect relevant evidence, or simply be seduced by jealousy or greed to behave sinfully.

However, Aquinas is of the opinion that the spark of reason cannot be extinguished so long as the light of the mind remains, which not even sin can remove. The underlying dimension of this perspective, taken up also by Rahner, is that there is no such thing as an ungraced nature. Wherever we find ourselves, in whatever circumstance, with whatever choices we are faced, the God-given possibility of choosing to behave well always remains with us. From one point of view, we may say that shame can perform the positive function of bringing us to ourselves. This encouraging thought offers an illuminating context in which to think through how best to behave when we come to believe that we have acted badly. It makes sense of the possibility that an apology can be the expression of a real sense of the good, its possibility the consequence of our failure to reason well enough to identify what we should have done—and could have done.

The fact is, therefore, that although we can never be completely satisfied, we can fulfill our responsibilities; we are morally responsible for our actions as persons. This is important for all our relationships and a normal assumption of our experience of others. Certainly, we hold other people responsible for their actions, which we place in a context that assumes their intentions toward us and beliefs about us. Strawson underlines the importance of this dimension when he says, "The central commonplace that I want to insist on is the very great importance that we attach to the attitudes and intentions towards us of other human beings, and the great extent to which our personal feelings and reactions depend upon, or involve, our beliefs about these attitudes and intentions" (Strawson, 2008, p. 6). Over and above the actual actions themselves, the intention or attitude that we associate with them is of paramount importance in our judgment of other people and their actions. Thus, depending on the intention or attitude that we attribute to the person in regard to his or her behavior, we will be (according to Strawson) resentful, grateful, or forgiving.

Interestingly, there is a parallel here with Jesus's remarks in the Sermon on the Mount in which he asks for a radical reordering of moral priorities. It's not a matter, he says, of simply refraining from adultery or murder; it is vital to understand that even considering doing so and planning it is itself evidence of a person's lack of virtue (Matt. 5:26–27). God sees a person's attitude and intention as vital. There is a connection here with virtue ethics.

This insight of Strawson is of particular significance in connection with the role of conscience in professional practice. As a client, I hold the professional lawyer responsible for the legal advice that he or she gives me in drawing up my will. But the lawyer's advice is given within a professional relationship that will only flourish if I believe that his or her advice is given with goodwill and a proper sympathy for my desire for the well-being of those to whom I intend to bequeath my property. The situation would be quite different if I thought that the lawyer's motivation was confined to the business of earning fees; how he or she comes across to me as a person is crucial. In reciprocal fashion, as a professional, I shall expect the client to be honest with me and not to be trying to use me (I employ the expression advisedly) in my professional capacity to implement an unscrupulous plan that will secure his or her unfair advantage. In both cases, I believe, above all, we want to be assured that we are dealing with persons of good character.

My conscience will threaten to bring me to my senses and awaken a realization not only that I can both behave well and behave badly but that I want to behave well and am dissatisfied if I do not try to do so. St. Paul is all too aware of this when he says, "I can will what is right, but cannot do it. I do not do the good that I want, but the evil I do not want is what I do" (Rom. 7:18b–19). He attributed this condition to sin: "Now if I do what I do not want, it is no longer I that do it, but sin that dwells within me" (Rom. 7:20). Sin is a concept that refers to my personal condition, my failure to recognize God's presence, not my professional malpractice, though false reasoning and a consequent habit of moral turpitude may lead me to wrong my client. I shall explore the concept further next. In order to satisfy my essential desire to be myself, a fully mature and responsible person, in the last resort, I need to be forgiven.

Forgiveness and Reconciliation

As humans, we desire wholeness: we do not enjoy the awareness of being a divided person, incomplete in the way we feel, think, and behave. Yet that seems to be our experience of ourselves. "Sin" is the term in which the Christian theological framework expresses our sense of incompleteness and inadequacy, our lack of awareness of God's presence. When the framework within which we conduct our lives excludes God, we are said to be "in sin." We are led to presume that we know more than we in fact know; that we have whole, even complete, picture, rather than partial pictures, of the world and the opportunities open to us; and that we know what to do when we don't: "It is the desire for 'wholeness' that draws us on in our best moments—wholeness as it touches us when life declares beauty; and then when beauty flashes the blinding coordination of each to its own" (Hollingworth, 2013, p. 8).

I have earlier referred to the experience of beauty as a wholeness that is healing because it reveals the truth and is rooted in justice. Chappell, following Nietzsche, makes an analogous point: "Seeing 'existence and the world' as beautiful is surely one way of seeing them as meaningful and worthwhile." Chappell goes on to talk of glory as another morally revealing term (Chappell, 2014, pp. 158–84). He says, "We might put it, with a little formality, like this. Glory is—typically—what happens when a spectacularly excellent performance within a worthwhile form of activity meets the admiration that it merits" (p. 160). Glory is something that we are free to desire and actually to work for, which involves us in a dependence on others; in a concern with facts (i.e., actual achievements) that are, strictly speaking, beyond our control; and in the approbation of others. It, along with the beautiful, gives meaning to life.

Moreover, in St. John's Gospel, "Glory" is a term used to indicate "the presence of God." The source of this desire for beauty, for glory, for wholeness is God, whose redemptive creativity inspires our curiosity and the search for meaning. God will not abandon us and leave us to our own devices; not even sin will utterly extinguish our sense of right and the good or our desire to be whole.

The pursuit of truth and the search for meaning has been a dimension of human aspiration throughout history. The world's meaning is implicit in this desire, for it owes its origin to God. Interestingly, St. Augustine takes up this theme from Seneca with whose work he was familiar, so the idea is not simply Christian but one grounded in human experience per se. Hollingworth in his intellectual account of Augustine's life refers to Seneca as the "Humanist Saint" and quotes him as follows:

> The maker is God; matter is the material; the form is the general character and lay-out of the universe as we see it; the model naturally enough is the pattern which God adopted for the creation of this stupendous work in all its beauty; the end is what God had in view when he created it, and that—in case you are asking what is the end God had in view—is goodness. That at any rate is what Plato says: "What was the cause of God's creating the universe? He is good, and whoever is good

can never be grudging with anything good; so he has made it as good a world as it was in his power to make it." (Hollingworth, 2013, p. 35)

Seneca's conversation was taken into the Christian theological framework, where it is treated as the God-given dimension of human experience that gives rise to the worthwhileness of confession and the hope of forgiveness. I use the term "worthwhileness" here because, as we have seen previously, Aquinas confirms that reason cannot be eliminated while the mind remains active, and the mind cannot be wholly extinguished by sin. My conscience actively reminds me of the real possibility of the wholeness that I desire. So my expression of apology and my desire to restore relationships may in turn stimulate a promising awareness of my personal failure and moral unworthiness. I use the term "promising" here because it can put me in mind of the dimension of human experience that must also be coped with if I am to become myself and again take up my responsibilities. The fact that I can choose to do so is God's gracious gift.

Of course, for the most part, we know that we are free to become more response-able and therefore potentially more responsible; in any case, we cannot eradicate our sense of right and wrong, even if the sense only emerges into consciousness from time to time. On reflection, our conscience will accuse us of wrongdoing and insistently require us to do something about it. But what can we do about it? How should we attempt to put things right when conscience tells us that we have wronged someone or behaved irresponsibly? We want to be reconciled, but forgiveness and reconciliation are independent experiences (Govier, 2002, pp. 141–57). Very particularly, as Chesterton says, those whose consciences prick them are in need of forgiveness; they want to be healed.

And when things go wrong, I shall want not just to be forgiven but to be forgiven by the person I have wronged. Such forgiveness can bring healing to the wronged person because, as Roberts understands it, implicit in forgiveness is the virtue of forgivingness (Roberts, 1995, pp. 289–306). A person who evinces forgivingness is able to overcome resentment, anger, and any desire for revenge: he or she is therefore free to seek good relationships with the offender, whatever the circumstances. The power of forgivingness, however, not only heals the forgiver, it liberates the wrongdoer thereby healing him or her too. This is important for if we take Strawson's insight seriously: it is the perception of the wronged person's resentment associated with the wrong done that has to be removed in order for me to feel forgiven. This is tantamount to the qualities of affectionate concern that are attributed to God: he heals and makes whole the person who is forgiven. God's forgiveness is personally renewing, not exclusively focused on objectively removing the fault.

The moral framework implicit within the Church's celebration of the lively relationship of God and the world provides the context for understanding good personal, institutional, and professional relationships. It is at one and the same time both practically reasonable and theoretically intelligible. It takes into account the wholeness of the person, body, mind and spirit; the nature of creation; and the God-given liveliness of human curiosity to explore it and come to terms both with it and with one's own self.

Acceptance of personal responsibility for ourselves and our actions is implicit in the doctrine of sin. The acknowledgement of sin, far from being a matter of despair, is the ground of hope and the healing root that stimulates profound gratitude. The realization that God has not removed himself from us despite our sin is a sign that we are already forgiven, even though we do not recognize it. It is this that gives us the confidence to tell ourselves the truth about ourselves in full knowledge of God's presence in order to enter into the already-existing relationship of God's acceptance for who we are and who we can become. The Christian Church provides a formal context in which, by confession and the receiving of absolution, we can learn what it feels like to be ourselves and accept the gift of God; above all, we know what it means to be a forgiven person and to recover the strength to forgive. The sacrament of penance informs the establishment and reestablishment of all broken relationships; the revelatory power of beauty is the healer.

The theological framework I have been exploring provides a dynamic and nourishing layer of interpretation through which to come to terms with what exactly is involved in picking up the pieces. The opportunity for a fresh start is grounded in the view of Aquinas that the desire for God cannot be ultimately extinguished in human life, which implies that it is not ultimately possible to be a human being and not want to inquire. Essentially, it is an ineradicable aspect of our humanity to want to put things right. It is worth recalling Rahner's point: "Our actual nature is *never* pure nature. It is a nature installed in a supernatural order, which man can never leave, even as sinner and unbeliever" (Rahner, 1966, p. 183). It is a point we can generalize: John Wesley, I remind you, that most Catholic of Methodists, affirms a similar sentiment when, in a sermon on Philippians 2:12–13, he writes, "No man sins because he has not grace, but because he does not use the grace which he has." There is always the opportunity, however dimly aware of it one may be, to respond to the world as creation, to "find oneself" and recover that lively sense of gratitude on which one's human nature depends. The sacrament of penance offers the healing experience of forgiveness, which liberates people to be themselves and live for others; it enlivens the sense of what it means to live freely as grateful people. We can aim reasonably to practice the good, but we are not defined by the purpose of simply trying to avoid the evil.

The peace of God's presence is dynamic: it is the beauty of his healing power incarnate in Christ. The positive infection of the gratitude we feel is caught by others through our dealings with them. It was G. K. Chesterton who wrote, "I would maintain that thanks are the highest form of thought, and that gratitude is happiness doubled by wonder."

Persons and Professional Identity

Of course one may say that this is all beside the point: what we are concerned with is *professional* practice. Moreover, if Marlynn Wei is correct when she claims that the reasons for the failure of the professional to apologize and therefore seek forgiveness from the wronged client are inherent in the norms of the profession, there are broader issues to consider beyond the personal recognition of individual wrongdoing: there is the culpability of the profession. Certainly we can see much of this in the attitudes of the public as expressed in opinion polls. We have apparently lost confidence in the police, politicians, lawyers, bankers, journalists, the military, teachers, and even the clergy. One can see why.

But that surely is the point: we have undermined the possibility of genuine professional relationships by disassociating them from *personal* morality. Such a separation is a cancer in the body politic: human well-being is not satisfied by compliance. Our consciences remind us, and we can be truly grateful. The recovery of trust in the professions depends on the rebuilding of confidence in the persons who become the professionals. Personal morality and public behavior are indissolubly bound together. I am a person before I am a member of a profession: I am a person who practices a profession. I can resign my professional role, but I can never resign my personhood.

Chappell is clear about the status of personhood. It is not the result of identifying criteria that we then apply to the creatures in front of us to see whether they are persons. The term applies only to human beings, not to seaweed or crocodiles. We treat a creature as a person in advance of determining sentience, rationality, self-awareness, and the rest of the personal properties. Thus, "a parent's attitude towards her child is always, basically, what Wittgenstein famously calls 'an attitude towards the soul.' (In other words, it is intrinsically second-personal.)" (Chappell, 2014, pp. 137–38). Indeed I think of myself first as a person responsible for myself and for all that I do before I think of myself as a teacher or a manager. Since I am a person, nothing can remove from me my responsibility for who I am, my character, or therefore what I choose to do, hence my need to know that I live in a world where I am forgiven, for which I can be truly grateful.

Conclusion

Humans, as Christians understand it, are made "in the image of God." In my earlier exploration of this idea, I suggested that what it implied was an ability shared with God to take responsibility. God accepts responsibility for his creation, which he is bringing into being by identifying himself with it through his gracious presence in Christ. The creation can assume everything that is of the Divine without compromise of either the nature of God or the nature of creation. For this reason, Christ is called both human and divine. Since he is made "in God's image," humans are able to accept responsibility for themselves and for their behavior and to give themselves wholly to the well-being of other persons without compromising their own senses of self. Indeed, by so doing, they grow in self-knowledge and in both ability and willingness to serve others. The trouble is that as humans, we do not believe it and are inclined to evade or sidestep our responsibilities, hence the essential need to confess and be absolved. The professional cannot, does not, cease to be a person when acting as a professional; indeed, doing what the professional does reveals the person he or she is, his or her character, and as Wittgenstein says, his or her soul.

Above all, therefore, we must conclude that in order to be good professionals, attention must first be given to us, our education to become virtuous persons of good character who know how to become response-able and responsible people. In my concluding chapter, I draw my argument together and look to the way forward.

Chapter 12

Conclusion
A Way Forward

Introduction

My argument is that the virtue of gratitude is liberating for individuals both as moral agents and as members of professions. The empirical evidence from positive psychologists supports the view that the virtue of gratitude increases subjective well-being and prosocial behavior (McCullough et al., 2001, pp. 249–66). A grateful person has the confidence to be curious about the world, to become more responseable, and potentially, therefore, to become more responsible. He or she takes up the conversation of the generations in order to endow the future with a legacy characterized by gratitude and the desire to understand, to act justly, and to be compassionate. To offer and accept the gift of service transforms the giver, the gift, and the recipient. It is of the essence of the pattern of human maturation that we learn to give appropriate attention to the many aspects of our experience, to bring them together, to share what we know, and to enjoy the inherent beauty of our world. An appreciation of the virtue of gratitude can reform a vocation and transform the personal relationships that underpin the experience of professional practice for both the professional and the client.

I have set the vision in a Christian theological framework not because I think that Christianity is the only possible framework that can be helpful; rather, my claim is that the theological framework presented in Christianity is a profoundly life-giving simile that stimulates the moral imagination and encourages a vision of the total context of professional practice. Its generality and inclusiveness, rooted as it is in God's redemptive creativity, makes it worth exploring: it can be revelatory. Our sense of gratitude is the embodiment in our lives of the gracious presence of God that leads us into the Real Presence of God himself.

I am reminded of Wittgenstein's remark, "A good simile refreshes the intellect" (Wittgenstein, 1980, p. le). But the intellect is informed not merely by reason but by feeling and emotion. A wholehearted expression of gratitude involves the whole of the self: I am a genuinely grateful person with all that that implies.

In this concluding chapter, I shall explore what I believe to be four of the essential features of the professional life. First, as a virtuous professional, I require awareness that I am a self; the professional is a person. Who I am, who I can become, and what my character is lies at the heart of my professional practice; I remain at all times and in every situation a person responsible for myself and for my professional practice.

Second, I require a sound liberal education in order to grow in response-ability. Only thus will I be able to act responsibly with gratitude for my inheritance and with the intention to leave a fruitful legacy for future generations. The art of open conversation is an integral ingredient, without which, my experience with be narrow and introverted.

Third, personal awareness and a sound general education are lifelong conditions for virtuous professional practice and must be attended to continuously. Professional competence is essential, but it is grounded in personal experience of the world: only as I keep that in mind will I remain free to understand and give attention to my professional responsibilities.

Fourth, I am aware of the happy prospect that as a person grateful for God's presence, I can accept that a professional life is a vocation to bear witness to the fact that the world is good.

In summary, we are concerned to be ourselves, to appreciate the totality of the context in which we operate, and to gain the liberal education and the professional skills necessary to act responsibly and serve the common good. Each of these features is involved with all the others. Moreover, none is ever completed. All involve a lifetime commitment.

I shall conclude by underlining the practical relevance of theological exploration and its encouraging potential for one's personal life and professional practice. Theological language is performative: to speak it is a reminder that our world is characterized by the presence of God. In particular, it points to the possibility of love, a relational term frequently neglected in professional relationships. Iris Murdoch notes the failure of philosophers to talk of love: "Contemporary philosophers frequently connect consciousness with virtue, and although they constantly talk of freedom they rarely talk of love" (Murdoch, 1970, p. 2). Yet she later writes, "We need a moral philosophy in which the concept of love, so rarely mentioned now by philosophers, can once again be made central" (Murdoch, 1970, p. 46). Within the theological framework I have outlined, our practice is informed by love because we are addressed as persons made in God's image by the God of love. The concepts of conversion and Resurrection declare the world to be loving and lovable.

The Self and the Liberation of Language

The professional is a self and remains such even when acting professionally. Language is a crucial ingredient of human inquiry but can, as Wittgenstein said, easily deceive us. Rowan Williams points to the deceptive use of one theological term: "One of the least helpful things in the history of Christianity is the way in which the word 'Catholic' has been turned into another tribal badge. The most important definitions of the word in the early Church stress that calling the Church 'Catholic' is a matter of grasping that it teaches the whole truth in a way that involves the whole person and is addressed to the whole of humanity" (Williams, 2013, p. vii).

We are made in the image of God and find ourselves when we reflect on our place in a world informed by the gracious presence of a loving God. Our world experience is one that can be truly called "Catholic": it offers "the whole truth in a way that involves the whole person and is addressed to the whole of humanity" (Williams, 2013, p. vii). When we lose sight of this, we can fall back on self-reliance and will have to work hard to recover the vision as we strive to be virtuous.

But we can be "brought to our senses." The sharpness of language in shaping an image can cause one to gasp and revive one's interest in a story that through familiarity has been emptied of meaning. Elijah, threatened with death by Jezebel, fled into the desert to find himself; he prayed that Yahweh would save him. He was unimpressed by fierce wind, earthquake, or fire, the conventional indicators of a theophany. But he was transfixed by what the Authorized (King James) Version calls "a still, small voice." The New Revised Standard Version is better: "a sound of sheer silence." Best of all, however, I think is the literal translation—"the sound of crushed silence"—which infuses the silence with vivid power: the sound of crushed silence (1

Kings, 19:11–12). (This translation was suggested to me by the Old Testament scholar Christopher North.) One not only apprehends intellectually what is going on but feels the shock: it expresses a revelatory, personally absorbing experience that at the same time affirmed Elijah to be in the presence of God. He recognized himself as he became aware of God.

C. S. Lewis wrote an account of his conversion from atheism to theism and theism to Christianity. He felt that he wanted something, but what he was looking for, he could not precisely say: he had no words for it. Then all of a sudden, he was surprised by joy. What is more, as soon as he had found it (or was found by it?), he was comfortable with who he was, was opened in a new way to the lives of others, and was gratefully alive to the delights of the world—natural, human, and divine. Lewis's experience of joy was, he felt, mutual: his joy for being found by God was reciprocated by God's joy for his return. The parable of the father and his two sons (usually known as the Prodigal Son), makes an analogous point: both father and the elder son share mutual joy as a result of their renewed relationship. The resentment of the compliant younger brother is intelligible: he has no joy, no sense of his forgiven self, and therefore is unaware of the presence of the living, affectionate God.

Gratitude, like beauty, can surprise us: it is not something we express after serious deliberation—"Yes, I see. Now I come to think of it, I am grateful." An expression of gratitude is more usually a natural, instinctive, spontaneous response to something that often takes us by surprise. Most particularly, when in the face of all our experiences—good and bad—we are "surprised" by the virtue of gratitude, we are transported by the vision of transforming love, beauty, and goodness that we glimpse in the world of God's creation. The therapist and his or her client (and I would say every professional) may experience a reciprocal virtue of gratitude as each learns wisdom from the other in their relationship. I am who I am and not another person, but I owe who I am to my relationships with others.

The Education of Character

Concern for my self is above all concern for my character, but when we consider what is meant by "character education," we are nowadays lost for words. And the words we were once accustomed to use are lost to us because of constant misuse. The quality of personal life takes much of its meaning from the experience of being loved and learning to love. But the use of the word "love" has become confusing: it is not easy to anticipate what one might be thought to be saying when one uses it. I was at one time responsible for a program of teacher education. The admission process involved an interview in which the assessment of the personal suitability of the applicant for the profession was a high priority. We wanted to get a feel for the person and his or her character. Why did this person wish to become a teacher? How would he or she handle a relationship with students?

I was therefore taken aback when a visiting member of the inspectorate remarked that many of the students whom he had asked why they wanted to teach had replied, "Because I love young people and want to inspire them to learn." I was told, orally, that loving children was not relevant when selecting students for professional training; what mattered was their subject knowledge and their ability to communicate it. This is true as far as it goes, but without access to the language of love and what it means, it says little about the process of education.

Knowledge of the discipline's subject matter is essential if one is to become a good teacher. Yet without a love of the subject, one is likely to fail to keep the knowledge current and alive; we have all experienced the teacher whose passion for the subject has died the death of a thousand repetitions! Moreover, a love of the discipline is essential if one is to acquire the skill to inspire students with a passion for the subject. One will hardly succeed in doing that if one does not also love the student whom one wants to inspire.

I believe the same is true in the life of every professional. Police officers who do not "love" their work will gradually lose a sense of what it means to be responsible police officers. Moreover, if they are to enhance their respect for justice, they must also find room in their hearts for the offender with some sense of "there but for the grace of God, go I." The doctor, the lawyer, the auditor must similarly be inspired with a love of their disciplines and love for the patient or client. This means that at some point during professional education, attention must be paid to the person—his or her self-knowledge, character, and appreciation of the meaning of the word "love." "Self-knowledge is something which shows overtly," Iris Murdoch says (Murdoch, 1970, p. 16). Self-knowledge is not contained within an inner life separate from one's public behavior. It informs our attitude toward life, our disposition, and therefore how we conduct ourselves in public society. It is the crucial influence on the capacity to love oneself, a term that is frequently misunderstood to imply selfishness.

Part of the problem arises from the fact that we have lost the ability to distinguish between the meanings of self-love explored by Aristotle

(Aristotle, 1984b, *N.E.*, 1169b). He asks "whether a man should love himself most or someone else" and recognizes that we, for the most part, regard the term "self-lover" as an "epithet of disgrace." It is assumed to point to someone as being selfish. Aristotle thinks there must be more to it than this, so he gives the matter further thought. He suggests that self-love should be well regarded when it refers to someone who is focused on things that are honorable and has, through the proper exercise of reason, the self-control to perform those things. The person, however, who loves himself or herself and grasps at wealth, public honors, and bodily pleasures, and focuses his or her life on fulfilling these natural desires, is indeed self-loving and selfish. In the former case, self-love includes the love of everything that is regarded as excellent by all and makes for the common good; in the latter case, one sets oneself apart from the world and takes of it what one can for oneself. In the sense that I used the concept of "person" earlier, the former is a person-in-relation whose self-love can for everyone's sake be copied by each person, thus contributing to the well-being of all; the latter is an isolated individual who believes that he or she will survive by depriving others of what each requires to live the good life.

The good person, argues Aristotle, can by means of his or her reason exercise self-control and in so doing, reveal his or her true self as self-loving in the best sense; the good person always does what his or her reason leads him or her to do, which is what is of good report. According to Aristotle, "Those, then, who busy themselves in an exceptional degree with noble actions all men approve and praise; and if all were to strive towards what is noble and strain every nerve to do the noblest deeds, everything would be as it should be for the common good, and everyone would secure for himself the goods that are greatest, since excellence is the greatest of goods" (Aristotle, 1984b, *N.E.*, 1169b).

Furthermore, it is therefore a mark of genuine friendship when someone reveals to another person destructive aspects of his or her character of which the other person had been hitherto ignorant. In this, as in other matters, it is the good person who is able to do many things for his or her friends, including die for them. All this may happen out of sheer love for a friend or some other noble end, such as the service of one's country or of human well-being in general. The point is that in so doing, this person is exercising genuine self-interest, for he or she is focused on what is good and true: he or she is serving the common good. Jesus, indeed, asks that we should love our neighbors as ourselves (Matt. 19:19). In the light of Aristotle's perspective, this is a profoundly insightful invitation. Only in loving our neighbors can we love ourselves; only in loving ourselves can we love our neighbors. And remember, our neighbors are all other persons.

The argument is significant for professional practice and illustrates clearly the centrality of self-knowledge and moral character. Both the good and the bad professional may choose to behave in a way that we should rightly call self-serving. The bad professional will act as a functionary, asserting rights as opposed to accepting personal responsibility, whereas the professional person of good character will choose to behave compliantly but, at the same time, commit himself or herself to "giving" the best personal service to the client. Both may be described as self-loving, but whereas the former sees this as being focused on his or her private interests, the latter is concerned with the common good and all that is consistent with such an ambition.

To get to this position is very difficult, Wittgenstein noted: "Nothing is so difficult as not deceiving oneself" (Wittgenstein, 1980, p. 34e). Jesus's teaching in the Sermon on the Mount emphasizes the importance of motivation and disposition as well as the actual practice of what is of good report. But in coming to terms with our true motives, we need help. What I say (and may well believe) I want to achieve in my life may conflict with what in fact, by my behavior, I actually seem to be trying to do, hence the vital importance of an honest friend who courteously points to my foibles and mistaken attitudes. The friend may be a fellow professional, but it is more likely that more direct, personal, positive criticism will come from a friend with a wider experience of life in society. It is regrettable that members of a profession tend to huddle together with members of their own profession and eschew more inclusive conversations with other professional persons.

There are reasons for this. A professional life is stressful with pressures on time. Further study, with all that it entails, is demanded if one is to retain qualification and continue to practice. But it is precisely these demands and the stress that arises from them that makes it vital to know oneself and possess the freedom to handle issues. A professional education program that pays little attention to this will inadequately prepare a person for his or her role. The consequence will be either burnout or a presumed safety by withdrawal into compliance.

To be free to know what it means to love oneself is the product of recognizing that one lives in a world to which God has given himself and in which one, too, as a human being made in God's image, can give oneself to the world for the love of God. The virtue of gratitude for what one has received, for the responsibilities entrusted to one, and for the opportunities afforded by the invitation to personally serve society in a professional capacity is a liberating experience.

Liberal Education

A professional requires a liberal education. Nussbaum, as we have seen, criticizes current formal education that focuses on economic expediency: it is, she says, literally valueless (Nussbaum, 2010). The "educated" person is straight jacketed, limited in imaginative and emotional sympathy, and actually reduced in professional competence. A liberal education is not an optional extra; it lies at the heart of a good education. Nussbaum especially commends the value of literature: "If the literary imagination develops compassion, and if compassion is essential for civic responsibility, then we have good reason to teach works that promote the types of compassionate understanding that we want and need" (Nussbaum, 1997, p. 99). The arts and social sciences, such as history, are ingredients of the formation of the character of every responsible citizen and *a fortiori* of a professional career.

Even in times of austerity, it is a false economy to unreasonably increase staff-student ratios in higher education. This has resulted in the virtual elimination of small seminar groups, thereby destroying a crucial personal dimension of the learning process. In such an interpersonal environment, skills of debate can be honed, new imaginative worlds opened up, ideas clarified, sharpened, or abandoned. The relevance of this process both for personal education and for professional practice is obvious.

Liberal education has also suffered as science has come to be regarded as the bedrock of real knowledge. A liberal education will, of course, include science and technology, even if that merely enables a person to be comfortable with the language of science and to be computer literate. There are two reasons for this. On the one hand, it is important for one to be capable—for example, as a lawyer who reads a brief that refers to scientific issues relevant to the case. On the other hand, only when one has some familiarity with the language of a discipline will one look for advice because one recognizes that one has insufficient knowledge to make a sound judgment.

Wittgenstein lamented an exclusive focus on science, as if poetry and music had nothing to teach people (Wittgenstein, 1980, p. 36e). He underlined the stimulus for self-knowledge and the moral imagination provided by these disciplines and indeed, he would agree, by a serious study of religious belief. The practice of a professional, be he or she a lawyer, doctor, priest, or businessperson, has purchase on life through its place in public understanding. Without awareness of this, the professional can do little more than try to satisfy the criteria provided by compliance. Yet we know that true satisfaction for the professional, as for other members of society, comes from personal commitment to the common good, for which nothing less than a sound liberal education will prepare one.

But we must not forget the role that a general education plays in the growth of self-knowledge. A sound liberal education will not only equip the professional to know facts about immediate experience in its various aspects but include a dimension that will enable the professional to cope with himself or herself. This is something that cannot begin in a crisis; it must be rooted in upbringing and the earliest phases of education. As the book of Proverbs puts it, "Discipline your children, and they will give you rest; they will give delight to your heart" (Prov. 29:17). "Discipline" is a term that can lead to misunderstanding. The Authorized (King James) Version seems, to me, better: "Correct thy son, and he shall give thee rest; yea, he shall give delight unto thy soul." "Correct" implies that a parent's duty is to point a child in the right direction, whereas the term "discipline" suggests punishment and parental control, which is unhelpful. The general education of the professional will include an element of correction that draws attention to the paramount importance of moral behavior and encourages a desire to serve the common good.

In formal education, moral standards are critical to a student's capacity to learn. Despite much public criticism of the behavior of the young, the largest survey ever undertaken of the attitudes, dispositions, values, and virtues of those between 3 and 25 years of age showed the contrary (Arthur, 2010). There is sound reason to believe that they have values on which a good society can be built and the common good celebrated. But an education system dedicated to serving the economy threatens the very moral values that serve the wider interests of society at large and the common good. For this to be possible, we need an appropriate language, stories, opportunities for open conversation, and even some attention to philosophical and religious language.

I have mentioned previously our suspicion of the use of words such as "love," yet we know that love points to an essential moral quality that we must learn to handle in a creative way. Terms such as "virtue," "community," "social responsibility," "public service," "sacrifice," and especially "self-sacrifice" represent concepts that should feature in moral discourse. The extent to which they have slipped out of public conversation provides further evidence of our reduced capacity to debate moral questions. Ill-defined concepts, such as dignity and self-respect, are readily discussed in relation to terminal illness, criminal conviction, and employment, but the suspicion remains that their use in practical decision making is precisely because there is no agreement about their moral significance. The same is true of concepts such as autonomy. Familiarity with the language of moral discourse must be developed in the process of preparing for a professional career; the seminar is an ideal context in which to pursue it.

Personal education and general education are both integral aspects of what we know as liberal education. The virtue of gratitude is the generous expression of the value we find in the development of character and the imaginative breadth of our educational experience. It embraces the fullest and deepest perspective in the Christian theological framework, which excludes nothing from our heartfelt appreciation of the goodness implicit in the creation. It encourages us to pursue the good, whatever our current experience, and awakens us to the fact that, as professional persons, we are committed to the well-being of society at large and care of the environment.

Professional Education

A liberal education and self-knowledge are mutually supportive and necessary conditions for personal and professional life. Indeed it could be argued that without them, one would have an inappropriate attitude toward the gaining of professional skills and therefore be ill-prepared when beginning a professional career. Learning to give attention to what matters, if one is to gain the knowledge and experience necessary to be a successful professional, is personally demanding. It requires openness to a wide range of disciplines and draws on a wide variety of experiences.

Every profession has, of course, its own specialist knowledge and particular skills. Programs that educate the professional will need to provide both knowledge and hands-on experience. But specialist knowledge and skills are not discrete; they need to be integrated with a broad range of complementary and complex disciplines in order to make sense and be practically effective. Architects have to have sufficient physics knowledge to manage the forces on which the safety of a structure depends, sympathetic insight in order to design a building that meets the client's needs, aesthetic sensibility in order to put in place buildings in which people will want to work, sufficient technical knowledge to know the potential of new materials, and relevant personal skills to be able to work in cooperation with quantity surveyors and accountants, among many other professionals. The civil engineer building a tunnel needs to make judgments holding together the information provided by geologists and soil engineers, the mechanical engineers who manage the drilling machines, and the companies who remove the spoil, while at the same time taking personal responsibility for the health and safety of everyone employed on the site.

What is more, none of this can be determined in advance and put into a fixed plan that is to be followed, come what may: every professional must take account of circumstances as they arise. This draws on personal maturity and the breadth of liberal education: it is not simply dependent on technical competence. Preparation for a professional career involves learning the relevant theory (most likely, theories) and attending to the business of learning through practice. Edward Schön describes the professional as a reflective practitioner (Schön, 1983 and 1987). He uses the expression to underline the fact that learning is neither theoretical nor practical but necessarily a matter of both theory and practice.

For the teacher, for example, a pedagogical theory is important, but its value depends on developing it in the light of adapting it to the needs of individual students and groups. We know, for example, that learning by repetition is a useful pedagogical technique, but only when it is combined with sessions of question and answer will the teacher know whether the student understands what he or she has memorized so as correctly to apply it.

The civil engineer will know the forces that he or she has to deal with in building a viaduct, but only through studying the attempts of earlier engineers will he or she be able to adapt that knowledge to take responsible account of new materials or new techniques of construction. The author knows that in writing a novel, he or she will not only need to find the prose style most suitable to his or her story but be willing—however clearly he or she had, in advance, worked out the way the story would go—to change its direction as the characters begin to take shape and influence the author's thinking. Rereading the story "so far," the author may realize that the doctor whom he or she had portrayed as having a fine bedside manner simply would not have spoken to the patient in the way he has written. Professional practice has a moral dimension that likewise involves the need to learn from both theory and practice. There is, it seems to me, no ethical theory that can simply be applied to a situation to draw a moral conclusion, a view shared by Chappell (Chappell, 2009). It is not simply that society changes over time, leading to new situations that no theory could have taken into account when it was formed but that the theories themselves, however carefully applied, lead to erroneous decisions.

Take, for example, the question of euthanasia. We can now live—or be kept alive—beyond our conscious capacity to make reasonable decisions. Living wills are increasingly common, but in the last resort, who should be given the authority to make decisions on our behalf? The medical profession faces this question daily. Is this person alive? In what sense is he or she alive? Has he or she what we would recognize to be a good quality of life? But such questions do not simply involve the medical profession, lawyers, theologians, ethicists, and other professionals; society at large has to find not just an acceptable answer but one that is consistent with a morality that puts love at its core.

The professional is concerned with truth: his or her purpose is to speak the truth to the client. In order to do so the professional will need, as Wittgenstein says, not just to be smart but to know that he or she is anchored firmly in the desire to know the truth. Indeed merely to become a cleverer lawyer, doctor, accountant, or priest will not of itself make one more likely to recognize the truth and to practice it. That will require self-knowledge and a liberal education, as well as deeper knowledge and professional experience.

As Wittgenstein said, "No one can speak the truth: if he has still not mastered himself. He cannot speak it;—but not because he is not clever enough yet. The truth can be spoken only by someone who is already at home in it; not by someone who still lives in falsehood and reaches out from falsehood towards truth on just one occasion" (Wittgenstein, 1980, p. 35e).

In other words, the professional must, as a person, love and give his or her full attention to the truth, for, as St. John affirms, it is the truth that makes us free.

Vocation

The virtue of gratitude can, I claim, open the professional to an awareness of what is inherited and what he or she can give to society through service in a chosen career. Gratitude does not live in a vacuum; it is important, therefore, that it feature as an element of every course of professional education. It is the key to the quality of the relationship that a solicitor or an accountant seeks to celebrate both personally and in professional practice. There is sound evidence, as we have seen, to support the view that a grateful person is open to wider opportunities of service and appreciative of a greater range of social relationships. The breadth and depth of gratitude is, above all, presented in the Christian theological framework that has informed the basis of this book: nothing is excluded. It is not, of course, the case that only Christians can appreciate this dimension of life. Aquinas, for example, celebrated the virtues of Aristotle, who was to him the preeminent outsider: "Everything Thomas does, he does for love of God who delights to make strangers, and even enemies, friends" (Decosimo, 2014, p. 1). To live with an inclusive perspective in a world that God sees is good and beautiful stimulates good professional practice because it is divinely personal and informing of good character.

A person may feel called toward a particular career: one may have a vocation. Properly understood, this implies that one has identified a career to which one believes one can give one's whole self in the service of the good society. We rarely hear such language now, but I sense that it is gradually gaining purchase again on our human sensibility. A vocation is not simply a matter of liking to do something because one likes it, because one finds that one has a talent for it, or because it will enable one to earn a good living. Of course it may, one believes, fulfill all those things, but the primary motivation for the career one is choosing is that it will fulfill one's sense of self because it satisfies an essential need if society is to flourish. In the second of Aristotle's senses of what it means to love oneself, it enables one to love oneself because one has rationally chosen to be a person who will identify himself or herself with what is excellent and of good report. In such a situation, one can, as Wittgenstein said, speak the truth because one is already at home in it and therefore loves it.

Medical courses will encourage the use of language that affirms the selfhood of every human being and refrains from reducing persons to cases. This is not only a moral necessity but a practical recognition of the fact that by so doing, the health of both the doctor and the patient will be encouraged. A doctor who maintains a liberal education will grow personally, thus extending the range of personal understanding and the capacity to empathize with the patient. The doctor will be compassionate, able to converse easily with a patient and therefore confirm in the patient's mind that he or she is being treated as an equal moral interlocutor. Recent research tends to support the view that even apparent unconsciousness may still leave a patient aware of the quality of the personal relationship he or she shared with the persons who care.

Doctors may protest that they have no time for "general education," including such things as reading short stories, taking an interest in astronomy, or doing things that seem, on superficial examination, not to contribute to their medical—scientific—knowledge. But that is to misunderstand the practice of medicine, let alone the nature of scientific inquiry. The medical profession is concerned to heal the person, not merely to cure the body. The truth on which doctors are focused is an open attention to everything that contributes to good health. Analogously, one can affirm the same of the teacher, the police officer, the lawyer, the accountant, and so on. One of the best educated people I ever had the good fortune to meet was a general in the British Army. He had not only a fine knowledge of military strategy and military history but also a passionate conviction that any military person who was seriously concerned with peacemaking needed constantly to deepen his or her understanding of human nature. History, literature, music, the visual arts, and conversation all combined to make him or her a person who would be a good general.

But let's be clear: none of this is of any value in the professional life unless there is a thorough specialist knowledge of the law, medicine, policing, military matters, teaching, banking, or whatever. As a professional, I must profess my discipline and practice my profession. My vital point is that not only is this professional competence not sufficient for good professional practice, but it is the easiest ingredient of good professional practice, hence the vital dimension that a sense of vocation adds to professional practice: serving society through meeting the needs of the client in whose presence one stands, when done well, serves the common good. Both professional and client are grateful for the personal service and the wider satisfaction of the common good. But in order to be able to go on serving the common good, one needs to be confident that one is living in the real world. So what is the real world?

The Theological Framework

The virtue of gratitude finds its nourishing context in the lively world of God's creation, in which we enjoy exploring our human nature as made in the image of God. Our real human world is one that is characterized by the gracious presence of God: love lies at the heart of our world as we experience it. Our gratitude, if it is to be life-giving, cannot be partial: it must embrace the whole of our world insofar as we can "see" it. I can only be truly grateful for the success of Manchester United Football Club if I am grateful for association football, and only grateful for association football if I am grateful for sport, and only grateful for sport if I am grateful for human being, and so on.

No matter with what experience we begin, we are led into the world of wholeness beyond.

We have, I believe, a view of the nature of our total environment, including ourselves in relation to it, which informs implicitly or explicitly our dispositions and attitudes toward life. But it will only be fruitful if we pay attention to it, keep it under review, and in the light of experience, work to make its meaning more explicit. If and when it reveals "reality," we will be able to find ourselves and draw life from giving it our full attention. Such a presumed real world is likely to be much more influential on our moral attitudes and commitment to the practice of the virtues than an attempt to embrace a moral theory and deduce how we should behave from strict adherence to it. Utilitarianism and deontology, for example, offer no moral consistency in the way that they can be applied. In any case, moral judgment is more than simply the accurate direction of rational thought.

I turn to Iris Murdoch again, for, following Simone Weil, she holds together the unity of human being and our capacity to "see" reality as the revelation of love:

> Will and reason . . . are not entirely separate faculties in the moral agent. Will continually influences belief, for better or worse, and is ideally able to influence it through a sustained attention to reality. This is what Simone Weil means when she says that "will is obedience not resolution. As moral agents we have to try to see justly, to overcome prejudice, to avoid temptation, to control and curb imagination, to direct reflection. Man is not a combination of an impersonal rational agent and a personal will. He is a unified being who sees, and who desires in accordance with what he sees, and who has some continual slight control over the direction and focus of his vision." (Murdoch, 1970, p. 40)

What the moral agent sees, according to Murdoch, is "reality," an elusive normative term to which we should not "try to give any single organised background sense" but that, provided its limitations are understood, may be used as a philosophical term: "What is real may be non-empirical without being in the grand sense systematic. In particular situations 'reality' as that which is revealed to the patient eye of love is an idea entirely comprehensible to the ordinary person" (p. 40). The reality revealed in the Christian theological framework is love, God's love in creation, a love that embraces the whole world and all people. It is an active love presented in the Christian understanding of the nature of God as Trinity—a lively, mutual, coeternal, loving relationship that human being is invited to share. The mutual self-giving of the divine nature is the image in which human being is made too: people will find their true natures and reveal themselves to others by giving and finding themselves in loving service. In so doing, they bear witness to reality, attention to which has nourished their will so that they want to do what their reason tells them they are capable of achieving.

"Love is knowledge of the individual," affirms Iris Murdoch (Murdoch, 1970, p. 28). In Christian theological terms, we could say that love is the knowledge of Jesus, the Christ in whom we see God's love in creation in our own likeness. But it is difficult to learn goodness from another person, so the simple question that has seemed to some to be the summary of Christian ethics—what would Jesus do?—is ridiculous. The "reality" to which Jesus draws our attention by his teaching, example, and self-sacrifice is the goodness of God, the Creator whose forgiving, redemptive, and loving presence reveals the nature of the creation for which he takes responsibility. The all-embracing range of his loving presence is expressed in the Christian Creed, which talks of Jesus's being with God, the presence of God with him in his life and death, his descent into hell, his Resurrection, and his ascension to the Father. There is nothing that is outside the love of God in creation. As St. Paul puts it, "For I am convinced that neither death nor life, nor angels, nor rulers, nor things present, nor things to come, nor powers, nor height, nor depth, nor anything else in all creation, will be able to separate us from the love of God in Christ Jesus our Lord" (Rom. 8:18–19). Hence we can, with God, declare that when we look upon the "real" world God has made, it is good: we can truthfully celebrate his "Real Presence."

However, notwithstanding this fact, we cannot simply read from the world what we should do if we are to behave well. There is no one whose example we must simply imitate. Indeed, were we to be no more than obediently imitative, we would not be acting morally; to act morally requires personal judgment. Much more important, "There exists a moral reality, a real though infinitely distant standard: the difficulties of understanding and imitating remain" (Murdoch, 1970, p. 31). The point is that we grow by small degrees through giving attention to reality and growing in the light of what we see. This is certainly a metaphysical perspective, but it is not unreal. Indeed what distinguishes the Christian from the Murdochian perspective on goodness is that its character is the lively, divine life of God himself, present in the world in the person of Christ, who inspires us and enters into our minds and hearts so that we can join our wills with God's and "will one will."

Sarah Bachelard points to Murdoch's claim that "many of our most profound moral differences are an expression of the fact that 'we see different worlds'" (Bachelard, 2014, p. 2). We might, following Wittgenstein, call them similes. But choosing between the "validity" of similes is not the product of rational inquiry; it will be a matter of choice but a choice informed by the whole of oneself. This is not a matter of blind choice; on the contrary, it implies a perspective on life that includes reason, aesthetic insight, feelings, and the emotions. It is unlikely to be completely developed at any time but to grow and be filled out in the course of one's life. Perhaps this is why Wittgenstein said that "a man's philosophy is a matter of temperament" (Wittgenstein, 1980, p. 20e). It might explain, too, why he should also say that when life becomes difficult, we think of a change in our circumstances while a change in our attitude does not cross our minds (Wittgenstein, 1980, p. 53e).

Changes in attitude are, however, of the essence of a maturing sense of what we believe to be reality and the development of the moral imagination with which it is associated. A breadth of experience, not merely of what we call "facts," will assist us in coming to terms with what we understand to be reality, at which point we shall want to reconsider our ethical stance and our place in the world. It is a matter of considerable importance analogous to religious conversion. As Lonergan reflects, "Religious conversion is a matter of being grasped by ultimate concern. It is other-worldly falling in love" (Lonergan, 1972, p. 240).

Formation of the ground of our theological perspective begins with the demand of truth. To repeat Wittgenstein's remark, "No one can speak the truth: if he has still not mastered himself. He cannot speak it; but not because he is not clever enough yet. The truth can be spoken only by someone who is already at home in it; not by someone who still lives in falsehood and reaches out from falsehood to speak the truth" (Wittgenstein, 1980, p. 35e). The search for God, for reality, for truth, for beauty, for goodness is a struggle that can bring suffering. Unfortunately, we have almost lost the willingness, let alone the ability, to struggle for the truth.

Our education is too bland: knowledge is accessed through mechanical processes, and even its links to more incisive perspectives are identified by technical maneuvers. Wittgenstein was right when he reflected, "I think the way people are educated nowadays tends to diminish their capacity for suffering. At present a school is reckoned good 'if the children have a good time' . . . Endurance of suffering isn't rated highly because there is supposed not to be any suffering—really it's out of date" (Wittgenstein, 1980, p. 71e). We are unprepared for the demands that we are required to accept if we are to attend to the reality that lies within and beyond our experience. Yet only by attending to it will we make the effort to inch toward the truth and freedom of our humanity, made as we are in the image of God.

Conclusion

In this book, I have argued that the sense of gratitude we enjoy finds nourishment in the Christian theological framework. Above all, our gratitude comes from the fact that we are made in God's image, which implies that we share the character of God and are free to give ourselves in service to one another, to the whole of creation, and thereby to God. Grounded in that tradition, we as professional persons will remind ourselves that what we think and do expresses our character both as people and as members of professions. We will appreciate our God-given capacity to be curious about the world of our experience in all its dimensions, to be grateful for what we inherit and share with others; our compassion will stimulate insight into the circumstances of others and widen our empathy. The shock of the beautiful will, from time to time, reawaken us to the wholeness of things, the metaphysical, and provoke opportunities for the recovery of hope, which will reengage us in a search for truth, justice, and love. There may be no way back, but there are ways forward inherent in the totality of our experience of the world, one another, and God. The professional, concerned to serve his or her client and society at large, has in a profound sense a vocation that the Christian theological tradition believes is the call of God.

For this transformation to occur, professional education will have to abandon a compliance culture and promote a culture of character virtues motivated by a sense of gratitude. Compliance, the mere obedience to rules and regulations, is not personally satisfying. As professional persons, we know this to be true. By placing ourselves consciously in the dynamic framework of Christian theology, we shall be alongside those who are trying in theory and practice to work out what it means to be made in the image of God—in principle, to share his character. We shall not achieve perfection, but we will be moved toward the truth and a vision of the divine reality, which is liberating. It is a vision for which we can be eternally grateful.

God is a source of energy, a loving presence on whom we can focus our desire for truth, goodness, and beauty. Awareness of God's presence focuses the will and informs the moral imagination. The

Resurrection reveals a new reality that shows us that we can be what, in our hearts, we know we want to be: "Finally, brethren, whatever is true, whatever is honourable, whatever is just, whatever is commendable, if there is any excellence and if there is anything worthy of praise, think about these things. Keep on doing the things that you have learned and received and heard and seen in me, and the God of peace will be with you" (Phil. 4:8–9).

A nourishing thought on which to reflect.

Bibliography

Biblical Quotations are from the *New Revised Standard Version* (NRSV; 1989, Oxford, Oxford University Press) unless otherwise indicated in the text.

Adams, R. M., (1999) *Finite and Infinite Goods*, (New York, Oxford University Press).
Agassi, J. B., (1974) "Objectivity in the Social Sciences," in Seeger, R. J., and Cohen, R. S. (eds.), *Philosophical Foundations of Science, Boston Studies in the Philosophy of Science*, Vol. 11, pp. 305–16.
Al-Khalili, J., and McFadden, J., (2014) *Life on the Edge: The Coming of Age of Quantum Biology*, (London, Transworld).
Anscombe, G. E. M., (1957) *Intention*, (Oxford, Blackwell).
Aquinas, T., (2006) *Summa Theologiae*, Vol. 2, (Cambridge, Cambridge University Press).
Aristotle, (1984a) *Metaphysics, Complete Works of Aristotle*, Vol. 2, trans. W. D. Ross, ed. J. Barnes, (Princeton, Princeton University Press).
———, (1984b) *Nicomachean Ethics, Complete Works of Aristotle*, Vol. 2, trans. W. D. Ross, ed. J. Barnes, (Princeton, Princeton University Press).
———, (1984c) *Physics, Complete Works of Aristotle*, Vol. 1, trans. W. D. Ross, ed. J. Barnes, (Princeton, Princeton University Press).
Arthur, J., and Nicholls, G., (2007) *John Henry Newman*, (London, Continuum).
Arthur, J., (2010) *Of Good Character*, (Exeter, Imprint Academic).
Augustine, (1907) *The Confessions of St. Augustine*, trans. E. B. Pusey, (London, J. M. Dent).
Austin, J. L., (1962) *How to Do Things with Words*, ed. J. O. Urmson, (Oxford, Oxford University Press).
Bachelard, S., (2014) *Resurrection and the Moral Imagination*, (Farnham, Ashgate).
Bellah, R., (2011) *Religion in Human Evolution*, (Cambridge, MA, Belknap Press of Harvard University Press).
Board of Directors of the Association of American Colleges and Universities (AAC&U), (1998) "Statement on Liberal Learning," (Washington, DC, AAC&U). October.
Broadbent, D. E., (1958) *Perception and Communication*, (Oxford, Pergamon).
Brown, R., Fitzmyer, J., and Murphy, R., (1995) *The New Jerome Biblical Commentary*, (London, Geoffrey Chapman).
Brown, W. S., and Strawn, B. D., (2014) *The Physical Nature of Christian Life*, (Cambridge, Cambridge University Press).

Bultmann, R., (1952) *Theology of the New Testament*, Vol. 1, (London, SCM).
Byron, W. J., (2012) "Gratitude: A One Word Summary of the Catholic Faith," *The Pastoral Review*, January.
Caldecott, S., (2012) *Beauty in the Word: Rethinking the Foundations of Education*, (Tacoma, Angelico).
Calman, K., (2001) "A Study of Storytelling, Humour and Learning in Medicine," *Clinical Medicine*, Vol. 1, No. 3, pp. 227–29.
Campbell, J., (2005) "Joint Attention and Common Knowledge," in Eilan, N., Hoerl, C., McCormack, T., and Roessler, J. (eds.), *Joint Attention and Communication*, (Oxford, Oxford University Press), pp. 287–97.
Catholic Church, (1994) *Catechism of the Catholic Church*, (London, Geoffrey Chapman).
Chappell, T., (2009) *Ethics and Experience: Life beyond Moral Theory*, (Durham, Acumen).
Chappell, T., (2014) *Knowing What to Do*, (Oxford, Oxford University Press).
Chomsky, N., (1986) *Knowledge of Language: Its Nature, Origin and Use*, (New York, Praeger).
Coakley, S., (2012) *Sacrifice Regained: Evolution, Co-operation and God*, Lecture presented in the Gifford Lecture Series, University of Aberdeen, April 17–May 3. http://www.abdn.ac.uk/gifford/about/2012-giff.
———, (2013) *God, Sexuality, and the Self: An Essay "On the Trinity,"* (Cambridge, Cambridge University Press).
Cohen, J. R., (2002) "Legislating Apology: The Pros and Cons," *University of Cincinnati Law Review*, Vol. 70, No. 819. http://scholarship.law.ufl.edu/facultypub/31.
Congar, Y., (1957) *Lay People in the Church*, (London, Geoffrey Chapman).
Corbally, C., (2013) Lecture presented at a speaker series sponsored by Dow Chemical, University of Charleston, Beckley, WV, March 26.
Cottingham, J., (2005) *The Spiritual Dimension: Religion, Philosophy and Human Value*, (Cambridge, Cambridge University Press).
Dawkins, R., (2006) *The God Delusion*, (London, Bantam).
de Botton, A., (2012) *Religion for Atheists*, (London, Penguin).
de Caussade, P., (1921) *Abandonment to Divine Providence*, (Exeter, Catholic Records Press).
Decosimo, D., (2014) *Ethics as a Work of Charity: Thomas Aquinas and Pagan Virtue*, (Stanford, Stanford University Press).
de Gruchy, J., (2001) *Christianity, Art and Transformation*, (Cambridge, Cambridge University Press).
Dennett, D. C., (1992) "The Self as a Center of Narrative Gravity," in Kessel, F. S., Cole, P. M., and Johnson, D. L. (eds.), *Self and Consciousness: Multiple Perspectives*, (Hillsdale, NJ, Erlbaum).
———, (1995) *Darwin's Dangerous Idea: Evolution and the Meaning of Life*, (New York, Simon and Schuster).
———, (2013) *Intuition Pumps and Other Tools for Thinking*, (London, Allen Lane).

Denning, Lord, (1954) *Packer v. Packer*.
de Stael, G., (1807) *Corinne*, trans. S. Raphael, (Oxford, Oxford University Press).
Diamond, J., (2012) *The World until Yesterday*, (London, Allen Lane).
Donne, J., (1946) *Complete Poetry and Selected Prose*, ed. J. Hayward, (New York, Nonesuch Press).
Donoghue, D., (2003) *Speaking of Beauty*, (New Haven, Yale University Press).
Dreyfus, H., and Kelly, S. D., (2011) *All Things Shining*, (New York, Free Press).
Dunn, J., (2000) *The Cunning of Unreason: Making Sense of Politics*, (London, HarperCollins).
Dworkin, R., (1977) *Taking Rights Seriously*, (London, Duckworth).
———, (1981a) "What Is Equality? 1. Equality and Welfare," *Philosophy and Public Affairs*, Vol. 10, pp. 185–246.
———, (1981b) "What Is Equality? 2. Equality and Resources," *Philosophy and Public Affairs*, Vol. 10, pp. 283–345.
———, (2000) *Sovereign Virtue*, (Cambridge, MA, Harvard University Press).
———, (2011) *Justice for Hedgehogs*, (Cambridge, MA, Belknap Press of Harvard University Press).
Emmons, R. A., and McCullough, M. E. (eds.), (2004) *The Psychology of Gratitude*, (New York, Oxford University Press).
Emmons, R. A., (2007) *Thanks! How the New Science of Gratitude Can Make You Happier*, (Boston, MA, Houghton-Mifflin).
Evans-Pritchard, E. E., (1934) *Witchcraft, Oracles and Magic among the Azande*, (Oxford, Oxford University Press).
Flanagan, O., (2002) *The Problem of the Soul*, (New York, Basic).
Flynn, G., and Murray, P. D., (2012) *Ressourcement*, (Oxford, Oxford University Press).
Ford, D. F., (2007) *Christian Wisdom: Desiring God and Learning in Love*, (Cambridge, Cambridge University Press).
———, (2011) *The Future of Christian Theology*, (London, Wiley-Blackwell).
The Forgiveness Project, (2010) "Mary Blewitt (Rwanda)," http://theforgivenessproject.com/stories/mary-blewitt-rwanda.
Frearson, J., (2014) "Business Reporter," *Sunday Telegraph*, September, pp. 6–7.
Fronda, E. S. B., (2010) *Wittgenstein's (Misunderstood) Religious Thought*, (Leiden, Brill).
Gittings, J., (2012) *The Glorious Art of Peace*, (Oxford, Oxford University Press).
Giubbilei, L., (2011) "Interview with Garden Designer Luciano Giubbilei," H. Gazeley, interviewer, Landscape Juice, http://www.landscapejuice.com/2011/11/interview-with-luciano-giubbilei.html.

Glock, H.-J., (1996) *A Wittgenstein Dictionary*, s.v. "Form of Life; Language-Game," (Oxford, Blackwell).
Glover, J., (1983) "Self-Creation," *Proceedings of the British Academy*, Vol. 69 (Oxford, Oxford University Press).
Good, J. A., (2005) "The German *Bildung* Tradition," http://www.philosophy.uncc.edu/mleldrid/SAAP/USC/pbt1.html.
Govier, T., (2002) *Forgiveness and Revenge*, (London, Routledge).
Greenfield, S., (2002) *The Private Life of the Brain*, (London, Penguin).
Gregersen, N., (2014) "Naturalism in the Mirror of Religion," *Philosophy, Theology and the Sciences*, Vol. 1, No. 1.
Griswold, C. L., (2007) *Forgiveness*, (Cambridge, Cambridge University Press).
Gutierrez, G., (1973) *A Theology of Liberation: History, Politics and Salvation*, (Maryknoll, Orbis).
Hahn, S., (1998) *A Father Who Keeps His Promises: God's Covenant Love in Scripture*, (Cincinnati, OH, Servant).
Hare, R. M., (1963) *Freedom and Reason*, (Oxford, Oxford University Press).
Hart, D. B., (2004) *The Beauty and the Infinite*, (Cambridge, Eerdmans).
———, (2011) *Atheist Delusions*, (New Haven, Yale University Press).
———, (2013) *The Experience of God*, (New Haven, Yale University Press).
Hauerwas, S., and Willimon, W. H., (1989) *Resident Aliens: Life in the Christian Colony*, (Nashville, Abingdon).
Hitchens, C., (n.d.) "Christopher Hitchens Quotes." Goodreads. http://www.goodreads.com/quotes/473894.
———, (2007) *God Is Not Good: The Case against Religion*, (London, Atlantic).
Hollingworth, M., (2013) *Saint Augustine of Hippo: An Intellectual Biography*, (London, Bloomsbury).
Hoogland, J., and Jochemsen, H., (2000) "Professional Autonomy and the Normative Structure of Medical Practice," *Theoretical Medicine*, Vol. 21, No. 5, September.
Hume, D., (1951) *A Treatise of Human Nature*, ed. L. A. Selby-Bigge, (Oxford, Clarendon).
Huxley, A., (1950) *Music at Night*, (Harmondsworth, Penguin).
James, W., (1950) *Principles of Psychology*, (New York, Dover).
Jeremias, J., (1969) *Jerusalem in the Time of Jesus*, (London, SCM).
Jewett, R., (1971) *Paul's Anthropological Terms*, (Leiden, E. J. Brill).
Kant, I., (1952) *Critique of Judgement*, trans. James Creed Meredith, (Oxford, Oxford University Press).
Kenny, A., (2004) *The Unknown God*, (London, Continuum).
Knight, C. C., (2007) *The God of Nature: Incarnation and Contemporary Science*, (Minneapolis, Fortress).
Kristjánsson, K., (2010) *The Self and Its Emotions*, (Cambridge, Cambridge University Press).

——, (2013) *Virtues and Vices in Positive Psychology*, (New York, Cambridge University Press).
Krznaric, R., (2014) *Empathy: A Handbook for Revolution*, (London, Random House).
Leahy, B., (1994) "Theological Aesthetics," in McGregor, B., and Norris, T. (eds.), *The Beauty of Christ*, (Edinburgh, T&T Clark).
Locke, J., (1947) *Essay Concerning Human Understanding*, Abridged, ed. R. Wilburn, (London, Dent).
Lonergan, B., (1970) *Insight: A Study of Human Understanding*, (New York, Philosophical Library).
——, (1972) *Method in Theology*, (London, Darton, Longman, and Todd).
——, (1985) "Natural Rights and Historical Mindedness," in Crowe, F. E. (ed.), *A Third Collection*, (New York, Paulist).
Machiavelli, N., (1935) *The Prince*, trans. Luigi Ricci, rev. E. R. P. Vincent, (London, Oxford University Press).
MacIntyre, A., (1999) *Dependent Rational Animals: Why Human Beings Need the Virtues*, (London, Duckworth).
——, (2009) *God, Philosophy, Universities*, (London, Continuum).
Mackey, J. P., (2006) *Christianity and Creation: The Essence of the Christian Faith and Its Future among Religions*, (New York, Continuum).
MacKinnon, D., (2011) "Theology as a Discipline of a Modern University," in MacDowell, J. (ed.), *Philosophy and the Burden of Theological Honesty*, (London, T&T Clark).
MacKinnon, D. M., and Holmes, J. D., (1970) *Newman's University Sermons*, (London, SPCK).
Macmurray, J., (1961) *Persons in Relation*, (London, Faber).
——, (1991) *The Self as Agent*, (New York, Humanity).
Mannion, G., (2003) *Schopenhauer: Religion and Morality, the Humble Path to Ethics*, (London, Ashgate).
Marx, K., (1875) "Criticism of the Gotha Programme," in Marx, K., and Engels, F., *Selected Works*, Vol. 3, (Moscow, Progress).
Maslow, A., (1968) *Toward a Psychology of Being*, (New York, Wiley).
McCullough, M. E., Emmons, R. A., and Tsang, J.-A., (2002) "The Grateful Disposition: A Conceptual and Empirical Topography," *Journal of Personality and Social Psychology*, Vol. 82, No. 1, pp. 112–27.
McCullough, M. E., Kilpatrick, S., Emmons, R. A., and Larson, D., (2001) "Is Gratitude a Moral Effect?," *Psychological Bulletin*, Vol. 127.
McDermott, T. (ed.), (1989) *Summa Theologiae: A Concise Translation*, (London, Eyre and Spottiswoode).
McGilchrist, I., (2009) *The Master and His Emissary: The Divided Brain and the Making of the Western World*, (New Haven, Yale University Press).
McIntosh, M. A., (2004) *Discernment and Truth*, (New York, Crossroad).
Mendenhall, G. E., (1954) "Covenant Forms in Israelite Tradition," *Biblica Archaeologica*, Vol. 17, pp. 49–76.

Merleau-Ponty, M., (1962) *The Phenomenon of Perception*, (London, Routledge and Kegan Paul).
Mobin-Uddin, A., (2002) "Gratitude to God Is at the Heart of Islam," *Columbus Dispatch* (Faith and Values), November 22. http://www.asmamobinuddin.com/Gratitude.pdf.
Mole, C., (2011) *Attention Is Cognitive Unison: An Essay in Philosophical Psychology*, (New York, Oxford University Press).
Monroe, K. R., (1996) *The Heart of Altruism Perception of a Common Humanity*, (Princeton, Princeton University Press).
Moore, S., (1967) *God Is a New Language*, (London, Darton, Longman, and Todd).
Murdoch, I., (1962) *The Bell*, (Harmondsworth, Penguin).
———, (1970) *The Sovereignty of Good*, (London, Routledge and Kegan Paul).
———, (1977) *The Fire and the Sun: Why Plato Banished the Artists*, (Oxford, Oxford University Press).
Newman, J. H., (1990) *The Idea of a University*, ed. I. T. Kerr, (Oxford, Oxford University Press).
Nozick, R., (1974) *Anarchy, State, and Utopia*, (New York, Basic).
Nussbaum, M., (1997) *Cultivating Humanity*, (Cambridge, MA, Harvard University Press).
———, (2001) *Upheavals of Thought: The Intelligence of Emotions*, (Cambridge, Cambridge University Press).
———, (2010) *Not for Profit*, (Princeton, Princeton University Press).
———, (2013) *Political Emotions: Why Love Matters for Justice*, (London, Cambridge University Press).
Nygren, A., (1969) *Agape and Eros*, trans. Philip Watson, (London, SPCK).
Pailin, D., (1982) "God and Creation: A Process View," *Epworth Review*, Vol. 31, January, p. 87.
Pakaluk, M., (2013) "Structure and Method in Appropriating Aristotle," in Hoffmann, T., Muller, J., and Perkams, M (eds.), *Aquinas and the Nicomachean Ethics*, (Cambridge, Cambridge University Press).
Passmore, J., (1974) *Man's Responsibility for Nature*, (London, Duckworth).
Peacocke, C., (2005) "Nature, Reflexivity and Common Knowledge," in Eilan, N., Hoerl, C., McCormack, T., and Roessler, J. (eds.), *Joint Attention and Communication*, (Oxford, Oxford University Press), pp. 298–324.
Pedersen, J., (1926) *Israel, Its Life and Culture*, Vols. 1–2, (Oxford, Oxford University Press).
Peer Review, (2012) "The Liberally Educated Professional," *Peer Review*, Vol. 14, No. 2, Spring.
Perkin, H., (1989) *The Rise of Professional Society: England since 1880*, (London, Routledge).
Perrin, N., (1967) *Recovering the Teaching of Jesus*, (London, SCM).
———, (1976) *Jesus and the Language of the Kingdom: Symbol and Metaphor in New Testament Interpretation*, (London, SCM).

Pew Research Center for Religion and Public Life, (2013) Telephone survey published December 30. http://www.pewforum.org/2013/12/30/publics-views-on-human-evolution.
Plato, (1963) Symposium: *The Complete Dialogues*, (Princeton, Princeton University Press).
Polanyi, M., (1958) *Personal Knowledge: Toward a Post-Critical Philosophy*, (London, Routledge and Kegan Paul).
———, (1966) *The Tacit Dimension*, (London, Routledge and Kegan Paul).
Popper, K., (1957) *The Spell of Plato: The Open Society and Its Enemies*, 3rd edn., Vol. 1, (London, Routledge and Kegan Paul).
———, (1968) *The Logic of Scientific Discovery*, (London, Hutchinson).
Pritchard, J. B., (1969) *Ancient Near Eastern Texts Relating to the Old Testament*, 3rd edn., (Princeton, Princeton University Press).
Putnam, H., (1992) *Renewing Philosophy*, (Cambridge, MA, Harvard University Press).
Rahner, K., (1966) *Nature and Grace, Theological Investigations*, Vol. 4, (London, Darton, Longman and Todd).
Rahner, K. (ed.), (1975) *The Encyclopedia of Theology*, s.v. "Beatific Vision," (London, Burns and Oates).
Rawls, J., (1972) *A Theory of Justice*, (Oxford, Oxford University Press).
Rees, M., (2013) "To the Ends of the Solar System," Lecture at the Hay Festival, Cambridge University, reported by Bignell, P., in *The Independent*, April 21.
Roberts, R. C., (1995) "Forgivingness," *American Philosophical Quarterly*, Vol. 32.
———, (2004) "The Blessings of Gratitude," in Emmons, R. A., and McCullough, M. E. (eds.), *The Psychology of Gratitude*, (New York, Oxford University Press), pp. 58–78.
———, (2013) *Emotions in the Moral Life*, (Cambridge, Cambridge University Press).
Ruti, M., (2013) *The Call of Character: Living a Life Worth Living*, (New York, Columbia University Press).
Sacks, J., (2002) *The Dignity of Difference*, (London, Continuum).
Sacks, O., (1985) *The Man Who Mistook His Wife for a Hat*, (New York, Touchstone).
Sandel, M., (1982) *Liberalism and the Limits of Justice*, (Cambridge, Cambridge University Press).
Saville, A., (1982) *The Test of Time: An Essay in Philosophical Aesthetics*, (Oxford, Clarendon)
Scanlon, T. M., (1998) *What We Owe to Each Other*, (Cambridge, MA, Harvard University Press).
Scarry, E., (2000) *On Beauty and Being Just*, (London, Duckworth Overlook).
———, (2011) *Thinking in an Emergency*, (London, W. W. Norton).
Schaper, E., (1983) *Pleasure, Preference and Value Studies in Philosophical Aesthetics*, (Cambridge, Cambridge University Press).

Schön, D. A., (1983) *The Reflective Practitioner*, (London, Temple Smith).
———, (1987) *Educating the Reflective Practitioner*, (San Francisco, Jossey-Bass).
Schopenhauer, A., (1969) *The World as Will and Representation*, trans. E. F. J. Payne, (New York, Dover).
Schwarz, D., (2007) *Aquinas on Friendship*, (Oxford, Oxford University Press).
Searle, J. R., (2004) *Mind: A Brief Introduction*, (New York, Oxford University Press).
Sennett, R., (2012) *Together: The Rituals, Pleasures and Politics of Cooperation*, (London, Penguin).
Shakespeare, W., (1955) *Julius Caesar*, ed. T.S. Dorsch (London, Methuen).
———, (1975) *As You Like It*, ed. A. Latham, (London, Methuen).
Silver, H., and Brennan, J., (1988) *A Liberal Vocationalism*, (London, Methuen).
Smith, A., (1976) *The Theory of Moral Sentiments*, eds. D. D. Raphael and A. L. MacFie, (Oxford, Oxford University Press).
Smith, N., (2008) *I Was Wrong*, (Cambridge, Cambridge University Press).
Sobrino, J., (1994) *Jesus the Liberator*, (London, Bloomsbury).
Solomon, M., Wilson, K., and Winter, T., (2014) *It Is Good to Give Thanks: Gratitude in the Abrahamic Religions*, http://www.jubileecentre.ac.uk/475/papers/insight-series.
Solzhenitsyn, A., (1970) "Beauty Will Save the World," http://www.nobelprize.org/nobel_prizes/literature/laureates/1970/solzhenitsyn-lecture.html.
Steiner, G., (1985) *After Babel: Aspects of Language and Translation*, (Oxford, Oxford University Press).
Strawson, G., (2004) "Against Narrativity," *Ratio* (new series), Vol. 17, December 4, pp. 428–52.
———, (2009) *Selves*, (Cambridge, Cambridge University Press).
Strawson, P. F., (1959) *Individuals: An Essay in Descriptive Metaphysics*, (London, Methuen).
———, (2008) "Freedom and Resentment," in Strawson, P. F., *Freedom and Resentment*, (Abingdon, Routledge).
Theissen, G. E., (2004) *Theological Aesthetics: A Reader*, (London, SCM).
Tillich, P., (1953) *Systematic Theology*, Vol. 1, (London, Nisbet).
Trevelyan, G., (1944) *English Social History*, (London, Longmans).
Turner, D., (2013) *Thomas Aquinas*, (New Haven, Yale University Press).
Tutu, D., (1999) *No Future without Forgiveness*, (New York, Random House).
von Balthasar, H., (1965–91) *The Glory of the Lord: A Theological Aesthetics*, 7 vols., (Edinburgh, T&T Clark).
von Ebner-Eschenbach, M., (1994) *Aphorisms*, trans. D. Scrase and M. Mieder, (California, Riverside).
Ward, N., (1967) *The Use of Praying*, (London, Epworth).

Wei, M., (2006) "Doctors, Apologies and the Law: An Analysis, and Critique of Apology Laws," *Student Scholarship Papers*, Paper 30. http://digitalcommons.law.yale.edu/student_papers/30.
Weil, S., (1951) "Reflections on the Right Use of School Studies with a View to the Love of God," in Weil, S., *Waiting on God*, (London, Routledge and Kegan Paul).
Wesley, J., (1872) "On Working Out Our Own Salvation" (Sermon No. 85), in Jackson, T. (ed.), *Sermons*, http://wesley.nnu.edu/john-wesley/the-sermons-of-john-wesley-1872-edition/sermon-85-on-working-out-our-own-salvation.
Williams, B., (1993) *Shame and Necessity*, (Berkeley, California University Press).
———, (2008) *Freedom and Resentment and Other Essays*, (Abingdon, Routledge).
Williams, R., (2013) "Foreword," in Duffy, E. (ed.), *The Heart in Pilgrimage: A Prayerbook for Catholic Christians*, (London, Bloomsbury), pp. vii–viii.
Wilson, J. A., (1969) "Myths, Epics and Legends," in Pritchard, J. B. (ed.), *Ancient Near Eastern Texts Relating to the Old Testament*, 3rd edn., (Princeton, Princeton University Press).
Wilson, K., (2006) *Learning to Hope: The Church and the Desire for Wisdom*, (London, Epworth).
———, (2008) *Dying to Live: A Christian Approach to the Matter of Mortality*, (London, Epworth).
———, (2011) *Methodist Theology*, (London, T&T Clark).
Winch, P., (1958) *The Idea of a Social Science*, (London, Routledge and Kegan Paul).
Wittgenstein, L., (1958) *Philosophical Investigations*, 2nd edn., (Oxford, Blackwell).
———, (1961) *Tractatus Logico-Philosophicus*, trans. D. F. Pears and B. F. McGuinness, (London, Routledge and Kegan Paul).
———, (1966) *Lectures and Conversations on Aesthetics, Psychology and Religious Belief*, ed. C. Barrett, (Oxford, Blackwell).
———, (1980) *Culture and Value*, trans. P. Winch, ed. G. H. Von Wright, (Oxford, Blackwell).
World Health Organization, (1986) "Ottawa Charter for Health Promotion," http://www.who.int/healthpromotion/conferences/previous/ottawa/en.
World Heritage Encyclopedia, (2014) *World Heritage Encyclopedia*, s.v. "Jugendweihe." http://self.gutenberg.org/articles/Jugendweihe.

INDEX

Adams, Robert M., 15, 67
Aeschylus, 22
agape, 47–48
altruism, 92
Anscombe, G. E. M., 1, 21, 87, 135
apology, 193–99
Aquinas, Saint Thomas, 10, 15, 20–21, 35, 38, 53, 66–67, 101, 103, 130–33, 135, 138, 155, 178, 198–99, 202–3, 213, 219
arete, 22, 104, 106
Aristotle, 1, 13, 23, 32, 41, 66, 91, 113, 135, 151, 169, 212, 219
aseity, 35, 43, 153
atheism, 158, 210
Augustine, Saint, 20, 22, 27, 201
Austin, J. L., 2, 94
authoritativeness, 40
authority, God's, 37–38, 47–48, 121–22, 149–50

Bachelard, Sarah, 162, 223
Balthazar, Hans Urs von, 4, 82, 132, 172, 183–84
Bellah, Robert N., 75
Bildung, 81
brain, 43–44, 59
Broadbent, Donald E., 129
Buddhism, 101–2

Calvin, John, 102
Chappell, Timothy, 201, 204–5, 228
Chomsky, Noam, 64–65

Christology, 140, 231
church, 24, 27, 45, 80, 106, 115, 122, 133, 149–50, 203, 209
Coakley, Sarah, 122, 125, 141
community, 39, 59–61, 106
compliance, 6–7, 10, 46, 91, 95, 109, 126, 188–91, 215
confession, 26, 103–5, 196–97, 202–3
Congar, Yves, 63
conscience, 198–200, 202
construal, 154, 157, 175, 190
contract, 115–16
Cottingham, John, 15
covenant, 76–77, 114–19
crucifixion, 40, 45, 157
curiosity, 39, 52–54

de Botton, Alain, 29, 92
de Caussade, Pierre, 47
de Gruchy, John, W., 16
democracy, 161
Dennett, Daniel, 70
Diamond, Jared, 59–60, 63
Donoghue, Denis, 171
Dunn, John, 149
Dworkin, Ronald, 191–93, 196–97

education, 79–82
Emmons, Robert, A., 2, 14, 93, 156
emotion, 1, 14, 42–45, 155–59
empathy, 98–101
equality, 96–97, 115–19, 148–50
Erasmus, Desiderius, 65

Index

Eucharist, 18, 26–29, 45, 89, 105, 152, 165, 184
evolution, 69–72, 122

falsification, 57
forgiveness, 102–4, 200–204
freedom, 33, 37–40, 45, 59, 71, 96–97, 102–3, 122–23, 141, 144
friend, 23, 32, 41, 91, 131–32, 212–13
Fronda, Earl, S. B., 130

Giubbilei, Luciano, 90
Glory, 95, 168, 182–83, 201
Grace, God's, 15–16, 21, 35–39, 54, 89, 131, 144, 199, 203
Greenfield, Susan, 142
Griswold, Charles, L., 100

Hauerwas, Stanley, 133
healing, 16, 18, 98, 103, 202–4
health promotion, 179
history, 72–77
Hitchens, Christopher, 55–56
Homer, 22
Hume, David, 32, 48

Image of God, 33–36, 39–40, 45, 47–48, 67, 92–93, 116, 131, 148, 197, 224
incarnation, 3, 45, 101, 119, 123, 137, 153
Islam, 9, 10, 19

James, William, 128
Jeremias, Joachim, 24, 95
Jewett, Robert, 36
Jugendweihe, 28
Julian of Norwich, 20
justice, 62, 65, 97–98, 104, 112–13, 160–61, 176–79

Kant, Immanuel, 17, 177
Kristjánsson, Kristján, 1, 31–32, 41–42
Krznaric, Roman, 65, 99

language, 63–65, 94, 171, 209–10
liberal education, 83–84, 214–19
liberation theology, 8
Locke, John, 128
Lonergan, Bernard, 10, 180–81, 190, 223
Lord's Prayer. See *Our* Father, The
lure, 55–56, 153–55
Luther, Martin, 9, 20

MacKinnon, Donald, 9, 30
Macmurray, John, 4, 91–92
Maslow, Abraham, 75
McCullough, M. E., 14, 93, 207
McGilchrist, Iain, 43
meaning, 152–55
Merleau-Ponty, Maurice, 43–44, 151
Mill, John S., 114
miracle, 17–18, 24
Mole, Christopher, 129, 135
Monroe, Kristen R., 92–93
moral framework, 10, 34, 203
moral imagination, 162, 207, 214, 223–24
Murdoch, Iris, 16, 21, 172–73, 209, 211, 221–23

Newman, John H., 30
Nussbaum, Martha, 1, 84, 92, 95, 156, 160–61, 214

omnipotence, 36–39
Our Father, The, 202, 39–40, 105–6

Pailin, David, 56, 67, 79–80
Pakaluk, Michael, 113
parable, 24, 38, 94, 9 6–97, 210
Passmore, John, 36
Paul, Saint, 18–19, 36–39, 96, 118, 120–21, 159, 183, 200, 222
peace, 26–28, 65, 204
Pentecost, 64
Perkin, Harold, 4
Perrin, Norman, 155
phronesis, 85, 169

Index

pity, 98–100
Plato, 23, 32, 104, 168
Polanyi, Michael, 44, 137
Popper, Karl, 57, 142–43
professional practice, 5–6, 141, 162–64, 182, 184, 189. 191, 196, 200, 204, 207–8, 218–20
professional society, 4–5
proud man, 23
Putnam, Hilary, 82, 130

Queen Elizabeth II, 86

Rawls, John, 97, 160–61, 176–77
reason, 100–102, 199, 202
reconciliation, 102–3, 193, 195, 200–204
reconfiguration, 23–25, 29
redemption, 16, 26, 130, 159
Redemptive Creator, 16, 68, 140, 157, 162
regulation, 6, 47, 85, 91, 126, 138, 190
remorse, 26
resentment, 103, 193, 202
Resurrection, 26, 36, 45, 81, 104, 157, 162, 209
revelation, 10, 101, 168, 179–81, 221
Roberts, Robert C., 1, 14, 34, 154, 175–76, 202
Ruti, Mari, 171–72

Sacks, Jonathan, 66
sacrifice, 27, 110, 122–23
Saville, Anthony, 172
Scanlon, T. M., 147
Scarry, Elaine, 170, 174–78, 184
Schafer, Eva, 172
Schön, Donald, 139, 217
Schopenhauer, Friedrich, 172–73
scientific method, 56–57
scrupulosity, 189
Searle, John R., 32

self-sacrifice, 68, 81, 126, 215, 222
Sennett, Richard, 85
Shakespeare, William, 99, 111
shame, 197–99
simile, 207–8, 223
sin, 20, 26, 38, 53–54, 64, 95–97, 100, 104–5, 118, 200–202
Smith, Adam, 14
Smith, Nick, 194–96
Solzhenitsyn, Aleksandr, 182
soul, 33–47, 135, 151–52
Steiner, George, 63
Strawson, Galen, 33
Strawson, Peter F., 31, 33, 99, 199–200

theological framework, 1, 2, 6, 13, 20, 31, 73, 82–83, 129–30, 137, 181–84, 196–97, 207, 220–24
theological inquiry, 3, 8–10, 13, 15–17, 29, 34, 70, 82–83, 130, 158
theological language, 2, 25, 43, 132, 208
Tillich, Paul, 15, 67
Trinity, 3, 17, 122, 130–32, 133, 148, 221
Turner, Denys, 40, 130, 151–52
Tutu, Archbishop, 122–23

vocation, 4–6, 30, 83–86, 90, 106–7, 123, 182, 218–20

Ward, J. Neville, 20, 28–29
Wei, Marlynn, 137, 142, 196, 204
Weil, Simone, 134–35, 221
Wesley, John, 54, 148, 203, 235
Williams, Bernard, 103, 197
Williams, Rowan, 209
Winch, Peter, 62
Wittgenstein, Ludwig, 33, 44, 62, 94, 132, 136–37, 152, 173, 205, 208–9, 213–14, 218–19, 223–24

CPSIA information can be obtained
at www.ICGtesting.com
Printed in the USA
LVOW04*1359290317
528913LV00010B/283/P